Madness IN THE Morning

Madness
IN THE Morning

Life and Death in TV's Early
Morning Ratings War

RICHARD HACK

New Millennium Press • Beverly Hills

ISBN: 1-893224-01-5

Printed in the United States of America

NEW MILLENNIUM PRESS
a division of New Millennium Entertainment
350 S. Beverly Drive
Suite 315
Beverly Hills, California 90212

10 9 8 7 6 5 4 3 2 1

To John-Bradley Minnich

Visions of rainbows and freedom from pain
My friend
Forever

CONTENTS

ACKNOWLEDGMENTS

Without a publisher, there is no book. My special thanks to Michael Viner, who characteristically refused to give up on this project when others had. He was also wise enough to pass along my first-draft manuscript to my editor, Shelly Kale. Shelly, I have learned from your input and appreciate your kindness.

Marilyn Richards opened her home and her heart to me during my many months of research on this book and endured my mess without the slightest fuss. Well, maybe just a little, but always with a smile. You are very special, Marilyn.

My sister, Joan, provided a warm bed for comfort and a large rottweiler as protection while I conducted interviews in New York, New Jersey, Pennsylvania, Maryland, and Delaware. Michael and Traci Henn, Richard Henn, and Cassandra Estepp provided additional research at the University of Delaware, Newark.

Ronald Kimani Saleh offered his hospitality in Washington, D.C., as well as his contacts within the District and the Library of Congress. You are a wonderful friend. Special thanks as well to Patrick Briggs, director of the Office of Presidential Inquiry, The White House. You know the reason why.

My thanks to Kallie and Cody, who taught me about unconditional love. And to Robert Elias Deaton, for his encouragement even on the snowiest days. Carole Ita White, actor, friend, and fiduciary advisor—there are no words to thank you for your friendship. Tony Melluzzo, who provided me with a daily dose of news from Maui, I treasure your gift of aloha. And a special nod to D. E. Eastman, who once again watched over Weezie the bird through endless months of early morning wake-ups. You have the job forever.

Warmest thanks to Lawrence P. "Skip" Carrington Jr., Los Angeles bureau chief of *TV Guide* magazine, who opened the magazine's reference library and welcomed me back to my old stomping grounds. To the staff at the Port Orange (Florida) branch of the Volusia County Library, not even the devastating fires of the summer of 1998 stopped you from helping. You made my life easy in a time of strife. Likewise to the staff of the Museum of Television and Radio, New York City and Beverly Hills. No fire, but no less heat.

Love to my parents, Anne and Joe Hack, who are there for me. Always.

And, finally, to the anchors, producers, crew, and staff of *Today,* *Good Morning America,* and CBS *This Morning*—past and present—who sacrificed much to bring viewers across this country the best in television anywhere: thanks for giving me a story worth telling.

PREFACE

I grew up watching early morning television. While my parents had a penchant for *The CBS Morning News* with its hard-line approach to delivering information, from the time I could reach for the TV dial, I favored *Today* with its view of downtown Manhattan through its studio window. Breakfast after breakfast, I sat with my bowl of Sugar Pops, completely captivated by the wonders I saw. I went through kindergarten watching host Dave Garroway and matured through a succession of anchors who replaced him, including John Chancellor, Tom Brokaw, Hugh Downs, and Barbara Walters. These men and women were my link to the world and became my extended family and loyal friends. Their problems became my problems; their joys, my joys.

After graduating from college, I joined the writing staff of *TV Guide* magazine and began looking at the early morning shows from a professional viewpoint. My extended family now became my interview subjects; their lives and loves the stuff of copy. Several years later, my career took its first bend and I moved to the show business bible, *The Hollywood Reporter,* as that trade paper's television editor. By this point, cable TV had grown into formidable competition for the networks, as MTV brought the disenfranchised Generation X back to their sets while their parents tuned in to commercial-free films on HBO.

Breakfast television had changed as well, with the addition of ABC's *Good Morning America* to that network's early morning line-up. The arrival of *GMA* turned what had been a skirmish to attract early morning viewers into an all-out war for ratings. It was a battle in which no holds were barred, and one in which lives were irrevocably altered. Throughout the next fifteen years and in over three thousand columns, I chronicled television and those who brought it to life, including the stars of those early morning shows, both in front of and behind the cameras.

When a television expert was needed on the air, I was flown in from Hollywood and found myself guesting on the very shows that had nursed me through adolescence and into a career as exciting as those I now joined. Through it all, however, I remained a fan. Even now, when I wake up to the themes of *Good Morning America, Today,* or CBS *This Morning,* I am surrounded by familiar friends and the excitement and information that two hours of daily, live production brings.

However, the success, the polish, the amazing ability of these early morning shows to bring their audiences breaking news, and with that the people who make it, come with a toll. The price that is paid by anchors, producers, and a vast supporting cast is a far more dramatic story than any that makes it onto their broadcasts. From back-stabbing scandals, drug-induced stupors, and international intrigue to lawsuits, labor disputes, and love affairs, this is a world unto itself, where madness in the morning is a way of life.

THE CURSE

It's as if some thick and omnipotent hand keeps pushing at you, daring you to break. There's a curse on this show that affects every aspect of your life, that no one can escape. No one.

—Dave Garroway, first host of *Today*

*K*evin Newman removed his wire-rimmed glasses and massaged the bridge of his nose. The tension gripping his back and shoulders had made its way to his head, pulsing a message of pain across the top of his skull with each fresh beat of his heart. Outside the window of Newman's New Jersey home, the frozen lawn and barren trees stood silent witness as he gazed across the yard, his mind lost in reflection.

It was January 3, 1999, exactly eight months since the newsman had taken over for Charles Gibson as the co-anchor of ABC's *Good Morning America*. Eight months that saw the ratings continue on a downward spiral that began long before Newman had joined the *GMA* family as its news reader a year earlier. Eight months that should have been the happiest, most exciting time of his life. Yet Kevin Newman was anything but happy. He had just received the call that he had anticipated as much as dreaded. He was being replaced as the host of *Good Morning America*, along with his co-anchor, Lisa McRee.

Only after hanging up the phone did Newman feel the tightening in his shoulders and the flush across his face. Each weekday for months, along with the show's script, came one or two newspaper articles projecting what changes would be made on the show, including rumors that Newman himself would be replaced. The politically savvy newsman was compared by the press and viewers alike to Matt Lauer, co-anchor of NBC's *Today*. While *Cosmopolitan* magazine labeled Lauer the "sexiest man on TV" for his matinee-idol good looks, Newman was busy fighting a suggestion by the network that he wear contact lenses instead of glasses to look less "intellectual." Formerly overweight and undermotivated, Newman had slain many personal dragons to rise to the top in his field, only to find that his lack of glamour and sex appeal seemed to be helping the competition.

As ratings on *Good Morning America* continued to slip, it appeared that even the perennially third-ranked *This Morning*, CBS's competitive entry, would top ABC. The unthinkable happened during the week between Christmas 1998 and New Year's Day. For the first time in twenty years, *GMA* fell to third place in the ratings, while NBC—with *Cosmo* man Lauer and co-anchor Katie Couric—was experiencing a seemingly unstoppable surge in popularity, with more viewers than *GMA* and *This Morning* combined. The resulting fallout from grumbling ABC affiliates caused the network to act sooner than many had projected.

Kevin Newman had neither met Dave Garroway nor knew anything about his "curse." Yet, if he had, he might have been tempted to agree. Certainly, since he had joined the *Good Morning America* staff, his life had seen its share of tragedy. His younger sister, Kelly, a police officer in Toronto, had died of cancer at the age of 34, only days after the newscaster began his job at *GMA*. She left behind a husband and a 1-year-old child. That memory was still fresh in Newman's mind when he was rushed on the air in late August 1997 to report on the shocking car crash that took the life of England's Princess Diana. His poignant reporting had impressed Americans and ABC News executives, who had rewarded his work by offering him the coveted *GMA* co-anchor spot.

A devoted family man, Newman had been slow to say yes. Before making any decision, he had felt compelled to discuss the opportunity at length with his wife, Cathy. They had met seventeen years earlier when they were both gofers at Global News, a regional television network in their native Canada. He would later tell the story of how he picked her up on their first date in a car he had borrowed from the network, the Global News insignia boldly printed on the sides. He thought it might impress her, and apparently it did, for the couple married a year later and eventually settled in New Jersey. Six months into his run on *Good Morning America,* another tragedy struck Newman and his family: Cathy was diagnosed with multiple sclerosis. The couple was handling the tragic news with a united front, supporting one another in what might become the biggest challenge of their lives.

Staunchly protective, Newman told few outside of his family circle. Yet, a part of America feasts on negative news, tracking it down with voracious aggressiveness, and as a result, it was only days before the *GMA* anchor received a call at his ABC office. A reporter for the *Star,* a supermarket tabloid, had gotten wind of the story and was telephoning to confirm the rumor. Faced with the disclosure of his wife's illness in a tabloid banner headline, Newman admitted to the reporter that while the diagnosis was accurate, he was proud of the way his wife was coping, that she had a very mild case of the illness, and that they were considering various drug therapies to contain the symptoms.

Newman's personal life had always been private property, his family off-limits to public scrutiny. But that was before—before his job at *Good Morning America,* before he became fodder for the gossip mill, before he was plunged into a war in which the team with the most rating points wins and the losers become yesterday's news. Now Cathy was preparing to fight the neurological disease she shared with 300,000 other Americans, including former Mouseketeer Annette Funicello, comedian Richard Pryor, and the wife of NBC newsman Stone Phillips.

Suddenly, Newman's extreme work schedule, one that saw him rising at 4:00 A.M. and getting to bed by nine, was no longer a detriment. Now his unusual schedule allowed him to accompany Cathy on medical appointments, just as his high-profile job allowed him access to the finest treatment available for her perplexing and incurable disease. Yet, the addition of this extra worry, coupled with his struggle to improve *Good Morning America*'s ratings, was clearly taking its toll.

There were reports that ABC's Entertainment Division was attempting to steal the program back from the network's News Division, which had overseen it for the past three and a half years. Infighting at the network centered on David Westin, newly promoted president of ABC News, who publicly pledged support of Newman and McRee. Yet, not even Westin could help but admit that the once top-rated morning show was "not where it should be." And despite repeated pronouncements that he had "confidence" in his anchor team, new rumors danced around the water cooler each day; the secretarial pool had even launched a lottery to see who could pick the exact date the Newman-McRee pairing would fall. Ironically, no January dates had been selected.

It was a loosely guarded secret that earlier Westin had pursued ABC newswoman Connie Chung to replace McRee during the co-anchor's first vacation from *GMA*. Chung's acceptance would have served as an on-air test of her chemistry with Newman in a possible anchor change. However, Westin actually had had an entirely different arrangement in mind. To be sure, he wanted Chung to join the program, but not as McRee's replacement. Rather, he was quietly devising a plan to *add* an anchor to the show, turning the duo into a trio of hosts.

When Chung rebuffed his offer, Westin next approached Meredith Vieira, who had generated attention as one of a quartet of hosts on Barbara Walters's ABC series *The View*. Vieira, too, turned Westin down, leaving the executive to rethink his inspiration. Fourteen years earlier, a different network had considered Vieira to anchor a different morning talk/news show, *The CBS Morning News*. At that time, Vieira was overlooked because network executives felt that her image was too straitlaced. They apparently were unaware that one night after partying heavily in Las Vegas, she had impulsively married an Elvis impersonator in a street-side chapel, only to later annul the marriage.

Now frantic to pull off a ratings miracle, Westin bypassed God and went straight to a diva—Diane Sawyer. A longtime friend of the news journalist, Sawyer had, only months earlier, hosted Westin's marriage to his third wife, Sherrie Rollins, at her home in Martha's

Vineyard. Although Westin didn't approach Sawyer about the possibility of taking the early morning post on bended knee, he might as well have. The situation at ABC News was dire. Profits at *GMA* had fallen to $50 million a year at a time when NBC's *Today* show was generating twice that amount.

While hardly jumping at the opportunity to throw herself on the live grenade that *Good Morning America* had become, Sawyer nevertheless saw the wisdom in not only being a team player, but also gaining a new audience among the early morning crowd. Charles Gibson, though not exactly eager to backtrack in a career that had been prospering since he had left the morning talk/news series, was not anxious to displease Westin, who had personally piloted Gibson's smooth transition into network news and was now calling him back to the cohost chair. Suddenly the pairing of Gibson and Sawyer—or Sawyer and Gibson, depending on whose agent one believed—took on a life of its own. Even the anchors managed to get swept up in the anticipation of what kind of program they might be able to deliver as a team.

To organize the new effort, Westin called upon ABC News vice president Phyllis McGrady, who was given the added title of executive in charge of *Good Morning America.* McGrady was the former executive producer of *Good Morning America* during its 1984 to 1986 seasons, who had quit to produce primetime specials for Barbara Walters. After producing the network's *Prime Time Live* series, she was now being brought onboard *GMA* with a mandate from Westin to "focus the show." According to McGrady, the series "still has a tremendous amount of strength, and a following."

Many at ABC would have agreed with her, but Michael Eisner was not among them. The chief executive officer of ABC's parent company, The Walt Disney Company, Eisner had so little faith in *Good Morning America*'s draw that he accepted a booking on NBC's *Today* to promote his 1998 autobiography, *Work in Progress.* Compounding the embarrassment to the *GMA* staff, Eisner remarked while speaking to Lauer's co-anchor, Katie Couric, about the book that he would "love it" if the Couric-Lauer combo would jump ship and move to ABC to host *Good Morning America.*

ABC spokeswoman Eileen Murphy commented, "Clearly, it was a

light remark meant to compliment Katie. David [Westin] has not changed his position on *GMA*. He has said all along that the program is not where we want it to be. However, at the same time he has expressed confidence in the anchor team and the executive producer to make those changes. He's not wavering on that." By January 1999, however, Westin's opinion obviously had altered. In addition to new hosts and a new executive in charge, he hired a new executive producer for the series—Shirley Ross, a senior producer for *20/20* and former producer of Sawyer's *Prime Time Live.*

The group inherited a show that had grown into the brunt of jokes. "What's the difference between the *Titanic* and *Good Morning America*?" the set-up asked. "The *Titanic* had entertainment."

If those at *Good Morning America* failed to appreciate the joke, the folks at *Today* were laughing out loud. Officially responding to the Sawyer-Gibson announcement, *Today* executive producer Jeff Zucker said he "welcomed the competition." Privately, he pointed to the wording of the *New York Times* headline announcing the news: OLD ANCHORS SEEK TO RESCUE ABC MORNINGS; RATINGS DIVE RESURRECTS GIBSON AND SAWYER. The 33-year-old Zucker found Gibson at 54 and Sawyer at 53 a little old for active combat, especially considering the Garroway "curse."

Zucker himself had firsthand knowledge of the malediction after having contracted colon cancer at the young age of 31. Matt Lauer also had been touched by "the curse" with the death of his father just months after he had replaced Bryant Gumbel as the *Today* cohost. More recently, however, Lauer was reported to have never been happier, a result of his October 1998 wedding to Dutch model Annette Roque.

The 40-year-old Lauer wed his 32-year-old bride in an afternoon service at a Presbyterian church in Bridgehampton, Long Island, with Bryant Gumbel as his best man. The former *Today* anchor had come to the wedding with his statuesque blonde girlfriend, Hilary Quinlan. It was Gumbel's most public appearance with the woman who was alleged to have contributed to the breakup of Gumbel's two-decade marriage to his wife, June. When Gumbel first became enamored with Quinlan, he was still hosting *Today* and adamantly denied her existence. According to Geraldo Rivera, Gumbel once had the journalist axed from an appearance on *Today* for reporting that the anchor was cheating on his wife.

"Bryant Gumbel is a wimp and a hypocrite," Rivera told radio host Don Imus while discussing the incident and challenging Gumbel to a boxing match to settle the score. Although Gumbel dismissed Rivera's challenge as a publicity stunt, after Lauer's wedding he could no longer deny the existence of Quinlan, who looked even younger and blonder surrounded by the springeri and pepper-berry garland of flowers in the church.

There are those who attribute the pressure of maintaining *Today*'s ratings to the disintegration of Gumbel's marriage. Dave Garroway's curse might have been a better explanation, if Gumbel's experiences after leaving *Today* were added to the scenario. Although Gumbel had signed a contract to host *Public Eye* on CBS at a reported $5 million per year, the series was canceled after a few months of disappointing ratings, leaving Gumbel showless for the first time in two decades.

For Katie Couric, who had lost her husband, Jay Monahan, to colon cancer nine months before Lauer's wedding, the ceremony was a rare opportunity for her to find some joy outside the confines of her family. In the months following Monahan's death, Couric had clutched at her home life as a sanctuary of relief from her pain. She finally chose to talk about her husband's death after five months of mourning while speaking at an awards luncheon for 1,300 businesswomen.

"How do you go on when fate delivers such a crushing blow that it causes permanent damage to your heart?" she asked. "I've often wondered. People ask how and why do you go on and do what you have to do," she continued. "I do it because I have two girls who are depending on me to show them what you have to do when life throws you a major curve ball." Away from the scrutiny of television cameras, Couric cried as she admitted that she had learned to believe that "everything I wanted was in my own backyard."

In an attempt to begin life anew, Couric subsequently moved out of the apartment she had shared with Monahan and into a new $3.6 million co-op. Yet she retained their white wicker bed, and still wore his wedding band on a chain around her neck. Each morning, she returned to sit next to Lauer and conduct business in one of toughest jobs in television.

The list of those who have tried and failed at early morning television is a long one, and now Newman and McRee were adding their names. While McRee, who had just learned that she was pregnant, consoled herself with the fact that she could rejoin her West Coast–based husband in Los Angeles while doing special reports for ABC News, Newman was jockeyed into a position as a correspondent on the network's late-night news series *Nightline*. At least they had jobs.

The early morning shows operate on a battleground that seldom pauses to forgive mistakes and never bothers to take any prisoners. It's a place littered with the fallen careers of many who have tried to wage the early morning ratings war only to find themselves expendable at the first sign of weakness. The names are familiar, if no longer the faces: Dave Garroway, the first human sacrifice, lost his sanity; David Hartman, his power; Kathleen Sullivan, her fortune along with her waistline; Joan Lunden, her marriage but not her happiness; Bryant Gumbel, his popularity if not his future. Add Lauer and Couric, Newman and McRee, and the story becomes one too laden with tragedy and drama to be mere coincidence.

This, then, is the story of those who launched a new television form and those who still breathe it life. Those behind the scenes as well as in front of the camera—their triumphs, tribulations, personalities, and wounds—all exposed in a remarkable story of determination, dedication, and, yes, madness in the morning.

CHAPTER ONE

THE MASTER COMMUNICATOR

*T*his is *Today.*" With those three little words, television was ushered into virgin territory. America yawned itself awake at 7:00 A.M. on the morning of January 14, 1952, to find Dave Garroway sitting behind an expansive oak desk, exuding enthusiasm for what NBC press releases had labeled "a revolution in the television industry."

Less revolt than experimentation, these first fledgling hours of the *Today* show were rough exercises in confusion that somehow only added to the spontaneity of the moment. From a glassed-in studio housed within the RCA Exhibition Hall on West 49th Street, Garroway began his morning broadcast surrounded by electronic equipment, cables, lights, maps, clocks, desks, typewriters, telephones, and record players in what the network predicted would become "the nerve center of the planet." Raw nerve center might have described it better.

"Well, here we are," said Garroway, "and good morning to you. The very first good morning of what I hope and suspect will be a great many good mornings between you and me. Here it is, January 14, 1952, when NBC begins a new program called *Today* and, if it doesn't sound too revolutionary, I really believe this begins a new kind of television."

At the very least, it meant a new life for Garroway. The low-key, large-framed, bespectacled 38-year-old broadcaster, who favored bow ties and argyle socks, was anything but modern and ahead of his time. The son of an engineer for General Electric, he had moved from town to town as a youth, gaining knowledge along with an inherent shyness, which worked well for a new audience that had yet to wipe sleep from its eyes.

Garroway moved through the intensity of the *Today* set, with its jumble of wires and frantic activity, as if floating above it. His six-foot-two-inch nimble frame launched itself silently, as if not to jolt his early morning audience at any expense. Dave Garroway of the gentle voice, calming demeanor, and unperplexed attitude welcomed viewers into a sea of high-tech gadgetry that threatened to swallow up all those who dared to venture outside his protective reach.

It had been an interesting ride that had brought Garroway to this studio on this morning. And it was as unlikely a scenario as the creation of the *Today* show itself. Seventeen years earlier, David Cunningham Garroway was newly graduated from St. Louis's Washington University with a bachelor of arts degree, having majored in abnormal psychology, astronomy, and landscape painting. Unable to find work, he drifted to Boston and finally landed a job the following year selling pistons to auto mechanics, a reach even for the most versatile of intellectuals.

Eager to pursue more lucrative employment, he joined forces with a friend of his father and published a softcover booklet of eight hundred of the most mispronounced words in the English language. Heading to New York in 1938, he began to sell the book—titled *You Don't Say . . . Or Do You!*—to schoolteachers, meeting with a modicum of success.

Housed at the local YMCA, he happened upon an old college chum who invited him to a party on Manhattan's trendy West Side. The lanky Garroway, who hated such events, was not eager to go, but finally agreed to assuage his persistent friend.

At the party, Garroway was introduced by chance to a woman who ran the guest-relations department of NBC, and was hired on the spot as a studio page at a salary of $15.85 a week. Despite the fact that it was less money than he received for selling books, Garroway later admitted that "the whole broadcasting business opened before my eyes." Of course, at the time broadcasting meant radio, and with his position as an NBC page came a uniform and an opportunity to enroll in the announcer's school that the network ran for its staff.

Discovering that he didn't have what his instructor called "a terribly commanding voice," Garroway experimented by mimicking his favorite announcers: Milton J. Cross, whose baritone voice welcomed listeners to the Metropolitan Opera, and Westbrook Van Voorhis, whose narration for the "March of Time" edged every word with the timbre of concern. He apparently failed to capture either, for the score on his final exam ranked him twenty-third out of twenty-four students in his class.

He did manage, however, to attract the attention of Adele Dwyer, whom he married the day after Valentine's Day in 1940. He also worked his magic on the general manager of NBC's Pittsburgh affiliate, KDKA, when the man came to New York looking for on-air talent. Garroway pledged to "risk any peril" to gain a spot on the station's line-up. The drama of his plea seemed to impress the general manager, who hired the young broadcaster as KDKA's special events announcer. At a salary of $30 a week, Garroway soon found himself reporting from a trestle of the 300-foot-high Swindell Bridge, broadcasting from a naval training submarine deep within the Ohio River, and soaring in a hot-air balloon above the Allegheny Valley.

While his skill at reporting was never quite appreciated as much as he hoped, Garroway was soon hired as a freelance broadcaster by WMAQ, the NBC affiliate in Chicago. And it was in the Windy City, in 1942, that he was called to active duty, joining the American forces fighting World War II.

Although the navy made him an ensign, it took only a single twenty-three-day maneuver to label the seasick deejay "not for sea duty." Garroway was dropped at the first port of call—Honolulu. There, while teaching in a yeoman's school for radio technicians in Pearl Harbor, he landed a night job for a Waikiki station as the disc jockey for a nightly 10:00–11:00 P.M. jazz show sponsored by a massage parlor that attempted to legitimize itself with the name The Body Sculpture Center of the Institute of Hawaii.

In the tranquility of paradise, Garroway used his on-air time to reflect on life and its meaning, and with it came the style that had long escaped him. As he remembered back to his favorite haunts in Chicago, the walks along the river, cruising the Loop, he lingered in the memories and brought his listeners—many of them also from Chicago—right along for the nostalgia.

"Old tiger," he thought out loud, "I miss those days." And he was not alone. Letters began to pour in from fans who needed to hear the gentle simplicity of his words. The response did more than raise Garroway's salary. It convinced the shy, retiring, complicated introvert that he had a future in broadcasting.

Armed with that knowledge, he returned to WMAQ at the close of the war and was hired to host a nightly program of jazz and rhumba music for $300 a week. *The 11:60 Show* aired each evening from midnight to 2:00 A.M. and provided Garroway with the perfect platform to wax poetic about every element of his existence.

"This is Garroway, David, going for some free-breathing records, like we do most nights about the witching hour, when the hands of your clock get so intimate," he began most broadcasts. "Yes, the ductile time of the day has come again, and we'll do it while you sit here, feet up, eyes closed, head back," he added, relaxing his audience even more.

His style was unusual enough to grab the attention of *Herald Tribune* reviewer John Crosby, who commented on Garroway's "distracted prose." According to Crosby, Garroway would toss out *bon mots* like "lissome and gauzy, incandescent and gruesome" with "no great interest in their connotations." To Crosby, that seemed to be a plus, as did Garroway's habit of calling his listeners "old delicate," "my so unfrowszy," or "old tiger eyes."

Not everyone was impressed, however. *Variety,* in its first review of the deejay, wrote that Garroway used "two or three adjectives where none would be best." Reviewers notwithstanding, the listeners in Chicago seemed unanimous in their praise of the newcomer's intimate style and relaxed cadence. Soon Garroway found himself hosting a daily afternoon deejay show as well as a Sunday night variety hour, in addition to continuing *The 11:60 Show.*

. . .

By 1949, television had begun to make inroads in the Chicago area with the arrival of a coaxial-cable connection to the networks in New York. With it came an offer of employment from NBC vice president Jules Herbuveaux, who wired Garroway: "Can you fill TV net 9–9:30 P.M. EST on Sundays?"

If Garroway hesitated slightly, it was only because his radio writer and best friend, Charles Andrews, thought that the future lay in radio, not the TV screen—which at the time was all of seven inches. Yet, not even the skeptical Andrews could refuse to go along with Garroway when he heard that he could earn $800 a week—and with that Dave Garroway, TV host, was born.

Sponsored by the linoleum company Congoleum-Nairn, the network's *Garroway at Large* turned the laid-back broadcaster into a star. With his now-familiar relaxed, folksy, esoteric style, Garroway introduced comedians, singers, magicians, and "anything else that has an act" for a half hour every Sunday night. *Herald Tribune* reviewer Crosby suggested, "He talks a low murmur, so low sometimes you can't hear him. In fact, the whole show is conducted almost in a whisper."

It was a time for celebration and easy living. Despite the fact that his marriage to Adele had dissolved in divorce, Dave Garroway moved in a circle of intimates that saw few close friends but many attractive women. Thanks to a shortage of expenses and an ever-expanding salary, the star indulged himself by buying several expensive classic cars, including a vintage Rolls-Royce and a 1937 XK100 Jaguar with alligator skin seats and dashboard.

Even as Walter Winchell was proclaiming *Garroway at Large* "big time all the way" and "the first show with a professional flavor," the increasingly popular host fought a nagging restlessness. Hit by an unexpected depression and unable to sleep, Garroway often spent his nights on a mechanic's sled, working on his cars until dawn. When his on-air performance began to suffer, he found a Chicago doctor who prescribed a "miracle elixir" made from Vitamin B-12, molasses, and liquid codeine. Referring to the magic potion as "The

Doctor," Garroway carried it everywhere and used it often. It was the beginning of a dependency on codeine that would shadow him the rest of his life.

In the fall of 1951, Garroway and "The Doctor" were joined on a cross-European tour by Charlie Andrews and Garroway's agent, William "Biggie" Levin. The trio traveled through Spain, France, and Scandinavia before driving to Switzerland. It was there, early one morning, that Garroway received the news: *Garroway at Large* had been canceled by NBC. Garroway later said, "Our sorrows melted twelve feet off the Matterhorn."

The popular series was a victim of its own success. Procter & Gamble had wanted the time slot for one of its own shows, and NBC capitulated. Jack Gould of *The New York Times* labeled the cancellation of *Garroway at Large* "grounds for genuine misgiving." Regardless, the series was history, and Garroway found himself taking a nosedive, financially and emotionally.

As he withdrew into the isolation provided by tinkering on his classic cars, and soothed his battered ego with the salve of "The Doctor" on an increasingly frequent basis, Dave Garroway found himself a star without a place to shine. Unwilling to return exclusively to radio and with no television show on the horizon, Garroway needed some luck to come his way. He found it in *Daily Variety* while having breakfast in the Pump Room, the restaurant in the Ambassador East, his residential hotel in Chicago.

The headline of the trade journal, left behind by a previous customer, blared forth the news that NBC was planning a radically different early morning series, to be called *Today*, that would strive to become America's "electronic newspaper." The article quoted NBC vice president Sylvester "Pat" Weaver as saying the show would keep Americans "in touch with the world" by every "means of communication yet invented."

The hyperbole sent a shiver of excitement through Garroway. All thoughts of breakfast were forgotten in the rush to phone his agent. While Biggie Levin failed to share Garroway's excitement over the program's prospects, he at least promised to arrange a meeting with NBC. What Biggie arranged was somewhat less than that. He managed to lay the groundwork to have Garroway's phone call accepted by Mort Werner, one of *Today*'s first producers.

On the promise of a dinner, Werner agreed to fly to Chicago and meet with Garroway, which he did the following week. There would be no Pump Room or a fancy lakefront restaurant for Werner, however. Instead, Garroway picked Werner up at the airport and drove him to his apartment, where the two ate cold baked beans from a can and became immediate fast friends. Night pushed into day, and as Werner watched the sun rise from Garroway's hotel window, he promised to sing the broadcaster's praises at 30 Rockefeller Plaza.

Despite Werner's enthusiasm, however, Garroway's hiring was not a certainty by any means. Pat Weaver wanted to jolt America awake, not shmooze them out of bed. "What we really wanted was a 'think-type' master communicator. Someone with experience in news and world affairs, like Russ Hughes," Weaver later admitted, referring to the staccato-voiced newscaster whose delivery mirrored that of Walter Winchell. "Dave Garroway was none of these."

Perhaps not, but after being invited to New York and reading a brief page of news bulletins for Pat Weaver and *Today*'s executive producer Abe Schechter, it took the network only two days to offer Garroway the job. With Charlie Andrews, his sports cars, "The Doctor," and a collection of bow ties in tow, Garroway moved to New York and into a penthouse at 710 Park Avenue and began to discover exactly what Weaver and his *Today* show were attempting to accomplish. His guaranteed salary: $2,500 a week.

In no small way, Pat Weaver's vision of a revolution in broadcasting was hinged to the latest electronic equipment of the day. It must be remembered that up until this point, television was basically an advertiser's medium, programmed to sell everything from soap to cars. The old concept was simple enough: provide the viewers with entertainment and, in between songs or comedy routines, sell them a Mercury or some Pond's Cold Cream.

Weaver saw things differently. He wanted to grab Americans fresh from bed and bring them news, sports, weather, politics, history, books, and heroism. Up until this point, the only thing viewers could count on seeing on their television sets at sunup was a test pattern.

So radical was Weaver's idea for his time that critics called the concept "Weaver's Folly," openly laughing in print that no one would be foolish enough to turn on their television sets before breakfast. That was, after all, a time period reserved for radio, with three-quarters of Americans listening before heading off to work, school, or housekeeping chores. Even other NBC executives had difficulty believing in the concept when Weaver first presented his plan—a series to be titled *Rise and Shine.*

In an internal NBC memo, Weaver attempted to sell his concept: "We cannot and should not try to build a show that will make people sit down in front of their set and divert their attention to the screen. We want America to shave, to eat, to dress, to get to work on time. But we also want America to be well informed, to be amused, to be lightened in spirit and in heart, and to be reinforced in inner resolution through knowledge."

Regardless of any initial doubt on the part of the network, Weaver's enthusiasm for the concept grew as the show—soon retitled *Today*—became a reality. He was thoroughly convinced of its logic and certain that America was ready for a "revolt in their living rooms over eggs and bacon."

Weaver was hardly characteristic of the average television viewer of the time. A magna-cum-laude graduate of Dartmouth with a degree in philosophy, Weaver had made his way up through the ranks of broadcasting, beginning in radio and moving into advertising and then on to NBC, where he conceived of the evening "spectacular"—productions so costly that no one advertiser could afford to cover the entire production. Instead, Weaver devised a plan to sell portions of shows, "participations" he called them, and in doing so created the form of television sponsorship that is used to this day.

Known later in life as the father of actress Sigourney Weaver, in the early fifties Weaver was one of the most creative programming executives in New York, spearheading NBC's first strong Saturday night line-up that included *All-Star Revue, Your Show of Shows,* and *Your Hit Parade.* Yet, even with enormous decision-making power at the network and a stable of fans among the top brass, Weaver had gone out on a limb to create *Today* and many were eagerly waiting for the branch to break. It almost did.

When the show went on the air the second week of January 1952, it was already two weeks behind schedule. Weaver had hoped to bring in his "revolution" with the New Year, but technical snafus with shortwave radio circuits and the street-level soundstage in the renamed Johnny Victor Theater made that hope little more than a dream. The delay, however, served only to heighten Weaver's enthusiasm for his "series of the future," and the executive made certain that everyone around him knew how excited he was. In December 1951 he wrote to his staff:

> We are about to inaugurate a new era in television programming. These words mean what they say. *Today* is a big undertaking in every sense of the word. . . . Seven to nine A.M. will be no "Siberia" as one columnist surmised; it will be the Sun Valley, Palm Springs, and Miami Beach of TV.
>
> We are building TV's first communication studio on the floor space of the RCA Exhibit Hall on 49th Street. The camera will see a working newsroom with printers, wire-photo, facilities for trans-Atlantic communication—every device needed for news coverage on the broadcast scale. . . .
>
> *Today* is in every sense a vast undertaking. It is a top-priority program. I urge you to destroy any mental image you have of just another morning program. We are building a program that will change the listening habits of this nation. We are setting standards that will bring distinction to every man and woman who joins in this project.
>
> The proudest order of journalists has always been that select group who made the old New York *World* [the award-winning newspaper] in its heyday. Now we are in an era

where newsprint has lost its force to the electronic wonder of television. I have a commission for each one of you. It is simply this: to make of *Today* not merely a good program but the finest news presentation in history. We have the resources. We have the opportunity. Now we go to work and do the big job.

The task ahead was taking place not only in the studio, but also upstairs in 30 Rockefeller Plaza, where an advertising sales staff was preparing to launch its own assault—this one geared not to viewers but to potential sponsors. Weaver attempted to enthuse the NBC sales staff with visions of a broadcast that was equally effective as a radio show. "We are going into something highly auditory . . . and encourage lack of interest in the picture," he wrote. He suggested that they pitch advertisers based on the value of "continuous association, of preparing advertising material which is good in either or both media—sight and sound, and sight or sound. We need not fear an uninteresting picture, as radio-trained men fear silence," Weaver asserted.

Television, with or without the picture. The very suggestion was enough to cause some to cry heresy, but to Weaver, the most important factor was the excitement, the anticipation of the event. "T-Day" he called it.

By the time Dave Garroway welcomed America to his version of a TV wake-up call, *Today* was still in the middle of a shakedown cruise that would not end for many months.

At Garroway's side were newscaster Jim Fleming and sports commentator Jack Lescoulie. With foot-long microphones cantilevered from cords around their necks, the team was free to move about its home-base set amid the myriad of electronic noisemakers—chief among them a teletype machine that would occasionally hammer to life, relaying to host Garroway the latest news. The plan was for Garroway to rush to the machine and be handed the "this-just-in" bulletin to share "hot off the wire."

Unfortunately, on the morning of January 14, the machines were humming but producing very little for an audience barely able to care. Gawking as if in overt awe at the equipment scattered throughout the studio, Garroway waited right along with America, hoping that some-thing—anything—would happen.

"This is the telephoto machine," he said at one point, passing by a rather bulky piece of machinery. "Anything coming in?" Garroway questioned the operator.

"Yes, the Twenty-fifth Division," came the response.

Viewers were left to wonder what that Twenty-fifth Division was all about, since nothing about the Twenty-fifth or any other division spilled forth. There were promises of cutaways: "We're still waiting for Secretary of the Army Frank Pace—expected any minute," a mystery voice said from off-camera. Pace never made it to the telephone and it was probably just as well. Chief of Naval Operations Admiral William Fechteler was not so lucky. He was cornered by a *Today* reporter in Washington as he walked toward the Pentagon. "How's the Navy going these days?" asked the young reporter.

"Guess it's all right," Fechteler managed to utter through his amazement at the sight of cameras outside the Pentagon at 7:00 A.M. "It was there last night all right, when I left it."

"Thank you very much, sir," the correspondent said in all seri-ousness, as the admiral hurried away. "Ladies and gentlemen, you have just heard from Admiral William Fechteler, chief of naval operations down here at the Pentagon in Washington. And now we return you to Dave Garroway in New York."

Garroway took viewers to the corner of Randolph and Michigan Streets in Chicago, an area even more asleep than those shivering through the windows at West 49th Street and Rockefeller Plaza. From Washington, weatherman Jim Fielder read the forecast for highs around the country. There were pre-filmed shots of a couple of ser-vicemen in Korea receiving greetings from their families, who were brought into the studio for the occasion. It seemed to matter little that they couldn't pick up the *Today* show in Korea, or west of Chicago for that matter.

Garroway's attempts to reach correspondents in Europe by phone were only slightly more successful. Having gotten through to NBC's man in Germany, Ed Hasker, Garroway asked, "Tell me the news in your part of the world."

"The big news is the weather," responded Hasker. "We had our first big storm of the year. We're really chilly."

"You're not alone," said Garroway, hanging up the line as if worried about the toll charges. He devoted little more time to Romney Wheeler, NBC's reporter in London, when he reached him long distance: "All we want you to do is start our next record."

"I hope it's 'Domino,'" said Wheeler, right on cue. "It's very popular over here." And with that, "Domino," a major hit sung by Bing Crosby and Doris Day, was played as Garroway tapped out the beat. Also on that first show, author Fleur Cowles plugged her new book, *Bloody Precedent*. The most interesting of the premiere guests, Fleur had a rapport with Garroway that hinted at his interviewing ease, although on this day, the style was never fully realized.

For the most part, *Today*'s premiere was a silly exercise in an abundance of nothing. More illusion than substance, it gave ample fodder to the critics, one of whom suggested that NBC do itself a favor: "roll over and go back to sleep."

One Weaver-inspired segment that attracted nearly universal criticism was "Today in Two Minutes." Weaver's initial concept was that Garroway would take viewers around the country via newspapers, reporting the headlines and showing photos. According to the *Herald Tribune*'s John Crosby, the concept failed miserably:

> "Today in two minutes," said Mr. Garroway and showed us the headlines of the day. INDOCHINA REBELS GET RED-BUILT RADAR GUNS: DOWN TEN FRENCH PLANES from the New York *Herald Tribune*. The Trend of the Day (a picture of Justice Douglas, who had said he didn't want to be President) . . . a picture of Jimmy Demaret, winner of the Bing Crosby golf tournament, being kissed by Bob Hope. . . . "That's *Today* in capsule. Cut to two minutes," said Mr. Garroway. "That is the day you are going to live." Having seen it, he implied we were better equipped to face the world, to

breast the slings and arrows of outrageous fortune. I don't know, though. About the only useful bit of information I gleaned from this capsule, repeated four times during the two hours, was a warning against inflammable sweaters, which I never wear anyway.

Crosby didn't like the rest of the show either, writing off the production as "an incredible two-hour comedy of errors, perpetuated as 'a new kind of television.'"

Janet Kern, writing in the *Chicago Herald American*, called the show "something without which TV can do very well." Jack O'Brien complained in the *New York Journal-American* that while the set looked like "a command post for an invasion," it didn't bring in much news.

The New York Times's Jack Gould watched a week's worth of shows before penning an opinion. And while not dismissing the series as others had done, he was dubious about its long-term possibilities:

> Television at breakfast. After weeks of preparations and communiqués, the National Broadcasting Company unveiled last week its much-awaited effort to add the hours between 7:00 and 9:00 in the morning to the television day.
>
> The two-hour marathon is called *Today:* its basic theme is the presentation of news in just about every shape, form, and manner possible, and its intriguing problem is to try to lure man, woman, and child to Channel 4 during the busiest and most confusing hours of the family's daily routine. . . .
>
> On the basis of its first four days of presentation, *Today* was a disappointment, albeit a disappointment which should not be too difficult to overcome.

Labeling Garroway "that leisurely gentleman from Chicago"; Fleming, "the erstwhile editor of that excellent radio program *Voices and Events*"; and Lescoulie, "sports specialist and general utility infielder," Gould went on to suggest that the complexity of the show added to the confusion.

With all the variety of equipment around them, the Messrs. Garroway, Fleming, and Lescoulie give the appearance of baffled fathers on Christmas morning who are intrigued with a new set of electric trains but are not quite sure how they work. . . . In short, *Today* is the slave rather than the master of its own inventiveness and ingenuity.

Everyone on the show is self-conscious and overawed by all the technical equipment. . . . The preoccupation with gadgetry makes for a program that the viewer must watch and cannot only hear; there's so much confusion on the show that a listener feels compelled to look to find out what's going on. When he does, it's often not worth the time. Old-fashioned radio has its points in the morning.

Indeed, one of the great problems of *Today* on its first week was its tendency to build to a succession of anticlimaxes. There was much hoopla about going to Washington, but what was shown? A parking lot, first empty and, an hour later, full. There was a melodramatic radio pick-up from abroad; it was snowing there.

While crediting Weaver with coming up with a concept that Gould labeled "a challenging experiment," he nevertheless cautioned him to "adopt . . . a healthy skepticism of publicity handouts, especially his own."

George Rosen, writing for *Variety,* was cautiously upbeat: "NBC on Monday (14) preemed its widely ballyhooed 7–9 A.M. *Today* television show, trailerized as a revolutionary concept in TV programming, designed to bring to the waker-upper a camera display of his morning newspaper, plus all the supplementary magazine-feature attractions. That it's novel, ambitious, and charts a new step in NBC's continuing quest for fresh patterns, there's no denying. In fact, radio in its most bullish days never dared venture into such gargantuan coin-splurging avenues of unorthodox programming."

Gould commended Garroway for his ability to "personalize the presentation and bring to it a human equation." Reaching into the future, he added, "This is lofty programming in the overall TV scheme;

even anticipating a day when early morning commuters will have access to the receivers on trains. It merits that kind of viewer and sponsor acceptance."

Unfortunately, advertisers failed to look into the same crystal ball. On the first broadcast and for weeks after, *Today* had but a single advertiser: *The Kiplinger Letter* was utilizing the show to introduce its *Changing Times* newsletter. While nationally *Today* was a tough sell, locally it was a different story, thanks to another Weaver innovation. In an effort to coerce reluctant affiliates to carry the new programming at an hour when most of them were still asleep, Weaver gave up five minutes of each half-hour segment to the affiliates to present local news and weather. During that time period, the local stations were permitted to sell their own advertisements, an extremely lucrative marketing tool with which Weaver could bargain.

By the end of week number one, the major players in this "revolution" were tired, irritable, and licking the wounds of their negative reviews—all except Garroway, who was somewhat praised by the critics and was doubly fortified by "The Doctor." Weaver, too, ended the week on a high—not so much because the show was a success, but more for having made it through "T-Day" plus four with his ensemble still in reasonably good shape.

Ever the memo writer, Weaver took to his typewriter once more. His own review of the series waited for his team on Monday morning. "You have done well in your first week," Weaver wrote. "I have just read through a large assortment of fan mail, most of the critical press reviews, some inter-department information on the subject, and what I can find of the reaction from the stations.

"As usual, the public, in part at least, has sensed what we are trying to do for them; while the critics find us preoccupied with the miracles that the public wish. The recurring 'mountains of labor and mouse emerges' note from the critics fails to realize that we bring mice to people who have only heard of mice hitherto, people whose letters thank us for showing them at last mice, for giving them a new horizon where mice will be commonplace. All this, before the fact that in addition to mice, we are and shall be bringing elephants."

Admitting he wasn't totally pleased ("we are far from doing it right"), Weaver pointed to the remote feeds in particular as an area that needed immediate help. "An interview should have a point," he declared, reminding everyone that a call to London to request a record was a call wasted.

The weeks ahead saw the expected shakedown of staff and equipment as awe gave way to familiarity and the *Today* show became less a three-ring circus and more a reliable source of morning news and information. Each week, the set became more refined as pieces of equipment originally placed out in the open were either eliminated or relegated to an off-stage position. And although the ratings for the program weren't rising in any official way, the crowds lining the windows of the Johnny Victor Theater became a daily reminder of *Today's* increasing popularity with viewers.

In the first weeks of the show, the all-male trio of Garroway-Fleming-Lescoulie was joined by a woman, Estelle Parsons. While she would later go on to win an Oscar for her portrayal of Blanche Barrow in *Bonnie and Clyde,* the then-struggling actress landed her first job in New York on the *Today* show as a production assistant at $75 a week. Her job was to phone the U.S. Weather Bureau in Washington, D.C., and relay weather forecasts to Garroway.

Although initially she was seen only in the background of the set, Estelle became a valuable asset to the on-air team, providing not only an attractive alternative to the all-male visages, but some clever and witty ad-libs as well. With increasing frequency, Garroway would reach a point in an interview or segment and call across the stage, "And what do you think of that, Estelle?" Reliably, the woman who later became known as the first Today Girl would shout out a reply, laced with charm, from the female perspective.

Soon, Estelle became a permanent fixture on the set, writing in her distinctive left-handed scrawl the weather in cities across America. It was snowing in Cleveland, drizzling in Kansas City, sunny in Los Angeles, foggy in Miami, and windy in Honolulu.

As the months passed, she took on more assignments, both in

and out of the studio. During the summer, she was even assigned to cover the presidential primary campaign trail of Senator Estes Kefauver, then famous for chairing the Senate committee investigating organized crime. Although Kefauver failed to gain the Democratic nomination, which went to Chicago's governor, Adlai Stevenson, Estelle Parsons entered the television history books as the first female political reporter.

Parsons also inteviewed Eleanor Roosevelt at New York's La Guardia Airport in the rain. The interview was so well received that the former First Lady was invited into the studio, and, again, Parsons was tagged for the assignment. Roosevelt, unused to the early hour, fell asleep on the air in the middle of her interview, only to wake with a start when Parsons prodded her with a follow-up question. Soon Parsons's salary escalated to $1,000 a week at a time when the average national income was $3,850 a year.

Despite her success, Parsons was forbidden to venture into exclusive Garroway territory—advertising. Amazingly, Garroway had the ability to sell anything. From underwear to garage-door openers, lawn sprinklers to fish food, he massaged viewers with his dulcet tones and reassuring gaze through horned-rimmed glasses perched just so. He moved like a cat through a maze as he maneuvered his audience from interview to commercial with never a hint that he was breaking stride. A conversation with a noted anthropologist gave way effortlessly with the move of a camera to Garroway's line "Of all the earth's inhabitants, man is the most likely [pause] to take a station break [pause] and we take one [a long pause as the camera moved in tight] right now."

For Weaver, Garroway became the essential pitchman: he not only delivered the goods on the air, but journeyed from advertising agency to advertising agency selling the show in person. Garroway spent many afternoons that first year accompanying Dick Pinkham to top firms along New York's Madison Avenue. Pinkham, a former newspaperman, had replaced Abe Schechter as executive producer early on in production and was handed the responsibility of getting some heavyweight advertisers into the *Today* line-up.

Garroway and Pinkham routinely delivered bags of unopened

Today show fan mail to the ad men and watched as they opened letter after letter, most praising the new program. However, although the public was obviously impressed, the advertisers remained reluctant to jump into something as new as early morning television.

Among the first national sponsors of note was *Time* magazine, which used the show to build its subscription base. Ironically, it was *Time* that, when discussing *Today* in print, continually referred to Garroway as a comedian, a tag that annoyed him thoroughly. "When was the last time I told a joke?" he questioned. In fact, Garroway went to great lengths never to make it appear that he was even mildly amused by the carnival continually swirling around him. Whether introducing Miss Concrete Block or Miss Dill Pickle, Garroway was the epitome of decorum, effusing graciousness without the slightest hint of any giggle lurking beneath his pursed lips. "Thank you, Miss Butter," he concluded one such interview. "For your beauty [pause] and your butter [pause], we are all very grateful." Without missing a beat, Garroway then moved across the studio and into a commercial for a pancake mix, asking his female viewers just as sincerely, "Ladies, did your pancakes fail to rise? Just look at this pancake mix," as he dropped mix into a sizzling skillet.

By the time *Today* celebrated its first anniversary, it ranked as the most popular daytime news program, with a million and a half viewers. Advertisers began to see the value in its unique audience. "The man who gets up in the morning and turns on *Today* is a new man," said Weaver, pitching potential sponsors. "He's been brainwashed by Mother Nature. . . . He's ready for anything."

Perhaps. But not even the "new man" of *Today* could foresee the new regular who would become the biggest ratings grabber of them all. He was three and a half feet tall, was covered in hair, wore diapers, and was about to make his mark on America.

CHAPTER TWO

THE CHIMP AND THE QUEEN

*I*n the third week of January 1953, J. Fred Muggs entered an elevator at 30 Rockefeller Plaza holding the hands of his trainers, Carmine "Buddy" Menella and Roy Waldron. The former NBC pages–turned–pet shop owners had recently paid $600 for Muggs, a 10-month-old chimpanzee still sucking formula from a baby bottle, who was brought into NBC casting for what Menella and Waldron hoped would be an opportunity to appear on the *Today* show.

Staffer Len Safir, who was the first to spot the chimp, went ape— literally. Safir was so enthused by the chimp's prospects that he pulled Dick Pinkham from a meeting to see the baby anthropoid and pushed to have Muggs make an appearance on the show the very next day. Pinkham agreed that the bizarre juxtaposition of the intellectual Garroway and the primitive ape might intrigue viewers, but not even he could have predicted the chimpanzee's effect on the ratings.

Dressed in shorts, T-shirt, and a beret, J. Fred mugged his way around the set and found his fans among children in record numbers. Previously not a part of the *Today* audience, children now waited patiently for Muggs to make his daily appearance. Their parents, now captive viewers, were introduced to the show as well. Ratings grew weekly on the strength of the chimp's pull, and despite misgivings from the country's critics, J. Fred Muggs became a *Today* show regular and an overnight star.

"Len Safir made like a hundred million dollars' profit for NBC," Pinkham later remembered. "Len said, 'If we put him on every day, the kids will see this little monkey, and their parents will realize there's wonderful news on,' and that's why the ratings went up."

While the series was now seen in forty cities (it was only on in thirty-one when *Today* first debuted), advertisers still had not demonstrated confidence in the program. J. Fred Muggs changed their perception, for with the chimp's arrival, the *Today* audience did more than grow—it developed into a fan club whose early morning ritual included watching the *Today* show.

The fifteen or twenty minutes' viewing time anticipated by Pat Weaver had grown: studies indicated that both men and women were eagerly spending forty-five to fifty minutes each morning in front of the TV screen. The breakfast meal was served on rolling carts in the living room, where most television sets were located, and the first TV tables were created from available furniture.

Pat Weaver now began to concentrate on improving other areas of the NBC line-up and brought in programmer John Herbert to oversee *Today*. One of Herbert's first responsibilities was hiring a full-time ad man to represent the program: onetime magazine and movie salesman Matthew J. Culligan. Wearing his trademark eye patch—the result of a World War II injury—Culligan set about to convince the still-fickle Madison Avenue crowd that the *Today* show had joined cornflakes as a staple of early morning Americana.

At about the same time, Jim Fleming became the show's first regular to leave the broadcast. Fleming, who fancied himself a newsman of the highest level, was frustrated by the antics of J. Fred Muggs and disgusted by the animal's importance to the program. He was replaced in the newscaster seat by Merrill "Red" Mueller, who lasted only thirteen weeks before tiring of the morning grind. In mid-1953, another new face appeared on the set—Washington correspondent Frank Blair, who reluctantly moved to New York to join Garroway's team.

Blair originally had been brought to Washington, D.C., in early 1951 by William McAndrew, NBC's general manager in the capital, to host an upcoming two-hour early morning news broadcast. When the network began pushing *Today,* McAndrew's show was dropped and Blair became *Today*'s Washington correspondent.

Blair arrived in New York to find that the *Today* show had settled into a smooth routine, albeit one that still suffered from technical glitches and dropped phone lines. He was slightly unnerved by the way the show was televised, due to the limitation of network feeds. The 7:00–8:00 A.M. hour was seen only on the East Coast. The 8:00–9:00 A.M. hour, a continuation of the show for viewers in the East, was the program's first hour for Midwest viewers on Central Time. In order to fill the second hour in the Midwest, the cast continued to broadcast from 9:00–10:00 A.M., repeating the interviews and news that had been originally televised.

Had *Today* done nothing else, its ability to react to breaking news of the moment was enough to set it apart from its chief competition, NBC's News Division. Since the show was run by the programming division rather than news, the two departments were under no obligation to cooperate with one another, and usually did not. To cover the news beat, *Today* often sent its own correspondent, Paul Cunningham, who would jockey with NBC newsmen for position.

One story that grabbed the network's interest, as well as the country as a whole, was the coronation of Queen Elizabeth II in June 1953. Elizabeth's father, King George VI, had unexpectedly died, leaving his eldest daughter to ascend to the throne. All three American networks covered the coronation using audio coverage provided by the British Broadcasting Corporation as well as still wire-photos. *Today* went one step further. The program interrupted its coverage of the coronation with spot commercials for General Motors, and Dave Garroway involved J. Fred Muggs in the proceedings.

Typically rambunctious that day, Muggs jumped over chairs and provided excellent opportunity for laughter in the midst of an extremely solemn and dignified event. Adding insult to British ire, Garroway sat down next to the frisky chimp and, wrapping his arms around him, said, "Ah, don't you wish that you, too, could be a king in a far-off land where you originated?"

The BBC made a formal complaint to NBC, first pointing to a

gentlemen's agreement against the use of commercials. It didn't help that the car ads used phrases like "queen of the road" and "a royal carriage." BBC executives' outrage over the "chimp incident," as they labeled it, allegedly "set back British supporters of sponsored television."

In private, Garroway thought the entire brouhaha was hilarious. But after the appearance of a *New York Times* editorial calling attention to "programs that transgressed the bounds of good taste again and again," Garroway publicly announced on television that any lack of taste was purely "unintentional."

The following month, the *Today* show seized on another unexpected opportunity, this time to showcase former President Harry S. Truman midway through his daily constitutional. Truman had stopped to peer through the windows of the West 49th Street studio when he was spotted by announcer Tom Naud, who raced out to the sidewalk and spoke on live TV to the retired politician.

After some banter about his walking pace, Truman looked through the window and asked, "What's that fellow doing with that baby in there?" Naud admitted that the "baby" was J. Fred Muggs, and the "fellow" was trainer Roy Waldron. Naud prodded Truman to join Garroway on the set, further demonstrating the spontaneity of the broadcast. However, Truman's walking partner, performer George Jessel, reminded the former president that he, Jessel, was signed to another network.* Not wanting to offend his friend, Truman thanked Naud and refused his offer.

Promotional opportunities were created more from necessity than function. With fifteen hours of live television to fill each week, the *Today* show was a ravenous beast that devoured creativity, novelty, and the mundane in equal portions. Attempting to capitalize on its own growing popularity, the series staged the "First Annual *Today* Hole-in-One Tournament." Televised from Chicago's Tam O'Shanter golf course, it attracted thirty-six golfing legends, including the 1953 PGA

---

*At the time, America's "Toastmaster General" had just signed with ABC to star in *The George Jessel Show,* a half-hour variety show that aired on Sunday evening.

champ Walter Burkema, Julius Boros, Jim Turnesa, Earl Stewart Jr., Dave Douglas, and Skip Alexander, plus entrants from six foreign countries. A $25,000 award awaited anyone who hit a hole in one. While no one copped the top prize, a golfer named Jay Herbert (representing the Kahkwa Club of Erie, Pennsylvania) walked away with $2,000 for hitting a four-iron drive within four feet of the cup on the sixteenth green.

By the time *Today* turned two, in January 1954, it was grossing $5 million from ads based on a viewership base of 1,719,000 people. Word began to filter out from CBS that the network wanted some of the early morning business. On March 15, 1954, CBS debuted *The Morning Show* with Walter Cronkite in the anchor chair. The newsman, already a veteran at the network, was hosting the popular *You Are There* program for CBS on Sunday afternoons. Unlike the *Today* show, *The Morning Show* was created by the CBS news department. As such, the emphasis was on information more than entertainment, though a modicum of fun ribboned through the headlines with regularity, thanks primarily to the Bil and Cora Baird puppets that costarred on the program.

In an effort to steal J. Fred Muggs's thunder, and not altogether unsuccessfully, the Bairds' newest conceit, Charlemane the Lion, snuggled up to Cronkite. While Muggs was unpredictable, Charlemane was under the extraordinarily skillful and creative hands of the Bairds, as were an assortment of other puppet characters that danced and cavorted to popular records introduced on the program.

Hard news became the onus of Charles Collingwood, whose Rhodes Scholar breeding and impeccable attire lent the show an air of sophistication and a certain formal presentation that was lacking in the *Today* show. An electronic weather map, manipulated by weather girl Carol Reed, made Garroway's weathercast marking pen look archaic by comparison. CBS's studio even took NBC's street-level concept one step further. Broadcasting from Studio 41 within Grand Central Station, the camera panned across the growing commuter frenzy, giving the show a unique vigor and vitality.

On opening day, Cronkite interviewed from Washington via

split-screen Stephen A. Mitchell, the chairman of the Democratic National Committee, and Secretary of the Treasury Ivy Baker-Priest. *Variety,* in its review of the premiere, labeled Cronkite a "relaxed, smooth-as-silk salesman" and the "centrifugal force from which the proceedings stem."

While *Variety* judged the show "a winning entry in the wake-up sweepstakes," it nevertheless thought that the series was a little too close to the "complexion" of *Today* for its own good. *Variety* failed to note that for the first time, a CBS newsman read a commercial over the air-waves. In this case, Walter Cronkite delivered a pitch for the new R. J. Reynolds Winston cigarette. Removing a cigarette from the red-and-white package, Cronkite placed it in his mouth, lit it, and, smiling into the camera said, "Ah, Winston tastes good as a cigarette should."

Soon after the second hour of *The Morning Show* ended, Cronkite was called into a conference of CBS executives and advertising agency executives, who lambasted him with stern adjectives and equally harsh glares. When told that the correct slogan for the new cigarette brand was "Winston tastes good *like* a cigarette should," Cronkite informed the assembled group that their slogan was grammatically incorrect. The agents looked at one another as if Cronkite had lost his mind. He was never asked to read another commercial on the show.

One thing that Cronkite *did* take pleasure in reading was a tongue-in-cheek telegram sent over from the *Today* show. It read: ABANDON HOPE ALL YE WHO ENTER HERE and was signed DAVE GAR-ROWAY, JACK LESCOULIE, AND FRANK BLAIR.

With fifty-four stations carrying its program, CBS had all the support it could muster, outnumbering NBC's *Today* by six outlets. Even so, NBC's *Today* easily beat *The Morning Show* by more than a full rating point during its first month on the air. However, for *Morning Show*'s executive producer Paul Levitan (who went on to produce a decade's worth of Miss America and Miss Universe pageants) and news editor Av Westin (who would later re-energize *ABC News* in the seventies), their pride came not so much in ratings, but in producing a seam-less show—one without all the technical flubs that continued to plague their competitors at NBC.

CBS's management was far less gracious. Five months into the series's run, Cronkite was replaced. He learned about his dismissal not through an official network communiqué or meeting, but via a gossip column written by Jack O'Brien, a Hearst Syndicate reporter. "CBS has finally gotten wise and is replacing Walter Cronkite on *The Morning Show* with that brilliant young West Coast comic, Jack Paar," O'Brien wrote. Cronkite had been handed the column by a pale-looking Charles Collingwood after their broadcast.

Although Cronkite's dismissal was finally corroborated, hours would pass before he finally got a network executive to confirm the rumor. With the entrance of Paar into the morning race on August 16, 1954, *The Morning Show* became the property of CBS's Entertainment Division, putting it on equal footing with NBC's *Today*—or so they hoped.

For its part, NBC was busy making money on its morning entry. With commercials now going for $4,000 a minute, the network had upped its gross take for the year to $8 million. Sponsors began to trip over one another in an effort to become part of the morning explosion. John Crosby, not about to let up on his criticism of *Today*, commented in his column in the *Herald Tribune:*

You get the idea that [*Today*] has at least 100 sponsors. Along toward the middle of the second hour here in the East—the first hour in the Midwest—the commercials come roaring at you one after another.

Jack Lescoulie will mix up some Amazo, "the fastest instant-mix dessert in the world," the sight of which at 8 o'clock in the morning will make you a little ill. Then a girl on film palpitates at us to eat more Florida grapefruit if we want to avoid winter colds. And Steve, the Alka-Seltzer urchin, tells us how to get fast relief from headaches, and Arlene Dahl blinks her pretty eyes and whispers the virtues of Pepsi-Cola, and Garroway sells toothbrushes and demonstrates a detergent and shows off a Polaroid Land Camera and—oh, brother!

All the money didn't go straight to NBC. Garroway got his cut, of course. He had signed a new six-year contract that guaranteed him $2,500 a week plus a percentage of the profit—estimated to be equal to another $2,500 a week. (By comparison, J. Fred Muggs was making do on $250 for his five-day stint.)

In addition, Garroway had been given a second series, a Friday night half-hour variety aptly named *The Dave Garroway Show,* which was carried by eighty-six stations on NBC. Outside of work, Garroway was making his own headlines by escorting TV's queen of commercials, Betty Furness, to private dinner parties. She was rumored to have knitted him forty-seven pairs of argyle socks.

As for CBS's effort, *Variety* found *The Morning Show* to be an "okay 30-minuter compressed into two hours. Anyone staying with it beyond half an hour ought to have his noggin examined." *TV Guide* magazine found more to like in Paar's premiere week and gave most of the credit to the host himself. "Paar, the perennial summer replacement, finally seems to have found a network spot where he can hang out his shingle on a year-round basis." While Charles Collingwood continued to deliver the news, those surrounding Paar elsewhere were mostly new, including singer Betty Clooney, pianist Jose Melis, and Cuban bandleader Pupi Campo. Producer Paul Levitan was replaced by Ted Fetter and David Heilwei. Av Westin continued as news editor.

On February 28, 1955, the *Today* show finally arrived on the West Coast, employing "instant kinescopes" to provide the feed. This meant an increase in revenues not only for NBC, but for the profit-sharing Garroway as well. Seemingly content with his life and career, Garroway began to stay up beyond his normal 8:00 P.M. curfew and to regularly entertain at his Park Avenue apartment. Among his guests were friend Pamela Wilde, his producer Bob Bendick, and Bendick's wife, Jeanne. Garroway managed to prepare rather exotic meals from his tiny Manhattan kitchen, which one visitor called "barely bigger than a hot plate."

In the pantry at the end of the kitchen, Garroway had hung a birdcage. Inside was housed a ceramic head that was sectioned off into areas of thought, such as love, understanding, hate, and sadness. Despite his outward appearance of contentment and his claim that this was the happiest period of his life, some suggested—Pat Weaver among them—that those elements of his mind were constantly at war with one another.

"Dave was always courteous and seemed to be in control," Weaver said, "but there was always 'The Doctor' in his pocket, and he seemed to be using it now more than ever. When I questioned him about it, he dismissed my curiosity by offering me some to try. I was always suspicious of what was in the stuff and never took him up on the offer."

Weaver may have done well to accept the offer. As creator of *Today* (and later *Tonight,* hosted by Steve Allen) and president of NBC as a result, Weaver should have been viewed as the most creative executive working in television. But David Sarnoff, who as chairman of RCA had founded its subsidiary broadcast unit NBC in 1926, had a major problem with Weaver. He wasn't his son.

Sarnoff had several sons and wanted *them* to occupy the executive suites at "his" company. As a result, in late 1955, Weaver was booted up to the largely ceremonial rank of chairman and Robert W. Sarnoff became NBC's president, essentially ending Weaver's dominance in programming.

About the same time, Estelle Parsons left the *Today* show to pursue her acting career on Broadway (she later claimed she was fired), and was replaced by Lee Meriwether, Miss America of 1955. To the naive Meriwether, the "family" of males who surrounded her on the series were surrogate fathers (Meriwether's own father had died just before she won the Miss America crown). "I had just finished the Miss America tour," she said, "where men are not really allowed in your life and you always had a chaperone at your left elbow. . . . Suddenly, I was doing a show where I got up at 4:00 A.M., worked with twenty men and eventually a chimpanzee."

About the same time, CBS, lagging ever more dramatically in the ratings, cut *The Morning Show* back to one hour, running from 7:00 to 8:00 A.M. In the 8:00–9:00 A.M. slot, the network introduced a children's program titled *Captain Kangaroo,* starring Bob Keeshan, the onetime Clarabel the Clown on NBC's *Howdy Doody.* (Also debuting that same day, in the afternoon on ABC, was *The Mickey Mouse Club.*)

While *Captain Kangaroo* was an instant hit and went on to last into the eighties, *The Morning Show* languished. Jack Paar had been having a rough time with the series, bickering with CBS executives and finding fault with the crew. The ratings on the show were hardly on Paar's side, however (in fact, the ratings numbers actually rose while Paar was on vacation and a comic newcomer named Johnny Carson filled in for him). By June 1955, Paar had been replaced by John Henry Faulk, a country humorist who drew upon a seemingly endless supply of folk stories. Faulk lasted on the program only four months. The folk raconteur became a victim of the anticommunist crusaders who black-listed him for what they claimed were communist ties.*

In Faulk's place, the network introduced a comic named Dick Van Dyke as host while bringing back Walter Cronkite—this time to the news desk—who accepted the post against his first instinct. Cronkite would later say that it was a "question of gold over pride." Producing the show was Dave Garroway's best friend, Charlie Andrews, who had left the *Today* show and was called in to save what remained of *The Morning Show.*

One of Andrews's additions was a rotating weather girl, who each day brought a sexy surprise to the viewing audience. The running fillip was initially embodied by a woman named Deborah Douglas, who first modeled a Jean Patou gown before pointing to the weather map with more or less accuracy. Despite a review in *Variety,* which called the show "much improved," the program's ratings indicated otherwise.

---

*Faulk had been cited for "communist activities" by a group known as Aware Inc. When he was dropped from the CBS line-up, Faulk hired famed attorney Louis Nizer to represent him and sued Aware. CBS newsman Edward R. Murrow donated $7,500 to pay Nizer's retainer. The case took six years to be settled, and Faulk was awarded $3.5 million. The trial was subsequently dramatized as an award-winning TV movie titled *Fear on Trial,* based on Faulk's book about his experiences, and broadcast on CBS in 1976.

Andrews did bring to the broadcast a professionalism that had been lacking. He also convinced ex-*Today* show newsman Jim Fleming to jump over to CBS and *The Morning Show* and even hired a new writer to prepare material for him. Her name was Barbara Walters, and at age twenty-seven, in her first job in broadcasting, she was beginning a career that would eventually take her to all three networks.

Charlie Andrews seemed willing to try anything to pull up the number of viewers, including a three-week, on-air tryout of a "diving" weather girl named Ginger Stanley. It was Stanley's job to don a bathing suit each morning in January 1956, and leap into a tank of 94-degree water, marking up her weather map while breathing through a hose. By February, the tank was gone and so was Stanley. Ditto for Van Dyke, Cronkite (again), and Charlie Andrews, as CBS did a total housecleaning of the entire morning series.

In their place was Will Rogers Jr. (son of the folksy comic), who struggled with hosting the newly renamed *Good Morning!* Previously, Rogers had been an actor, a United States congressman, and a magazine publisher; he seemed ill-prepared for his debut, nervously approaching his material. Helping him smooth the way were veteran CBS newscaster Ned Calmer and weather girl Pamela Good. They were what *Variety* called "nice, pleasant people."

Nice as they were, however, the CBS show seemed tame compared to *Today,* whose viewers had learned to expect the unexpected from Garroway. One morning, while delivering one of his frequent monologues on life in the city, Garroway noticed a man dressed in a gorilla outfit through the studio window. He alerted his viewers and a cameraman to the gorilla, who, it turned out, was wearing a sign that read J. FRED MUGGS IS MY LONG LOST SON. Yet, as soon as the camera got the gorilla in a tight close-up shot, the beast turned his back and revealed another sign. This one screamed KING KONG—MILLION DOLLAR MOVIE—WOR-TV—ALL NEXT WEEK. Before anyone had realized it, the NBC network had given free advertising to New York's biggest independent station.

Perhaps more importantly and in character, when the cameraman attempted to block the shot and refocus, Garroway stopped him.

"No, no, no. Leave it on," Garroway instructed on the air. "We should have known better, but he tricked us fair and square, so they may as well get the plug."

The man in the gorilla suit was an actor named George Gathrey; he was hired by WOR publicity chief Dick Jackson to pull the stunt. So impressed was Jackson by Garroway's reaction that he invited the host and Muggs to plug *Today* on WOR-TV. It was an invitation that Garroway never accepted.

Occasionally, the drama on the *Today* show was produced by tragedy, such as on the evening of July 25, 1956. A little after 11:00 P.M., the Italian luxury liner *Andrea Doria* was broadsided by the Swedish-American liner *Stockholm* in the foggy waters just south of Massachusetts's Nantucket Island. Within hours, the *Andrea Doria* sank to the bottom of the Atlantic at a depth of 225 feet, taking forty-six of her passengers with her.

Early the next morning, Mary Kelly, a staffer and occasional reporter on the *Today* show, received word of the collision and talked her way onto the Coast Guard cutter *Evergreen*, which was heading out to the scene. When the cutter arrived off the coast of Massachusetts, it encountered the *Ile de France*, a cruise liner that had picked up the SOS call from the *Andrea Doria*'s captain, Piero Calamai. Kelly boarded the *Ile de France* and returned with the rescued passengers to New York.

As Kelly discovered, among those pulled from the Italian luxury liner was Hollywood film actress Ruth Roman, who had been traveling with her three-year-old son, Dickie. Roman had been separated from her child, now presumed lost at sea, and was hysterical. While doing her best to comfort the actress, Kelly happened upon another survivor who recognized her from her television appearances. The man had shot an 8-millimeter home movie of the listing *Andrea Doria* and gave it to Kelly for use on the *Today* show.

When the *Ile de France* finally docked in New York, Kelly buffered Ruth Roman from the onslaught of news reporters, offering her sanctuary in the *Today* show suite at the Warwick Hotel. Later that night, Kelly learned that Richard Roman Hall was safe; he had been discovered among the rescued who were picked up by the *Stockholm*. Although Roman was too emotional to appear on the *Today* show, Kelly made an on-air appearance herself, relating her story to Garroway and showing the exclusive *Andrea Doria* home movie.

Making the program all the more unusual was the scheduled appearance that day by Jayne Mansfield. The actress, who was yet to make her mark in films, was aware of the benefit of appearing on television. She was set to do a scene from George Bernard Shaw's *Caesar and Cleopatra* with Jack Lescoulie, and tragedy or no tragedy, was not about to give up her spot.

Across town at CBS, *Good Morning!* was faced with covering the big news story as well. Series producer Michael Sklar sent Barbara Walters to cover the disaster. The woman who would become cohost of *Today* in the next decade managed to prove her worth even as a newcomer. She convinced thirty survivors from the *Andrea Doria* to appear exclusively on *Good Morning!*

Even with its unopposed dominance in the market, the *Today* show continued to tinker with its presentation. Lee Meriwether, *Today*'s Women's Editor (as the Today Girl was briefly known), left the program to become an actress and was replaced by former big-band singer Helen O'Connell. Helen would occasionally lip-sync to some of her old hits and brought a touch of classy nostalgia to the program, but it didn't come without a price. A perfectionist in her presentation and appearance, O'Connell was particularly tough on the crew, which was already being pushed to the wall by the unpredictable behavior of J. Fred Muggs.

The chimpanzee, now five and a half, was becoming increasingly hostile to both Garroway and the show's guests, often biting the host and knocking over pieces of the set. According to producer Bob Bendick, "Muggs would jump up into the lights and tear everything to pieces. A chimpanzee when he gets older is an enormous beast. After a while, we couldn't trust him any longer." Even Garroway was given to taking swats at the animal when the camera was turned off.

When the animal knocked the March of Dimes poster child off of her chair with a powerful backhand to the head, the producers replaced him with a new chimp—Kokomo Jr. Muggs's trainers, Waldron and

Menella, were outraged at the chimp's firing and filed a multimillion-dollar suit against NBC and Garroway that was later settled out of court.

While NBC issued a formal release that J. Fred Muggs had "decided to terminate his contract with the *Today* show in order to extend his personal horizons," they had anticipated a public outcry. In the four and a half years he had been on the program, Muggs had traveled worldwide to open supermarkets and shopping centers, made public appearances at zoos and conventions, and rivaled Garroway himself in fan mail. By the time he appeared on his final broadcast, Muggs was earning upwards of $1,300 a week, only slightly less than Helen O'Connell.

TV Guide seized upon the opportunity and, tongue planted firmly in cheek, offered some editorial advice to *Today*'s producers on how to keep Kokomo from turning into another raging Muggs. "First, he should never be permitted to see his ratings," said *TV Guide*. "Second, he must not be given an opportunity to ad-lib or to deviate in any way from the script. Our third suggestion is that his salary should be banked by his manager, that Kokomo should be given a weekly allowance for bananas and other goodies, but that he should be excluded from all salary negotiations."

Mr. Kokomo had a tough act to follow and never managed to recapture Muggs's popularity. In his book *The Today Show,* Robert Metz wrote: "Mr. Kokomo . . . was to Muggs what a tank town bum is to Muhammad Ali. During his short reign, Kokomo never hit the newspapers—even those provided for his pit stops."

Regardless of its problems, the *Today* show had the now-wavering support of NBC, which was far more than *Good Morning!* received from its network. Although the CBS entry managed to equate itself well in covering the news, it lacked the spontaneity of *Today;* it lacked a host as unique as Garroway; and it lacked many viewers. Now broadcast from a small set hidden far away from the public, *Good Morning!* had almost no budget and was competing with a show that had its network's unlimited resources. Ultimately, CBS executives were unwilling to throw more money into a losing enterprise. The network canceled *Good Morning!* and on April 5, 1957, officially abandoned early morning programming altogether, leaving the *Today* show uncontested once more.

By this time, even the most reluctant observers were forced to admit that *Today* had altered America's morning viewing habits. The network had expanded to 132 stations, all of which were eagerly carrying *Today* and benefiting from its continuing five-minute local cutaways for news and weather.

Yet as good as things seemed on the surface, the reality at NBC was altogether different. For one thing, Dave Garroway had married his frequent dinner guest, Pamela Wilde. What should have been a cause for the *Today* host to celebrate became instead another unnerving issue, as Garroway clumsily attempted to cope with a wife who was often more depressed and paranoid than he was.

Pamela Wilde was the daughter of a Hollywood movie executive. She had spent most of her growing years in Paris, where she eventually met and married the Marquis de Coninck, who fathered her first two children. Prior to her marriage, the waiflike woman had a brief career in the ballet and later as a stage actress (including a role in the 1946 Broadway production of *Lute Song,* starring Yul Brynner).

Garroway was first introduced to Wilde in 1954 at the Mount Kisco, New York, home of producer Billy Rose, and while it may not have been love at first sight, he was said to have been pleasantly amused by her ability to make polite conversation. After their marriage on August 7, 1956, the couple moved with her son and daughter into a brownstone on East 63rd Street near Madison Avenue, where an increasingly paranoid Garroway had a bomb shelter installed in the basement.

Always suspicious of communist activities, Garroway had convinced himself and anyone who would listen that there was a serious chance of a Russian nuclear attack on Manhattan. As a result, he stocked his bomb shelter with food and water and kept a loaded rifle in the corner to fend off any unwanted visitors who might try to crash his survival party.

As his nuclear neuroses grew, Garroway took to spending more and more time with his classic cars, "The Doctor" as his only company. On the set, he was becoming increasingly difficult to handle, the result of a nagging conviction that he was losing his appeal to the average American. Since Garroway had never been able to determine exactly why his fans considered him a star, he was unable to stop what he saw as his waning popularity. Adding to this paranoia was the loss of Pat Weaver, who suddenly resigned as NBC chairman after a disagreement with David Sarnoff over the activities of his son Robert. Garroway felt that his mentor had deserted him, and he vainly tried to replace Weaver, primarily with *Today*'s staff writers.

While the world continued to see a mellow and nostalgic, if slightly eccentric, friend on the air, there was little "peace" for the man who daily held up his hand and signed off with that single word, palm turned toward the camera. He feared the uncertainty of the world around him, a changing place that put a premium on the fast-paced and the hip and wrapped it in the parlance of rock and roll.

On January 7, 1958, Nelson Rockefeller appeared as a guest on the show, reporting on the growth of the Soviet military. A report published by the Rockefeller Brothers Fund predicted that the Russians would gain military supremacy of the world within two years if the United States did not act to circumvent it. As an indication of Garroway's own concern over the matter, he offered to send out copies of the report to any viewer who wrote in and requested one. The network was bombarded with responses; over two hundred thousand letters were eventually received.

In March, Garroway invited Leo A. Hoegh, the administrator of the Federal Civil Defense Department, on the show to alert Americans to get a "preparedness card," a pamphlet that gave information on how to survive an atomic attack.

Americans were drawn into the nuclear scare willingly. The specter of annihilation was very real given the heat of the Cold War, and those on the set of NBC's *Today* knew that many members of its early morning audience actually tuned in each day to find out if "it" happened—"it," of course, being an attack by the Russians. The timing was near perfect. With a recession souring the economy and the bite of taxes stinging more than ever, the Russian threat was perfect fodder to take viewers' minds off of their own problems. *Today* producer Jac Hein capitalized on the mood of the country and played into it.

Unfortunately, with the economy in a tailspin, the windfall advertising boom the show had benefited from began to evaporate. By the end of 1958, what was a $10 million gross was now cut by more than half. In an effort to recoup costs and return *Today* to some position of profit, NBC readjusted its policy of allowing affiliates to keep all the dollars from ad sales in the local breakaways at five minutes before each half hour. To make up for pulling dollars from the pockets of its local stations, NBC gave them four one-minute spots within the course of the two-hour broadcast. To cue local stations, Garroway would announce the now-familiar line, "This is *Today* on NBC."

Other changes were occurring as well. With videotape technology now replacing kinescopes, on October 6, 1958, the show dropped its third hour (shot live for the Midwest and West Coast) and replaced it with video of the two-hour broadcast. (Even with this change, however, half of the country was still watching part two ahead of part one, a concession to tradition.)

When Philco, the television manufacturer, complained about RCA's unfair competitive advantage—its sets were seen on television in the background of the RCA Exhibition Hall—NBC's parent company advised the network to make other plans for studio space for the *Today* show. As a result, NBC moved the broadcast upstairs in the RCA building to the windowless but larger Studio 3-K.

Studio 3-K was the most modern studio of its time, with more electronic gadgetry, rear-screen projection, elaborate lighting, and a "sponsor area" for doing commercials. Among the guests on the show during its first week in Studio 3-K were Jackie Cooper playing jazz, Gypsy Markoff playing the accordion, and thirty debutantes on their way to the Versailles Debutante Ball in France.

Charles Van Doren, the scholar and educator who had won big bucks as a contestant on NBC's *Twenty-One,* joined *Today* regulars as the resident wise guy. He was promptly pulled aside for esoteric conversation with Dave Garroway, who liked to "explore and extract" bits of trivial information from the egghead. Doren's duties on the show included reading classical literature and poetry, and he approached his role with an energy that quickly managed to build him his own legion of fans. Toothy actress and frequent game show panelist Betsy Palmer also joined the regulars, replacing Helen O'Connell as the Today Girl, and was periodically reduced to tears by the erratic behavior of Garroway, who one day collapsed in her arms.

The host was now seeing poltergeists in the basement of his house and confided to several members of the crew that ghosts were playfully rearranging his tools each night. Garroway was also convinced that he was being targeted by the communists for extinction and placed microphones in the mouths of the stone gargoyles that stood watch on either side of the front door to his brownstone—all the better to listen to the conversations of passersby who, he remained convinced, were plotting against him.

In October 1958, Garroway took an extended leave of absence from the program for what his doctors labeled "physical exhaustion." He did not return to the program until November 24, when he walked back on to the set wearing a black homburg, swinging a cane, and smiling ear to ear. For a moment, it appeared as if the old Garroway was back.

"I've missed you," he told the audience. "Been away a long time. But I got a lot out of the past month. I got to know my children. I met my wife again, and I didn't meet myself coming home. I read a lot of books I never thought I'd get the chance to read and I found out something really important to me. I did a great deal of nothing. I filled up my days with nothing and I found that I wasn't cut out for 'nothing'— so let's get back to work."

In April 1959, the show went to Berlin for a series of segments that *The New York Times* labeled "outspoken and illuminating." Called the "Berlin Reports," the features were produced by Bob Bendick and were reported to have "inspired the democracies and their citizenry to the crisis confronting West Berliners."

In a traveling mood, the entire show and its regulars went to Paris at the end of the month, causing even the most sophisticated Frenchmen to stop and perplex at the spectacle. It wasn't so much the allure of show business, or even the thought of being caught on American television that challenged their senses. It was the sight of Dave Garroway tasting the finest in pressed duck offered by the maître d'hôtel of the Tour d'Argent—or, rather, what happened next. Without missing a beat, the host lumbered across the room to face a handsome chafing dish in which water was boiling. Using silver tongs and with arms akimbo, Garroway carefully withdrew a swatch of DuPont nylon carpet from the bubbling liquid and extolled the virtues of its nearly indestructible fiber. On another show, while walking down the famed Champs-Élysées extolling France's military victories, he paused beside a nearby table to demonstrate the latest Presto pressure cooker.

Such live commercials were taken in stride by *Today*'s regular viewers back home, with the exception of members of the National Association of Broadcast Employees and Technicians (NABET), who called a work stoppage when word reached them that French technicians were used in the recording of the Paris footage. On Monday, April 28, 1958, the *Today* show failed to air as NABET crews pulled the plug on the broadcast for its entire two hours. The program was eventually shown the following day, with supervisory personnel handling the technical aspects of the network signal.

The NABET strike created by *Today*'s Paris adventure lasted seventeen days. Critics were quick to point out that NBC may have had cause to question whether it was all worth the effort. *Daily Variety* reported that "buffs of travel shows won't find much to cheer about in this Parisian peregrination." Among the guests on the show were Brigitte Bardot, Jacqueline Joubert, Miss TV of France, and Miss Blue Bell, whose dancers formed the kickline at the Lido de Paris.

Once back on local soil, the *Today* show attempted to give the impression that it was business as usual. However, events suggested otherwise. Garroway, who was stressed to the point of immobility, refused to budge on issues until his demands were met. The exact necessity of the moment was immaterial since his fussing was accommodated without question. By this point, the host had the power to hire and fire at will everyone—from the executive producer to the custodian who cleaned the private bathroom in his office. Not wanting to lose their jobs, most of the *Today* staff spent as much time humoring Dave as performing their jobs. That included producer Bob Bendick.

Eager to preserve what remained of Garroway's fragile mental health, Bendick decided to end live production of the *Today* show and replace it with a taped version prepared on the afternoon of the previous day. When NBC released the news to the press, it was accompanied by formal statements that the afternoon taping of the program would open up the scope of available guests.

"There are more things happening at four in the afternoon than at seven in the morning. We'll be able to cover many stories that we could not do before, including activities on the West Coast," Bendick attempted to explain. What no one was mentioning was the fact that for years the show had filmed interviews as talent became available. Mary Kelly and others had gone on location and interviewed celebrities, who answered questions, appropriately dropping in Garroway's name as if responding to him. On the air, Garroway would ask the question; through split-screen, it appeared as if he were talking directly to the stars.

Bendick's explanations to the press notwithstanding, it was Garroway's shaky emotional condition that was at the root of the switch away from live production. Yet not even the safety net of tape was enough to prevent the truth from becoming evident on the air. For fans of *Today,* the real-life drama was only beginning to unfold.

CHAPTER THREE

THE BREAKDOWN

*C*harles Van Doren had won $129,000 on NBC's primetime game show *Twenty-One* by unseating the current champion, Herbert Stempel. Van Doren struggled through question after question, haltingly, his face skewed in perplexity, his popularity rising with each grimace. Having converted his *Twenty-One* victory into a television career, he made several guest appearances on a variety of programs before being signed as a regular on *Today*. Van Doren's celebrity on the program, evident from his first appearance, grew to the point at which he filled in for Dave Garroway when the host went on his summer vacation in 1959.

After his defeat on *Twenty-One,* Herbert Stempel publicly accused the game show of being rigged, claiming that Van Doren had been supplied with the answers to his questions. While executive producers/creators Jack Barry and Dan Enright chalked Stempel's complaints up to "sour grapes" and Van Doren emphatically denied any wrongdoing, Stempel persisted.

At first with quiet determination, then ultimately with loud resound, Stempel pushed his message to a New York grand jury and subsequently to a special House subcommittee investigation. However, *Today* fans loyally supported Van Doren, and in October 1959, Garroway himself went public. Unequivocally defending his coworker in an on-air statement, Garroway wept as he described the aspersions cast on his colleague.

Unfortunately that same day, Garroway and producer Bob Bendick learned that Van Doren—his conscience now getting the better of him—had written a letter to NBC admitting that he had, indeed, been given the answers to questions on *Twenty-One*. Although Garroway had time to pull his statement of support out of the show before it was broadcast the following morning, both he and Bendick thought it best to allow *Today* to run unedited.

NBC suspended Van Doren on October 8, 1959. On the morning of November 3, he was fired from the network for his role in the cover-up. Garroway again felt compelled to make an on-air statement and that same afternoon delivered a highly emotional testimonial to his former colleague. Stating that Van Doren had "wronged himself," Garroway added that he still felt "warmly" toward the game show winner. Suddenly, overcome with emotion and tears, Garroway broke down on-camera. "What more do you want me to say? I can say I'm heart-sick."

The show was abruptly cut off and went awkwardly to a commercial break. As pandemonium broke out on the set, a hysterical Garroway walked out of the studio. Jack Lescoulie finished the last half hour of the broadcast, stating simply that Garroway was "too overcome" to continue and had gone home. Amazingly, Bendick made the decision to run the tape, complete with Garroway's on-screen breakdown.

NBC executives were fully aware of Garroway's increasingly unpredictable emotional condition. They also knew that part of *Today*'s popularity hinged on that very instability. Viewers never knew what Garroway might do or say on the broadcast, and the more erratically the *Today* host behaved, the more they enjoyed the show.

Florence Henderson, who became the fifth Today Girl just after the Van Doren incident and later went on to greater fame as Carol Brady on ABC's *Brady Bunch*, quickly learned about Garroway's impulsive behavior. One of her first assignments was to model the latest fashion in rainwear, which she did, twirling an umbrella and offering a rendition of "Singin' in the Rain." Suddenly, midway through the song, a stream of water poured down on Henderson, who was only partially protected by the umbrella. At the song's end, the camera panned up to find Garroway standing on a ladder, reading a book and holding a garden hose aimed in Henderson's direction.

Henderson, whom Garroway himself described as having "an indefinable quality of awareness," didn't get flustered in dealing with the increasingly difficult host—although she did nearly run him over while attempting to demonstrate a toy car during a taping one afternoon. She proved to be an attractive and agile foil for Garroway and eventually handled location pieces and interviews for the show, not always with universal success. On one occasion, she was assigned to interview a Japanese author about her book on floral arrangements. After Henderson asked her first question, the woman simply smiled and said nothing. As the one-sided interview progressed, it became obvious that the woman didn't speak or even understand English. With the laughter of the crew in the background and precious little else to do, Henderson paged through the book, showing photos of the exotic arrangements.

In early 1960, Henderson decided to concentrate on stage work and was replaced as the Today Girl by Beryl Pfizer, a journalist whom Garroway once spotted on a bus and declared to be the "perfect female." Garroway loved the way Pfizer moved across the set when she arrived one day to audition. "Gossamer and ethereal" was the way he put it; the next day, she was hired.

Pfizer seemed to have a calming effect on Garroway. The Master Communicator would stare at her as if in a trance, and at times was caught on-camera in mesmeric enchantment. Lulled into a false sense of security, Bob Bendick decided to press his luck and take the *Today* show on the road one more time. The chosen spot was Rome, complete with ancient splendor. Unfortunately, Bendick elected to send Jack Lescoulie, not Beryl Pfizer, to join his host.

At first things went smoothly. Garroway took viewers on tours of the Appian Way, the Via Veneto, the Colosseum, the Piazza del Popolo, and the Spanish Steps. The show was even shot inside the Basilica at the Vatican, and on Good Friday, April 15, 1960, Americans were treated to a rare glimpse of the interior of St. Peter's Cathedral.

One highlight of the week took place at the Forum, where Garroway recited Marc Antony's funeral oration in front of Caesar's tomb as the sun was quickly setting below the hills in the west. Writer John Dunn attempted to direct Garroway, but the host wasn't in the mood to cooperate and began pulling rank. Frustrated, Dunn threw up his hands and threatened to pack up his bags and head back to New York.

Bendick, who was listening in on the conversation through headphones from the production truck parked nearby, approached Garroway in a rage. He lambasted the host for delaying the production as daylight was fading. Garroway became quiet and somber, saying only, "Okay then, let's get on with it."

Garroway's silence was the host's way of dealing with anger. Rather than scream at Bendick, Garroway became unnaturally docile; he would find a more appropriate time to handle his feelings. That moment came a little over a month later in Los Angeles, where Garroway was covering the 1960 Democratic National Convention. In a chance meeting with NBC president Robert Kintner at the L.A. airport, Garroway vented his anger with Bendick during the Rome shoot. He wanted Bendick fired. Kintner obliged. Right there in the airport's concourse, Kintner telephoned his office and informed his assistant that Bendick was history.

Bendick's dismissal occurred during a crucial moment in *Today's* history—a time of intense activity for the program. In addition to the Rome shoot, the series had followed presidential hopefuls John Kennedy and Hubert Humphrey through their political handshaking and stumping as they crisscrossed the country; provided an analysis of the results of the Wisconsin primary with political commentator Marvin Agronsky; featured a two-hour report on the racial problems in South Africa (complete with remote footage); interviewed Vice President Richard Nixon; and covered both the Paris summit and the national conventions.

Today's viewers were now more than loyal—they had come to depend on the show to provide them with an informative beginning to their day. In a critique in its June 11, 1960, issue, *TV Guide* equated the *Today* show to a "bosk where flowers bloom and maidens gambol in the dreadful wasteland of daytime network TV."

Into this place of outward idyllic play and internal frustration and turmoil stepped producer Robert "Shad" Northshield, who had worked at the *Chicago Sun-Times* and had produced public affairs programs for ABC. The daily dramas he faced at *Today* were both unexpected and unbelievable. Yet, Northshield picked up the saber of leadership and marched forward—sometimes blindly, always courageously.

Northshield had inherited a show that was all reputation. By now, some 11,500 guests had crossed the threshold of the *Today* studio; workers who had begun with the program were beyond caring. Garroway's mood swings and insecurities were searing the workplace with uncertainty, not only about job security, but also about his ability to get through even the most routine program. Jack Lescoulie had become so bored with the program that his bits were actually video suicide bombing missions of the most effective sort. (According to Thrya Samter Winslow, writing in *Variety,* "When Lescoulie does the interviewing, the program falls with an unbelievable thud—he has a way of draining the personality from even a seemingly robust individual—almost an art in TV dullness.") Northshield's first job was to boost morale and galvanize the cast and crew.

As he set about restoring order and a chain of command, Northshield gained the respect of Garroway, who saw in the producer a man with the creativity of Pat Weaver. Now wildly vacillating between the mellow blur of codeine and the frantic high of insecurity, Garroway needed to prove to himself and to NBC that he could be effective as something more than a "wake-up jockey." In his current contract, Garroway had a provision for a primetime special, and he immediately began to envision a program that would allow him to showcase his talents as a self-styled storyteller.

Unfortunately, in reality, Garroway was no longer able to summon the warmth that memory brings. His nostalgic reflections of the past were lost in a quagmire of mental confusion and emotional vulnerability. Garroway hoped that a well-written script might replace

what he was no longer able to bring spontaneously to the set and per-
suaded Northshield to work on the production. The producer, eager to
reinforce his own network position, accepted the challenge and
brought in longtime friend Andy Rooney to write the hour, a show to
be titled *Dave's Place.*

Styled as a souvenir of Rockefeller Plaza, and replete with all the
stories and legions that abounded there, Rooney gave *Dave's Place* his
touch of wit and offbeat sarcasm. However, while well written, the
script was impossible copy for Garroway to digest and he ripped it up
in a fit of frustration. Believing that writers from the *Today* show would
have a better grasp of his style, Garroway looked to his staff; eventually,
veteran scripter Bud Lewis wrote an acceptable draft.

Unfortunately for Garroway, the finished product was neither
well received nor critically acclaimed. If anything, it seemed to reinforce
his singular role in early morning programming. Additionally, Northshield allowed the special to run shamelessly overbudget—the budget
in this case coming directly from Garroway's pocket. Ultimately, Garroway's disappointment translated into a pink slip for Northshield,
who was dumped on the day after Christmas 1960.

While Northshield's new year began rather shakily, so too did that
of his replacement. Producer Fred Freed had come to the now-
renamed *Dave Garroway Today Show* from CBS, where he had produced documentaries, but was familiar with NBC production through
an earlier stint on the network's *Home* show. While he would later gain
fame for producing NBC's "American White Paper," at this moment he
was occupied with cleaning out and replacing much of the longtime
Today show staff. He was also running interference between the network and Garroway, who was renegotiating his new contract and
demanding an ever-changing list of conditions.

Although there were discussions of returning the *Today* show to
live production, Garroway's fragile emotional stability made that more
a concept than a reality. Now nicknamed "The Big Spooky" for his random and often unexplainable behavior, Garroway besieged Freed with

requests any time of day or night, even scrapping entire show line-ups only hours before deadline. Adding to Garroway's pressure were the episodes of severe depression plaguing his wife, Pamela. Under the care of Dr. Henry Horn, Mrs. Garroway longed to return to the days when her husband romanced and captivated her with stories of Chicago and Waikiki during World War II. But those days were lived now only in her quiet, solitary moments of reflection.

On Friday, April 28, 1961, Garroway was tinkering on one of his classic cars at his summer home in Westhampton, Long Island, having left his wife and children at home in the city, where he claimed rascal poltergeists continued to rotate his undershorts. Tuning a carburetor required a fine ear and Garroway listened closely to the sound of the antique engine. Ignoring the ringing of his telephone, he concentrated on adjusting a sticky set-screw. Only after he was satisfied that the engine was purring optimally did he pick up the phone and hear the news: his wife had committed suicide with an overdose of barbiturates. Pamela Wilde de Coninck Garroway was dead at the age of 33.

Although shaken, Garroway took his wife's death much as he had taken their marriage—without overt emotion. He took a week off from the program, but when he returned, his nerves were raw, his tolerance low. One day, on-camera, he lost his temper so violently that NBC president Robert Kintner was forced to make a public apology.

The *Today* show's newest writer watched all the melodrama unfolding without comment. She was young, attractive, energetic, and named Barbara Walters. Hired by producer Fred Freed on a thirteen-week trial basis at the Writers Guild's minimum wage, which in those days meant a couple of hundred dollars, Walters was initially assigned to work with "The Face." That was the nickname given to a tall, chestnut-haired model named Anita Colby, who was signed to do an insert spot sponsored by S & H Green Stamps.

Colby had a thick Boston accent, cultivated and performed with aplomb for effect. She was more than beautiful—she was smart, connected, and talented. Her first appearance on the *Today* show, on April 12, was remembered as much for Walters's contribution as her own. "Barbara had this marvelous gift. She would slave for hours perfecting a script that in turn would make me look good," Colby said. "Every detail had to be correct. If it wasn't, she would kick herself for her oversight."

Walters knew that she had only a few weeks to make her mark on the *Today* staff. After Pamela Garroway's suicide and the host's subsequent return to the program, every day was another drama of unpredictability. Renewing his attempts to negotiate a new contract and driven to prove his worth, Garroway insisted that the shows be produced live once again, in an effort to return spontaneity and excitement. However, the status quo would continue for several more weeks, until Friday, May 26, when Garroway lay down on the studio floor in front of a camera and refused to budge or do another show until NBC conceded to his demands and signed a new multiyear contract.

Given the uncertainty of Garroway's health and his vacillating behavior, an ultimatum was hardly welcomed. The network notified Garroway that his contract would not be renewed. In an effort to spare the longtime host any embarrassment, the network's official news release indicated that Garroway had resigned from his position in a letter sent to Robert W. Sarnoff and Robert Kintner, then chairman and president of NBC, respectively.

According to the release, Garroway intended to resign on October 31 or "before, should we agree to an earlier date." There was much praise of his contribution to the *Today* show and a suggestion that other productions with NBC were being discussed. In truth, no such discussions were taking place.

"This interruption in television work is in my mind simply a preparatory period to ready myself for a new and more effective effort in the future to make what contribution I can to peace," Garroway suggested. While stating that he regretted his resignation, he said that he had come to realize that for ten years, he had been doing all the talking. "I want to start looking, thinking, and listening to people," he said. "Even more important to me, I want to be the best father I can be to three beautiful and exciting children during a critical period in their lives. Our family needs each other now more than ever."

Coincidentally, as Garroway made his announcement of resignation, the current issue of *TV Guide* was singing his praises. In a review of *The Dave Garroway Today Show,* Gilbert Sildes wrote, "The triumph of the Garroway show is that it rises above more faults than you can count. And it is a triumph of character and temperament and intelligence—all Garroway's." Pointing to the grab bag that *Today* had become, Sildes gave credit to the host for making the series work as well as it did. "Over this, Garroway, who likes to appear owl-eyes and simple at times, presides with an easy skill. He seems always sympathetic—but you become quickly aware of one thing: no one puts any buncombe over." No one, except perhaps Garroway himself, who had succeeded in fooling the public yet again.

Dave Garroway's final *Today* broadcast aired on June 16, 1961. In an effort to limit the damage to the program caused by a change of hosts, NBC decided to turn the selection of Garroway's replacement into an on-air talent hunt. The four candidates for Garroway's host position were announced as John Chancellor, then the network's Moscow-based news correspondent; Edwin Newman, NBC's European correspondent; and Ray Scherer and Sander Vanocur, who covered the Washington beat. NBC News, long annoyed at not being in control of the *Today* show, promptly made a move to bring the program into its fold under the watchful eye of veteran NBC News chief William McAndrew.

John Chancellor got the nod for week number one of round-robin television, and his on-air audition was so successful that McAndrew decided to go with Chancellor almost immediately. For the news correspondent, the word that he had gotten the job was received as a mixed blessing. He loved the increase in salary—from $32,800 to $100,000 a year, but he did not love the thought of being compared to Garroway—a man who had been boxed, wrapped, and placed on a pedestal by every reviewer in the business.

Even *Saturday Review* magazine, long respected for its independence, firmly placed itself in Garroway's corner when it published an article by Robert Lewis Shayon. Shayon reported that Garroway had taken to sending copies of the book *Excellence* by John W. Gardner to friends as a goodbye token. He quoted a passage from the book in which Gardner states that we must all reach for self-discovery in an effort to be our best. "To interrupt a successful career for such a quest," said Shayon, "is an act of integrity. One hopes the medium will do a bit of questing of its own while he takes his hard-earned sabbatical. Yes or no, with or without added wisdom, television will need 'Dave Garroway Tomorrow.'" Perhaps. But what it got was a reluctant John Chancellor and a reorganized *Today* show.

Chancellor was born on the North Side of Chicago and was a desultory student. A high school dropout, he got his equivalency diploma while serving in the army. After the military, he became a student at the University of Illinois, but dropped out of that school as well. He joined NBC as a summer intern after having been hired, fired, and rehired at the *Chicago Sun-Times,* which he later quit.

Few who saw this newsman behind the desk that Garroway built could have guessed that prior to joining NBC News he had also worked on a tugboat on the Illinois River, an orderly in a hospital, a book wrapper at Brentano's, a dishwasher, a busboy, a waiter, and a loader of big rigs. When the *Today* show called, Chancellor's mother was the executive housekeeper at the Conrad Hilton Hotel in Chicago. His father had died years earlier.

Frank Blair, who had taken over the news desk in *Today*'s second year, was in for an even bigger surprise. He was suddenly pulled off the desk to replace Jack Lescoulie, who was pushed out by the boys in the News Division as "not one of us."* Blair was therefore placed in the awkward role of playing second banana to a stiff Chancellor, who was adjusting to his new role. Meanwhile, Edwin Newman, now out of the running for the host position, was thrown a bone and made *Today*'s official news reporter. If NBC had tried to pick a more strained, lackluster trio, it would have been hard-pressed to do so.

---

*The official NBC release at the time noted that Lescoulie had resigned, explaining that since the *Today* show was now being done live, Lescoulie would prefer to concentrate on taped projects.

• • •

In its first week as the "new" *Today,* the show struggled to cover the Berlin crisis, a Tunisian crisis, and a space launch. Producer Fred Freed was under so much pressure to deliver that he came down with chickenpox and was out of commission for a month and a half. When he finally was well enough to return to the program, he discovered that he had been replaced by Shad Northshield, who had been fired only six months earlier. Chancellor had worked with Northshield previously and begged him to return to the front line. This time, when Northshield agreed, it was on his own terms. When he returned to *Today,* he took a firm hold of the production.

One of the people to benefit the most by Northshield's return was Barbara Walters. Northshield had first met Walters during her short time at CBS's ill-fated *Morning Show,* which he helped produce. Now in charge of revitalizing *Today,* he saw in Walters's energy and creativity an opportunity to enlarge the scope of the program.

To Northshield, Walters had the ability to become "every woman," and give a female slant to what had increasingly become a male-oriented news broadcast. Walters's first piece for Northshield—about biking in Central Park—was broadcast in early July. She introduced the segment from her seat on a two-wheeler.

The following month, Northshield sent Walters to Paris for three weeks to cover the fashion shows of couturiers Dior and Maxime, and on August 29, she was officially introduced by Frank Blair to the *Today* show audience. Walters's coverage of the fashion shows was upbeat, colorful, and professional. It was the first step of many for the aggressive, yet surprisingly naive Walters and another instant success for Northshield, who was succeeding in motivating his cast and crew.

Not even Northshield, however, could get John Chancellor to loosen up and become human. The newsman felt a responsibility to the News Division to be dignified and authoritative. On the air, he came off looking pinched and uncomfortable. Actually, Chancellor *was* uncomfortable. He hated being thought of as a "performer."

Pushed into doing publicity for the program, Chancellor tried his best to play the role of star and give the impression that he liked sharing the microphone with the Today Girl. "We feel that people will think that, since the news department took the program over, we're going to run a two-hour news show or a *Meet the Press* sort of thing," he told *The New York Times* in August. "I think there's a great value in having a pretty girl on the screen in the morning." After reading the article, Chancellor became nauseated.

Yet, the veteran newsman's predicament was easy compared with the one in which Frank Blair had been placed. As Jack Lescoulie's replacement, Blair was expected to do comedy skits. He vainly attempted to make himself into what his network required. However, the audience for the series began to disappear, and so did *Today*'s advertisers. The show's sponsors had already voiced their unhappiness when Chancellor refused to do commercials—one of Garroway's best talents. In the end, no one was satisfied—not the stars, the network, or the fans.

According to Chancellor, just weeks into his run at *Today* he went to see NBC News chief Bill McAndrew and demanded his release from the show. Chancellor said that McAndrew agreed to his request but asked him to keep it to himself until a suitable transition could be made on-air. Chancellor gave the news head his promise. Soon thereafter, however, McAndrew came down with hepatitis; it would be six months before he returned to his office at NBC. By that time the series had lost 25 percent of its advertisers and was limping along, a damaged image of its former self.

On Friday, January 12, 1962, the *Today* show celebrated its tenth anniversary. The big news of the day was that Dave Garroway, rested and seemingly in good spirits, returned to the roost with Jack Lescoulie. Also along for the ride were all eight former *Today* show producers: Abe Schechter, who had retired; Dick Pinkham, now at Ted Bates advertising agency; Mort Werner, who had moved on to head NBC programming; Robert Bendick, Gerald Green, and Fred Freed—all of whom produced for NBC News; Jac Hein, in independent production; and, of course, Shad Northshield. One thing was abundantly clear: the *Today* show ate up producers. And in a few months, Northshield would find that it was his head on the platter—once again.

First, however, Edwin Newman would face the firing squad in May 1962. Then, at the end of June, both Northshield and Chancellor got the NBC boot. Officially, Chancellor was given a chance to resign his post and actually stayed in the host chair until his successor arrived on the dawn patrol. Having had ample time to prepare for the on-air changes, NBC already had their newest *Today* show host under contract. They had given the nod to the announcer on *The Tonight Show*, an amiable man named Hugh Downs.

When he first heard about the possibility of being named the new host of *Today*, Downs had the normal reservations about the early hours. Yet, a move from the fringes as an entertainment announcer to center stage as the anchor of an NBC News–produced show was the type of lure against which the threat of bloodshot eyes could not compete. Downs accepted happily and needed only to get out of his contract with NBC's *Tonight Show*. As it turned out, it was a move easier said than done. *Tonight* was going through its own crisis at the time. Jack Paar had left the show the preceding April under a cloud of controversy caused when he took the show to Berlin just a month after the erection of the Berlin Wall. While there, Paar taped a segment in front of the Brandenburg Gate and, with American troops in the background, openly expressed his view of the situation. Under pressure, Paar resigned as host of *Tonight*, and Johnny Carson was hired to replace him.

Unfortunately, Carson—who was hosting the ABC game show *Who Do You Trust?*—was not able to end his own contractual obligations until October. Not wanting to leave *Tonight* with no familiar face, Downs was told to remain on until the end of August while a variety of guest hosts treaded water as temporary fill-ins. Then, in the network version of musical chairs, Ed Herlihy* replaced Downs as announcer on *Tonight*, while Downs replaced Chancellor as host on *Today*.

Downs's first outing on *Today*—September 10, 1962—was a low-key affair. The highlight of the program was a tribute to the new host, highlighting scenes from his home life with his family and his wife,

---

*Herlihy was *Tonight*'s temporary announcer until Ed McMahon joined the show with Johnny Carson on October 1, 1962.

Ruth. The writer and producer of the segment was Barbara Walters. The program would have a lasting impact on Downs and prove to hold the key to Walters's future.

By the time Hugh Downs turned up for his first day on the job, Al Morgan, the newest candidate to take over as *Today*'s executive producer, was already well established. Morgan had come to *Today* after a career that included writing for NBC's *Home* show, where he first worked successfully with Downs, who was the program's announcer. Morgan left *Home* to write novels, including the bestseller *The Great Man*, which he subsequently turned into a feature film starring Jose Ferrer.

Morgan later asserted that he returned to the TV "racket" only after serving up a list of "impossible demands" to NBC. "To my surprise, they said yes to everything, including an outrageous salary, and I found myself in charge of the show." As Morgan arrived, so too did Jack Lescoulie, back in for another run playing second fiddle. Frank Blair was happily reassigned to the news desk.

Beryl Pfizer, who had left the show as the Today Girl after six months, was replaced by Robbin Bain, whose single claim to fame was being a former Miss Rheingold. When Bain exited shortly after Christmas 1961, actress Louise King began a brief run in the job and was holding down the post when Morgan was named executive producer. At the time, King and John Chancellor were engaged in their own on-air, off-air battle of personalities, which Morgan actually seemed to encourage in the hopes of injecting some energy into the lagging morning show.

Morgan wanted to return spontaneity to the series, a quality that had been all but forgotten during Chancellor's heavy-handed news-oriented broadcasts. The first move Morgan made toward effecting the transition was moving the show back onto ground level and returning the series's backdrop to the "Window on New York." Since the old RCA Exhibition Hall continued to feature the company's television sets, an alternative site was found directly across 49th Street in the office of the Florida Development Commission.

Today inaugurated its new studio on July 9, 1962. Each morning the Florida folks would move their posters of oranges and sunshine, mannequins dressed in Day-Glo swimwear, and a live parrot named Jungle Jim into a storage room to make room for *Today,* replacing the props after the show had completed its 7:00–9:00 A.M. run. Although small, the space allowed fans and passersby alike to view the internal workings of the program and share in the on-air excitement.

With the show's studio space revitalized and its host and second banana in place, Morgan turned finally to the Today Girl position. Morgan realized the advantage of catering to females who might continue to watch the program long after their husbands went off to work and the kids were packed up for school. He saw the Today Girl as the perfect opportunity to get the kind of chitchatty family atmosphere back on the set and had the perfect candidate in mind.

Pat Fontaine was a weather girl from St. Louis who offered youth, charm, and a giddy enthusiasm that impressed Morgan. Hugh Downs was anxious to have input in the selection process and asked to meet with Fontaine before she was hired to get a sense of her personality and how well they might work together. While Morgan agreed and arranged to introduce the two over lunch, he neglected to tell his new anchor that he had already offered the job to Fontaine. As Downs tells the story, "Over lunch Pat let slip a revealing fact—how grateful she was to Al for locating a house for her in the New York area." Morgan's failure to bring Downs into the hiring process would set a tone that would continue for the next six years as each attempted to assert his control over the final look of the broadcast.

When Barbara Walters had heard about the on-air Today Girl opening, she applied for the position but was rejected by Morgan. He saw her as a talented writer but questioned her on-air personality and diction. Undaunted, Walters quietly continued to write and produce segments, waiting for her next opportunity to gain increased experience and airtime. That moment came in a period of national mourning, during coverage of the funeral of assassinated President John F. Kennedy.

Barbara had gotten her initiation into the Kennedy clan in March

1962, when she had convinced Shad Northshield to allow her to cover Jacqueline Kennedy's official visit to India. Originally planned as a small state visit, the national interest in Mrs. Kennedy soon turned the trip into a major production that lasted eleven days and covered three countries. Northshield was quick to give Walters the nod based on her enthusiasm, but as she set foot in India Walters realized that she was in over her head, with precious little in the way of resources at her disposal. Despite her promise to Northshield to gain a one-on-one exclusive interview with Mrs. Kennedy, Walters was faced with an impossible task. Not only had the First Lady specifically expressed her intention to do no interviews at all—save one with her dear friend Joan Braden, who had gotten an assignment to cover the trip from the *Saturday Evening Post*—but also there were a couple of dozen other reporters along on the trip, each eager for the same opportunity.

It was only by literally drawing attention to her inexperience and her need for help that Walters scored what was an amazing coup. Taking pity on the newcomer, the First Lady's social secretary Letitia Baldrige pleaded with Mrs. Kennedy on Walters's behalf and managed to score the reporter a few precious, private minutes with her. The resulting interview and Walters's on-air narration of it was both professional and entertaining. Her next meeting with Mrs. Kennedy, however, would be far less enjoyable.

The assassination of John Kennedy not only plunged the nation into emotional turmoil, it stretched the limits of the network news organizations to provide nearly round-the-clock coverage. All entertainment programming was canceled as television kept its vigil along with the country, bringing the tragedy into the homes of viewers across America and the world. On the day of the funeral, Walters was assigned to the Capitol's rotunda, where the body of the president lay in state.

As the White House entourage delayed making its way to the Capitol, the camera focused on Walters, who calmly and effectively filled viewers in on a variety of facts that seemed to come effortlessly off the top of her head. In actuality, Walters had researched, rehearsed, and carefully prepped herself for the exposure in front of millions of citizens who hung on her every word.

Several months later, with the same seeming lack of effort, Walters donned a bunny tail, ears, and a pink satin suit to present a report from inside the Playboy clubs at the height of their popularity. "It was the first time I knew she had a figure," Downs commented. Not only did Walters have one, she wasn't afraid to show it if it brought her some precious on-camera exposure.

By spring of 1964, it was obvious even to Morgan that Pat Fontaine was not working out on the show. Where he had hoped for easy conversation, Fontaine gabbed. According to Morgan, she was the "quintessential out-of-town personality." When word reached Walters that Fontaine was out and the search was on for a new Today Girl, she once again stood at the head of the line. Once again, she was rejected.

This time, Morgan searched the ranks of established movie actresses who could bring the same kind of fan loyalty and professional style that Helen O'Connell had previously brought to the job. His first choice was Maureen O'Sullivan. O'Sullivan, who had made her imprint in Hollywood playing Jane to Johnny Weissmuller's Tarzan, had returned to work in a Broadway play titled *Never Too Late*, and had impressed Morgan during a guest spot on *Today*.

Hugh Downs was on vacation when O'Sullivan was hired and only learned upon his return that, once again, he had not been consulted in the hiring of the Today Girl. Downs was livid at this maneuver by Morgan, who was no longer making any effort to hide his disdain for his anchor, openly referring to Downs as "the laziest man on television." Barbara Walters wasn't pleased by O'Sullivan's hiring either, yet she returned to the grindstone, doing the research and producing the copy that O'Sullivan would ultimately read on the air.

While giving O'Sullivan every opportunity to prove herself, Downs was continuously appalled by the actress's lack of television savvy. She infrequently drew on her Hollywood background to bring a unique element into the *Today* conversation, although when she did, the air became electric. During an interview with Irving Shulman, who had just written a biography of Jean Harlow, O'Sullivan became assertive and questioned Shulman's research and veracity. Based on her own personal friendship with Harlow, she contradicted several of Shulman's stories from the book.

Downs enjoyed the interchange, but those moments were far too rare, and the on-air relationship between Downs and O'Sullivan disintegrated into a strained partnership that saw little give and generous amounts of take on both sides. What neither Downs nor Morgan realized was that O'Sullivan was taking heavy doses of prescribed tranquilizers that were affecting her ability to concentrate. Before joining the *Today* family, O'Sullivan's husband had died. She went through an extended period of mourning under the care of a physician.

Finally, after only a few months on the air, O'Sullivan was fired. She got the news almost accidentally over dinner from an NBC vice president while covering the Democratic National Convention in Atlantic City. O'Sullivan was furious at the off-handed way in which she was dismissed and vented her frustration on any and all who would listen. In *TV Guide,* she described her role on *Today* as "asinine." She said, "It's not enough to sit there and smile every day with nothing to do. The show is simply no place for a woman."

Barbara Walters could not have agreed less. When she heard that O'Sullivan was leaving the program after only four months, Walters went to Morgan to plead her case for the third time in less than two years. This time, however, she had something she lacked on her previous pitches—Hugh Downs's support.

Reluctant to make another mistake, Morgan agreed to give Walters a chance. Although he was still unconvinced of her on-air presence, he knew that he could at least place the blame on Downs should Walters fail to make the grade. Yet, Downs knew something that Morgan didn't. He had watched Walters carefully during their time together and knew that no one would work harder to achieve success as an on-screen talent. Not even Downs could have predicted, however, the extent to which Walters would go to achieve fame and power, and the effect her debut would have not only on early morning television, but on women on TV as well.

THE LORD-KNOWS-WHAT

*B*arbara Walters had waited rather impatiently on the sidelines for over three years. Now that she had what she was quietly labeling "a chance of a lifetime," she was not about to waste the opportunity. She began to pull in favors and call up contacts in an effort to ensure her success.

Walters had grown up surrounded by celebrity. The daughter of Lou Walters, a nightclub owner and showman, her solitary childhood was one graced with travel and privilege. Yet, by the time she was about to assume her new role on *Today*, Barbara Walters was no longer "daddy's little girl." Through a series of bad business dealings, Lou Walters had lost most of his fortune, and his daughter Barbara took up the role as breadwinner in her family.

Unbeknownst to her coworkers, Walters was supporting both her parents and her mentally disabled sister, Jacqueline, who was living at home and working at Miami's Hope School. If NBC had only a passing acquaintance with Barbara Walters–writer/producer before her on-air assignment, the network was about to be introduced to Barbara Walters–TV personality in a major way. She had retained Ray Katz, a tough personal manager, to represent her, and Katz structured an initial deal that would set the tone for all future negotiations. At a time when the average annual income in the United States was under $6,000, Walters's salary was $1,000 a week.

Walters was married to Broadway producer Lee Guber and lived in a three-bedroom apartment on West 57th Street across from

Carnegie Hall. Yet, a lovely home and a high-profile marriage were hardly enough for Walters, whose career was of increasing importance in her life. Seemingly, no sacrifice became too great, no assignment too difficult. The end justified the means and, to Walters, having her face in front of millions of viewers each morning was everything she had hoped for and dreamed of.

No longer content to report women's features, Walters began to conduct celebrity interviews, using her contacts to seek out the rich and famous. She scored an exclusive interview with First Daughter Luci Baines Johnson, which opened the door for a subsequent interview with her mother, Lady Bird, as well as coverage of the Johnson sisters' White House weddings. Friend Truman Capote talked on the record. So, too, did Princess Grace of Monaco.

On location, Walters went to schools, parks, and hospitals. When New York's public health officials reported a 10 percent jump in the rate of tuberculosis infection, Walters filed a detail report from the Will Rogers Hospital and O'Donnell Memorial Research Labs at Saranac Lake, New York. Suddenly, Barbara Walters was everywhere.

Walters hired a public relations firm and proceeded to plan a media blitz. She wanted America to realize that she had arrived. *TV Guide* headlined her arrival: "I'M A LORD-KNOWS-WHAT." The point of the article was that the Today Girl of old was now merely a memory. "She isn't a 'star,' she isn't a 'celebrity,' she isn't a 'personality,'" *TV Guide* suggested. "As Barbara herself defined it in a hasty phone conversation with a researcher, 'Now that I'm a Lord-knows-what,' would you mind doing this little job for me?'" The article ended with the prophetic "If the viewer mail continues to be as enthusiastic as it has been, girl-reporter Barbara Walters might gradually grow from 'Lord-knows-what' into full-fledged morning star." And "girl-reporter" Walters had every intention of seeing that happen.

As Walters's publicity machine rolled into position, the *Today* anchor, Hugh Downs, was stunned into the realization that having opened the door for a coworker, he was now being eclipsed by the brouhaha surrounding her arrival. When *Life* magazine headlined BAR-BARA WALTERS OF *TODAY* SHOW LOOKS SHARP—AND IS EARLY TO RISE,

WEALTHY, AND WISE, featuring a large photo of Walters, with Hugh Downs in profile off to the side, the star knew he had to deflate some of the puffery, and do it quickly.

Barbara was instructed to turn down the burners on her over-heated publicity campaign; she obliged immediately. While she was only too happy to find herself quoted and exploited in the press, and was thrilled at being recognized by fans on the street, she knew enough not to upset the power behind the popularity—the network that made it all possible.

Although Walters was seamless on the air, off-screen things weren't quite as perfect. Her marriage was beginning to falter, due largely to the overwhelming amount of time required to keep her career growing and glowing. Not even the adoption of a baby girl, named Jacqueline after her sister, would slow her drive for fame. She hired a cook from Jamaica and a nanny from France. Miss Walters was a mama, if not exactly a hands-on one.

As her workload increased, her available time for family shrank, and international travel cut into her home life even more dramatically. The first television program broadcast from Europe via satellite on May 3, 1965, aired on NBC and featured Walters. "I can hardly believe I'm here," she gushed, beaming from Paris and the balcony of Yves Mon-tand's apartment on the Boulevard Saint-Michel. From his command post in Brussels, Al Morgan was in control of not only Walters's feed from Paris, but also Hugh Downs's in London's Westminster Abbey, Jack Lescoulie's from Holland, art correspondent Aline Saarinen's at the Forum in Rome, and Frank Blair's on the Capitol steps in Washington, D.C. Children from the various countries welcomed viewers in their native tongue with "Good morning, this is *Today.*"

The event was so significant that it was introduced by the Pope speaking from the Vatican, and was followed by the Changing of the Guard at Buckingham Palace. Because the guards rotated assignments on the hour, Morgan talked an officer assigned to the palace into drop-ping his rifle, effectively delaying the changeover of soldiers for the two minutes and ten seconds that were allotted to the Pope's address. Morgan later said that the soldier, whom he had met in a bar, was anxious to cooperate so that his regimen of the Palace Guard could be seen by his aunt, who lived in Nebraska. The aptly named Early Bird satellite brought *Today* live into Omaha and all across America, and the world's newspapers noted the fact.

Soon after the Early Bird launch, Senator Robert Kennedy was preparing to go on the *Today* show for an interview with Walters about his political future. As usual, the Florida Development Commission had moved its displays into storage to allow the *Today* set to occupy its "Window on New York." This day, however, Jungle Jim the parrot was left uncovered in a corner and decided to speak.

"What's your name?" the parrot asked.

"Robert Kennedy," the senator answered, absorbed in his notes.

"What's your name?" the bird asked again.

"God damn it, I won't tell you again!" Kennedy screamed, getting even more heated when he looked up and saw no one. Charging over to Barbara Walters, who was preparing to go on the air, Kennedy railed in fury, pledging never to do the show again. "You people don't know how to treat a guest," he said.

At the time, NBC had more pressing problems than Robert Kennedy. The network found itself in court defending its past advertising practices. In a New York State courtroom, John Andreadis was on trial, charged with false advertising. Andreadis, under the name John Andre, was the promoter of a product called Regimen, a weight-reduction tablet that was launched by Dave Garroway on the *Today* show.

"Now we'll meet Dorothy Bryce, another Regimen girl who dared to lose weight before millions!" Garroway had pledged, gesturing toward a somewhat slim mother of three from Westchester County, New York. Garroway was unaware at the time that Mrs. Bryce was an actress who was paid $17,701 by Andreadis to starve herself—losing twenty pounds in four weeks—and be weighed every Monday on the NBC series.

Smiling into the camera, the proud woman had responded, "Right, Dave. Here's my 'before' picture, one I'll never forget. . . . I was

173 pounds and size 18 before I learned about the Regimen Tablets way to lose weight. Millions saw me weigh in each week on the *Today* show as I lost 25 pounds in six weeks. . . . You know, reducing the Regimen Tablets way, I ate what I liked—just not so much. Actually left satisfied, on a fraction of the calories I use to eat, and pounds tumbled off."

Garroway, equally enthusiastic, had added convincingly, "Regimen Tablets! A completely new, clinically proved drug combination to help you reduce." Now, in court, the former *Today* host heard that two years before he had put his own good name behind the product, medical testimony before a congressional committee investigating the tablets had labeled them "worthless." Additionally, the federal post office had issued a mail fraud order against the manufacturer. Eventually, both the manufacturer and its advertising agency were found guilty of making false claims on the *Today* show.

Helping to clinch the case was footage of Jack Lescoulie grinning his toothy smile and adding, "Dorothy, you look sensational. How do you feel?"

"Wonderful!" Mrs. Bryce had responded. "And what a pleasure to be trim again. I can't praise the Regimen Tablets way enough!"

"You may not lose as much as Dorothy," Lescoulie had advised *Today*'s viewers. "You may lose more!"

In September 1965, the show once again lost its "Window on New York"—and its fans the opportunity to wave to the folks at home—as *Today* moved into Johnny Carson's old *Tonight* show studio, which was vacated when Carson moved with *Tonight* to Los Angeles. At the same time, NBC was moving into all-day colorcasts. To continue using the ground-floor studio space would have required the network to commit a quartet of color cameras to that studio alone. Unable to justify the expense, NBC executives moved *Today* upstairs in 30 Rockefeller Plaza, into a windowless yet fully equipped facility.

On the new set, even the most casual viewer could observe the competition between the on-air personalities. While Downs and Walters had developed an easy and nonthreatening rapport, Jack Lescoulie was beginning to feel left out. The man who had appeared on nearly every *Today* show (except during his one-year exile) was annoyed. He began to glare openly on the air. When Downs would toss him a line, instead of responding, he would just stare back with contempt.

When Lescoulie had returned to the *Today* show in July 1962, he had believed that his seniority would make him the star of the broadcast. As it became evident to everyone—including the insecure announcer—that he was far from central to the success of the program, Lescoulie became an angry, openly hostile man. The "Lescoulie situation," as Morgan called it, came to a head during a shoot in the U.S. Virgin Islands. For all its exotic appeal, the location wasn't well equipped for a shoot of *Today*'s magnitude. At one point the series's remote unit, which Morgan said was approximately the size of a "bus and a half," rolled off the deck of a tanker into the St. Croix harbor and blacked out the entire island.

It was a poor moment for Lescoulie to create a fuss. After discovering that he was spending more than anticipated, the announcer went to Tom Sternberg, *Today*'s unit manager, to demand more expense money. Sternberg, a Princeton graduate, was already juggling the budget to stretch the money allotted from the network and bluntly turned down Lescoulie. The announcer dashed off a heated memo to the NBC hierarchy with a blatant threat: if Lescoulie ever saw Sternberg on the *Today* set again, he would refuse to go on-air.

At this point in his career, Lescoulie was earning $175,000 a year. He was considered an expendable talent by many of the NBC brass, and written threats did nothing to improve his standing in their eyes. It was only weeks later, during a special three-hour *Today* broadcast, that Lescoulie made good on his promise. Arriving early, he noticed Sternberg talking to a cameraman. He immediately turned and walked out of the studio, leaving Downs to handle the entire broadcast on his own. When Lescoulie arrived at NBC the following morning, he was handed his discharge notice. To take his place, Morgan hired former baseball catcher Joe Garagiola, whose arrival heralded what many consider to be *Today*'s finest years.

Garagiola had a reputation as an all-around good guy. With bald head and twinkling eyes, the onetime play-by-play announcer for the

New York Yankees was hardly handsome. But he was affable and asked the kind of direct, knee-jerk questions with a truck-driver bluntness that endeared him to viewers and colleagues.

There was a genuine respect and affection within the Downs-Walters-Garagiola-Blair team, each talent adding a unique strength to the whole. Barbara Walters once remembered a oft-repeated Garagiola line: "There's no such thing as a good Amos and a bad Andy," adding, "We were kind to one another."

The on-air talent moved as a team, feeding one another; yet all four shined independently. Much to his credit, Hugh Downs allowed the others to share in his key light. He was, after all, the designated anchor of *Today*, a position that in the past had meant the ability to rule with a dictatorial authority. It was not so much that Downs didn't make his star status known. After hearing that Johnny Carson had a private bathroom in his office, Downs insisted that one be installed in his as well, despite the plumbing nightmare that developed as a result. For months his office was in disarray as engineers fretted over the most efficient way to bring water and drainage into the location.

Still, it was Downs's nonchalance that encouraged the on-air growth of Walters, and to a lesser degree, Garagiola. In return, they helped Downs in his areas of weakness, particularly during interviews, when he sometimes seemed unwilling or unable to move beyond any question that wasn't written in his script.

Downs occasionally did become surprisingly aggressive in his on-air commentary, and no more so than during the 1968 Democratic National Convention in Chicago. As the *Today* cameras recorded the images, demonstrators clashed violently with Chicago police on the streets surrounding the city's convention center.

America had been polarized by the Vietnam War and the deaths of its soldiers during the Tet offensive. President Lyndon B. Johnson had declined to run for another term and passed the scepter of authority to his vice president, Hubert Humphrey. Antiwar candidate Eugene McCarthy had challenged the vice president and the administration's military policies, setting the stage for the demonstrations that would shock most Americans, *Today*'s correspondents among them.

As the Chicago police attempted to quell the demonstrators by using tear gas and nightsticks, the remote staff of the *Today* show was caught in the resulting violence. Most suffered the effects of tear gas. Aline Saarinen was maced and struck. While Chicago's mayor, Richard Daley, went on NBC and labeled the demonstrators "terrorists" whose only purpose in coming to Chicago was to "assault, harass, and taunt the police into reacting before television cameras," Hubert Humphrey made an appearance on *Today* blaming both sides. Claiming to have been threatened with assassination "half a dozen times," Humphrey defended Mayor Daley by asking, "What is the Mayor of this city supposed to do about that? Every one of us were threatened and had to be under heavy guard. Now that doesn't make you feel very happy."

Uncharacteristically, Downs was so shaken by what he witnessed in Chicago that he read a prepared statement on-air that Al Morgan had written soon after the attack. He labeled the Chicago police force "far worse" than the term "pig" assigned to them by the protestors. In addition, he personally paid for food to be distributed to the demonstrators.

It was one of the few times that Downs and Morgan actually agreed on anything, and it would be the last. In September 1968, while renegotiating his *Today* contract, Downs refused to re-sign for another three-year hitch unless Morgan was fired. NBC executives calculated that it would be simpler to replace *Today*'s executive producer than its host and capitulated, unceremoniously dumping Morgan despite having just re-signed him to a new three-year deal as well.

Morgan learned about his dismissal only when he received a call from a friend who had read about it in the trade paper *Daily Variety*. Morgan was at home at the time, fasting during the Jewish holy day, Yom Kippur. After confirming that the article was accurate, the head of NBC News reassigned Morgan to a dutiless position within the production ranks and basically paid off the remainder of his contract. Several months later, Morgan would write about his six years at the *Today* show in *TV Guide*. He likened running America's early morning news broadcast to a quote by Orson Welles when he completed shooting *Citizen Kane*: "It's the greatest set of electric trains in the world." Morgan talked of the "pride of raising Barbara Walters from a cub," referred to the "good humor of Jack Lescoulie," reflected on the "professionalism and decency of Joe Garagiola and the major contributions of Paul Cunningham and Aline Saarinen," and never mentioned a word about Hugh Downs.

Taking Morgan's place was Stuart Schulberg, the brother of Oscar-winning screenwriter Budd Schulberg *(On the Waterfront)*, who arrived on the *Today* set with the full knowledge and approval of Downs. The host later labeled the executive producer "highly literate and a warmhearted man." Among his strengths, the most instantly notable was his accessibility. While Morgan had always watched the show from the comfort of his bedroom, Schulberg was in the trenches with the rest of his troops at 6:00 A.M. each day.

Unlike Morgan, when Schulberg arrived at *Today*, the series was well oiled, well reviewed, and well watched. Viewership now topped seven million. Hugh Downs was publicly billed as the star of the broadcast, but not even the network could continue to ignore the mounting attention in the press received by Barbara Walters. Often, it seemed, she was far more famous than those she was assigned to interview, despite her official billing as a reporter on the program.

There was still little in the way of competition for the *Today* show and certainly none for Walters. Early in 1963, CBS made a halfhearted attempt to re-enter the early morning arena, from 7:30 to 8:00 A.M., with *The CBS Morning News*. The network hired a new reporter named Mike Wallace to anchor the series. Wallace had begun his career as a game show host of NBC's *The $100,000 Big Surprise*, but had moved into news via an interview show that bore his name and was televised on ABC for a couple of seasons.

In September 1966, Wallace left *The CBS Morning News* to take on other assignments at the network's News Division (*60 Minutes* was still two years away from debuting). Replacing him on the program was Joseph Benti, a seasoned newspaper columnist and reporter. Benti was still in place two and a half years later, on March 31, 1969, when the network decided to expand the show to run from 7:00 to 8:00 A.M., in what was the first regularly scheduled hour-long network newscast. Benti lasted in the position until August 31, 1970, when John Hart, who had previously been a correspondent on the show, took over the reins of the anchor desk.

During this entire time and for several years more, the thrust of *The CBS Morning News* would be limited to covering those news stories that had developed during the previous night. The network felt that viewers had a need to be informed rather than entertained at that early morning hour. It was a concept that pleased the "old boys club" of newsmen still running the division, who kept a photo of Walter Cronkite talking to the Charlemane the Lion puppet to remind them of mistakes gone by.

If those at CBS News laughed at the liberal way the *Today* show mixed entertainment with journalism, they would find nothing funny about the ratings leadership that NBC continued to enjoy in early morning broadcasting. During an average week in 1971, *The CBS Morning News* managed to generate a rating of 1.5. Translated, this meant that 20 percent of the viewing audience (or 2.6 million people) were tuned to see John Hart in New York, assisted by Bernard Kalb in Washington, D.C. By comparison, NBC's *Today* was generating a 5.9 rating. A full 35 percent of available viewers were tuning in to *Today*—4.7 million of them. It didn't matter that *The New York Times* had called CBS's effort "one of the best news hours on television." The facts were easy enough to read in the advertising ledgers of both networks: NBC was offering what the majority of people wanted (NBC went as far as to say "needed") to see when they first opened their eyes to daylight.

At the end of April 1971, Hugh Downs inadvertently gave CBS something around which to rally by announcing that he would leave the *Today* show when his contract expired on October 11. After nine years on the program, Downs had simply grown tired of the hours and the routine. The easygoing demeanor that Dave Garroway had long tried to assume but that Downs had more comfortably worn lent a sincerity to the announcement.

When Downs said that he didn't need the energy of New York, but instead longed to watch the sun set over the hills of his Arizona home, there was a truth in his voice that no one doubted. Even so, those on the *Today* show were genuinely sad to see him leave his TV family, and viewers flooded the program's offices with letters of goodbye.

With Downs's announcement came the additional news from NBC that newsman Frank McGee would become the new *Today* show host. At the time, McGee had been co-anchor of *NBC Nightly News* for nine months and was a favorite of NBC News president Reuven Frank.

What was fascinating to CBS about the appointment of Frank McGee was that he was a newsman. It suggested that just as *Today* had swung hard toward news with the arrival of John Chancellor, so too would it now with McGee behind the anchor desk. It would be "news against news," the way CBS analyzed it, and the network immediately began making plans to alter its own broadcast to compete more effectively.

As *The CBS Morning News* regrouped for an all-out attack, the *Today* show was making surprising headlines. TODAY SHOW GUEST ATTACKED, the popular *New York Daily News* reported on July 6, 1971. The accompanying story went on to relate the saga of Mrs. Cynthia Wedel. It seemed that Mrs. Wedel, president of the National Council of Churches, was leaving the City Squire Motor Inn in Manhattan for a scheduled appearance on *Today* when she was forced "at knife point" from an unmanned elevator, tied up, and robbed by a masked assailant. Mrs. Wedel was able to free herself in time to make the program, the *Daily News* stated.

Days later, it was George Jessel who was complaining about being robbed, this time of his right to speak, and once again the *Today* show was center stage. On Friday, July 30, Jessel was making an appearance on *Today* to announce his retirement from show business "except for a few speeches," when newsman Edwin Newman retired him permanently. Jessel had arrived for the telecast attired in a self-described "U.S.O. uniform" decorated with medals and a variety of ribbons. He was being interviewed by Newman, who was asking him about his visits to various military bases overseas.

Jessel responded that he found the morale of the troops high and then added: "But of course, when you pick up *Pravda,* uh . . . *The New York Times* . . . you generally see, oh, they're all full of dope and killing children, drunk."

Ignoring what seemed to be a reference to communist propaganda in the *Times,* Newman continued the interview, only to encounter another Jessel reference to communism. "You pick up a paper, you know, *Pravda,* uh . . . *The Washington Post* . . . and you see 'hundreds die of pollution,'" Jessel said.

At this point, Newman interrupted the performer, known as America's Toastmaster General, and told him, "You are a guest here, but I don't really think very much of this talk about *Pravda*—excuse me, *The New York Times; Pravda*—excuse me, *The Washington Post.* I think that's silly. I do. Thank you very much, Mr. Jessel," he said, adding that calling legitimate newspapers communistic was a "serious matter."

Jessel attempted to argue that he did not mean it "quite that way," but before he could say another word, Newman cut him off with a station break. When the show returned, Newman apologized to the viewing public. "I'm a little sorry about that incident. I hope I did the right thing, and I guess the best thing to do at the moment is to forget about it."

During the minutes after the *Today* show signed off, NBC's switchboard lit up with calls from over 1,240 viewers. Most were in support of Newman, who declined to comment directly about the incident after the broadcast, saying that he felt Jessel's comments were "disjointed and frankly infantile."

"I don't think he should have treated me the way he did, treated me like a bum and kicked me off his show," Jessel told *The New York Times.* "I think he should have been kinder to me. But I know that newsmen feel strongly about newspapers just the way I feel strongly about actors. So I forgive him the way one forgives the blindness of a departed owl."

NBC News president Reuven Frank issued an official network response: "Edwin Newman handled an unfortunate occurrence with dignity and dispatch, and NBC News feels he acted wisely and in the best possible taste to correct a live broadcast situation that seemed to be getting out of hand."

· · ·

On October 11, 1971, true to his word, Hugh Downs retired from *Today*. The first hour of his last broadcast recounted his nine years on the series, which, like Downs himself, was low-key and humble. There was a sense of transfer of power as the incoming Frank McGee started work immediately and interviewed Senator Hubert Humphrey. Then the set was pushed back and the punch bowl was filled, as cast and crew sang "Auld Lang Syne."

Yet, even as Downs was driving to his home in Carefree, Arizona, the following week, the executives in the CBS News Division were preparing to capitalize on his departure. Executive producer Richard Clark was hired by CBS to "transform and revitalize" its early morning news hour. Building on the theory that viewers don't care to see "an hour of blood and thunder fresh out of bed," Clark intended to introduce softer features into the CBS news hour—still news, but with more human interest: "the news wrapped in an attractive, easy-to-swallow-with-the-orange-juice package."

Arriving at a time when much of the hard news that was broadcast over the CBS early morning telecast concerned hunger and oppression in India and Pakistan, Clark commented to *The New York Times*, "You can't help wondering how many people we've got throwing up in their cornflakes at 7:15."

Clark devised a plan to deliver the news in a more conversational tone, with John Hart hosting from New York, Nelson Benton in Washington, D.C., and Bernard Kalb reporting from the field. Getting high marks from school officials, Clark also planned on televising children's news with Punch and Judy puppets and reporter Marya McLaughlin. The plans were a radical departure from anything that had been previously attempted on any network, and were viewed as CBS's only hope of breaking through its stalled ratings climb.

If the executives on the *Today* show were at all concerned, their anxiety did not translate on-air. Frank McGee settled into his role as the series's host with a certain disgruntled complacency, making no secret of his view that compared to co-anchoring *NBC Nightly News*, his assignment on *Today* was a considerable comedown, and of his hope that he would soon return to the evening shift. McGee had actually guest-hosted the program when Hugh Downs was on vacation and, while doing a good job in the anchor seat, did not particularly enjoy the responsibility.

What McGee *did* enjoy, however, was emphasizing his own importance on the program, especially to Barbara Walters. In her determination to gain a foothold on *Today,* Walters was not content to wait for assignments; rather, she aggressively pursued interviews and surprised many with her ability to land exclusives.

She delighted in gaining access to the inaccessible—from Prince Philip to Richard Nixon, from former Secretary of State Dean Rusk to Henry Ford. And she was the only woman who was invited to report on Nixon's visit to Peking on U.S. television. "This is Barbara Walters," President Nixon said to China's Prime Minister Zhou Enlai. "We're just breaking her in."

If McGee was threatened by anyone on the *Today* show, it was Walters. She was as hungry as he was established, and he was willing to do anything short of putting his hand over her mouth to keep her in her place. Previously, Walters had been encouraged by Downs to join in interviews, asking the kind of questions that he was too timid or too polite to broach. Under McGee's early reign, Walters was not allowed to ask *any* questions. In fact, she was specifically forbidden to join in during McGee's interview of any Washington personnel. It would take several years before Walters was able to break through the prohibition and only then after she had created such a stink that a truce had to be arranged by the president of NBC News. Walters could join in an interview session, but only after McGee had asked the first two questions. He also had to ask the final one, making it seem as if he were in control.

By the time *Today* moved past its twentieth birthday and into the latter part of 1972, Walters's marriage to Lee Guber was all but finished, another victim of "the curse" that the show places on nearly all those who manage to be touched by its power. In October, Joe Garagiola became a casualty of the grind as well, announcing his decision to leave the program because of the early morning hours. "By one o'clock you're like a rubber band," he stated, describing the daily stint on the

Today show as tougher than double-headers in August. Gene Shalit, who had previously done occasional book reviews on the program, took over Garagiola's role in early January 1973.

With his handlebar mustache, out-of-control hair, and off-center sense of humor, Shalit seemed a strange choice for the nervous, intense Schulberg to make to replace the low-key Garagiola. Many feel that it was Shalit's adaptability that was his strongest suit. And as the on-screen tension developed between McGee and Walters, he could always be called upon to play the buffoon.

If Garagiola's departure was to weaken *Today*, CBS stood to reap the benefits. *The CBS Morning News* was still limping along, a distant second in the morning sweepstakes, and CBS News president Richard Salant knew that he could wait no longer for executive producer Richard Clark's experiment in diversity and multiple anchors to charm America. When the CBS affiliates met for their annual meeting at the Century Plaza Hotel in Los Angeles in May 1973, Salant revealed to the broadcasting executives that John Hart and Nelson Benton would be reassigned within the CBS News organization and a new team—one male, one female—would be hired to replace them as early as August.

The new show was going to continue to be "essentially news-oriented," Salant said, "but we hope it will be faster-paced, more urgent, more departmentalized, with special emphasis, on as regular a basis as possible, on matters of interest to the consumer." On tap to become the program's executive producer was CBS News national assignment editor Lee Townsend.

Salant admitted to disappointment at the failure of *The CBS Morning News* to generate ratings. "There comes a point, regrettably, when we have to face the harsh realities—that we were on dead center, and our support was eroding. The decision to try something new was a hard one, but it had to be made."

CBS wasn't the only network looking hard at the early morning arena. During its own affiliate meetings later the same month in the same hotel, ABC announced that it, too, was developing an early morning show to compete with *Today*. While there was no comment on CBS's difficulty in topping *Today*, one ABC executive preferred to think of an early morning news show as an image builder. "It will look good on [the affiliates'] FCC reports," she said.

Image was on CBS's corporate mind as well when the network revealed in June that *Washington Post* reporter Sally Quinn would cohost its new *Morning News* show. Quinn had no prior television anchoring experience, but was characterized by *The New York Times* as being "well known in Washington as a witty and rather caustic commentator on political personalities and the social scene." Hughes Rudd, a veteran correspondent with the network, would join Quinn on the program.

At first critics reacted to the news with mild disinterest, but as the show's August 6 debut grew near, they found their tongues. It was to be "Sexy Blonde vs. the Iron Butterfly," according to one journalist who attempted to create a feud between Quinn and Walters where none existed. In Walters's own backyard, *New York* magazine tried to fan the flames by hyping Quinn's image as a feminist's worst nightmare. "'Powerful people say things to women they would never say to men, especially over a martini,'" Aaron Latham wrote in *New York,* quoting Quinn. "'If a Senator is putting his hand on my fanny and telling me how he is going to vote on impeaching President Nixon . . . I'm not so sure I'm going to remove his hand.'"

In reality, Quinn provided her own worst publicity by her embarrassing on-air performance. In its haste to rush the show to the air, no one at CBS had thought to school Quinn on broadcast technique. She was literally pushed into a chair and expected to read a TelePrompTer with no preparation. Additionally, there was little attempt to tone down her well-known caustic wit.

The New York Times critic Albin Krebs wrote, "Mr. Rudd and Miss Quinn intend to give their show a folksy, informal flavor by indulging in ad-lib comments on the news and feature items presented. Yesterday it was demonstrated that they'll have to be prudent about what they say."

After a segment that glumly reported on the plight of migrant child laborers, Quinn quipped that she once picked strawberries but had to quit "after half an hour." She then giggled into the camera that the $3,000 a year that a migrant family makes would last less than a week in New York, adding an anecdote about trying to buy a steak the previous weekend.

Later in the broadcast, after a segment in which correspondent Marshall Efron ate a salad made with dollar bills, since "real lettuce was more expensive," Quinn held up some clean singles, noting that they had been washed after the taping. "Which proves," she added, "that you can launder money without sending it to Mexico."

Considering her lack of preparation and the fact that she was suffering from a bad case of the flu, it was even more amazing that Quinn showed up for the debut telecast at all. At 5:00 A.M., having forced herself out of her sickbed, she collapsed on the floor of the studio and was rushed to the hospital, only to be released in time for the news hour and giving new meaning to the adage "the show must go on."

Despite *Today*'s generous lead in the ratings, NBC executives were genuinely worried about CBS's Quinn-Rudd pairing—the first attempt to duplicate the *Today* magic with any diligence. Executive producer Stuart Schulberg decided to counter the hype that CBS was generating among female viewers by taking *Today* on location—all of ten blocks away—to the Plaza Hotel. He staged a fashion show in the Palm Court, offered jazz courtesy of Duke Ellington, and provided some tips on correct tennis form. *The New York Times* reviewer, having taped the program for comparison to *The CBS Morning News*, found that "compared to the CBS show, [*Today*'s] pacing was dolorous, if not downright torpid."

It was true that *Today* had begun to take on an increasingly obvious malaise, mostly due to a grim Frank McGee. What viewers didn't realize, however, was that McGee's determined expression was due to far more than an uncomfortable association with Walters. The series host had been diagnosed with bone cancer shortly before he moved over to the early morning shift. Initially the disease caused little pain and no outward symptoms. But as the show entered the spring of 1973, McGee's condition was worsening. He didn't inform Schulberg or any of his coworkers, but he did begin to realize that his life was coming to a close.

Frank McGee had married his childhood sweetheart, Nialta Sue Beaird, in 1941. After raising two children, their world had become a comfortable if predictable place. Sue McGee was content with that status. Frank McGee was not. And in April 1973, he decided to do something about it. Suddenly, after thirty-two years of marriage, he told his wife that he was leaving her for another woman. He didn't mention her name.

Mamye Smith was a production assistant on the *Today* show and had an infectious laugh that splashed its own special brand of happiness whenever it appeared. When she was around Frank McGee, it appeared quite often. Mamye was fond of McGee, proud of his work, impressed by his diligence, and surprised beyond belief when, one day over lunch, he confessed he loved her. He was a gentleman from Monroe, Louisiana. She was a black woman from Brooklyn.

The affair was replete with the makings of a scandal and could have easily spelled doom for McGee's career. But given his life expectancy, he elected to place happiness before his career. McGee had a long-standing dislike for racial prejudice. It was during his coverage of racial friction in Montgomery, Alabama, that McGee first attracted the attention of NBC's chairman and chief executive officer, Julian Goodman, who later assigned him to cover the integration crisis in Little Rock, Arkansas. To Frank McGee, there was only one race—the human race—and he proved it conclusively by sharing what remained of his life with Mamye Smith.

The *Today* staff, outwardly congratulatory, was privately shocked at the pairing of the coworkers, who temporarily moved into Budd Schulberg's empty apartment in New York City. A month later, they moved into a co-op in Gracie Plaza at 89th Street and York Avenue. Each morning they walked together the two and a half miles to Rockefeller Plaza and each evening made their way home on foot as well in an effort to keep Frank's body moving and his disease at bay. While

McGee's wife remained silent in their Manhattan home, Frank and Mamye made no secret of their love—going out to restaurants, night-clubs, and the theater.

By early 1974, Frank McGee began to experience pain in his back. Not wanting to alarm Mamye, he kept his discomfort private, increasing his reliance on pain medication. Outwardly his movements began to slow, but there was little else to suggest that his life was ending.

During the second week of April 1974, McGee developed what he thought was a bad cold. He was experiencing chills and a high fever and informed his doctor, who suggested he go to the hospital emergency room. On the morning of April 11, despite his illness, McGee insisted on going to work, but as soon as *Today* was finished, he checked himself into the Columbia Presbyterian Medical Center. He died six days later of pneumonia, a complication brought on by his multiple myeloma. At his side was his daughter, her husband, and Mamye Smith.

The sudden death of Frank McGee sent the *Today* show into shock. Barbara Walters announced his passing on the air to a stunned viewing audience. On *The CBS Evening News,* Walter Cronkite said, "Behind Frank's soft-spoken, almost courtly, manner one sensed char-acter and integrity of iron." Walters did not agree. After attending the memorial service for McGee at the Frank E. Campbell Funeral Home on Madison Avenue, she telephoned her agent, Lee Stevens, to alert him to place a call to NBC.

The network apparently had overlooked a seemingly insignificant clause in the three-year contract that Walters had signed the previous July. In addition to guaranteeing her $400,000 a year, the contract stated that should McGee leave *Today* for whatever reason, she would be named cohost of the broadcast. Amazed, but in hindsight hardly surprised, the network had little choice but to oblige the rising star. Just five days after McGee's death, NBC announced Walters's new status on the program.

For Walters, it was the reward for ten years of tireless devotion to the show and her career. What she had lacked in training, she had made up for in discipline, making this moment in her life all the more meaningful. She had no peers among female journalists. After only five months on *The CBS Morning News*, Sally Quinn had self-destructed and had quit the program to return to newspaper reporting, this time for *The New York Times*'s Washington bureau.

Yet, Walters was not about to rest on her laurels. While newsman Garrick Utley temporarily filled in for the late Frank McGee, the search began in earnest for his replacement, and this time Walters intended to see that she had specific input in the selection process.

Officially, a trio of men in charge—Julian Goodman and Herbert S. Schlosser, respectively chairman and president of NBC, and Richard Wald, president of NBC News—made the choice of whom to place in *Today*'s hot seat. The men created a shopping list of candidates, mostly comprised of NBC newsmen. On the first draft were Tom Snyder (then hosting NBC's *Tomorrow* show); Tom Brokaw (stationed at the White House); veteran newscasters Edwin Newman, Douglas Kiker, Floyd Kalber, and Garrick Utley; and newsmen Jim Hartz (WNBC, New York) and Jess Marlow (KNBC, Los Angeles). Looking outside their own ranks, the trio added the names of Dick Cavett, Bill Moyers, and Harry Reasoner.

Of the initial group, Reasoner and Newman were passed over because of their age. The executives wanted to bring a younger newsman into the *Today* family in an attempt to improve the demographics of the ratings.* Bill Moyers was contacted, but turned down the position. Dick Cavett was eliminated because of his mostly entertainment background.

With the remaining candidates all in-house NBC employees, another on-air talent hunt began. Each potential host was given a week to rotate in and out of the *Today* host chair. As each candidate completed his tryout, Walters presented the executive trio her written evaluation. Walters liked all the men, but initially was leaning toward Tom

---

*In 1974, *Today* was attracting a majority of viewers in the 40–68 age range. Advertisers prefer to reach 18–48 year olds.

Brokaw, who had shown a fascinating and heretofore hidden sense of humor. Tom Snyder, who many thought was too abrasive to work with Walters, also scored high with the cohost, and for a while it appeared that both men had the inside track.

The last to try out for the *Today* spot was WNBC's news anchor Jim Hartz, who viewed his inclusion in the group as more of a courtesy than an actual audition. In truth, the NBC executives did feel that Hartz's experience was a bit limited for the high-pressure *Today* spot, but agreed to wait until they saw how he performed before making a final decision.

At that point, Tom Brokaw was the leading candidate and was actually in active discussions with Wald about taking the post. Brokaw was hesitant for a number of reasons. First, he loved covering the White House for NBC and saw his role in Washington as a far more important position than hosting an early morning news/entertainment series. Second, he absolutely refused to do commercials of any kind, viewing them as a compromise of his journalistic integrity.

During his audition week, Jim Hartz illustrated amazing versatility and a surprisingly warm camaraderie with Walters, who later gave him the highest marks. Another major plus for Hartz was his willingness to do commercials.

By mid-July, the network was tiring of the audition process, which had been ongoing for three months. Viewers, too, were beginning to show their discomfort at the musical chairs and changing faces that flashed before them weekly. Pressed to make a decision, the trio finally agreed on Hartz and surprised him with the news while he was playing in a charity softball game in upstate New York.

Hartz was sworn to secrecy until the news could be formally announced, and broke his word only to tell his wife and his friend, weatherman Frank Field. NBC finally announced its decision ten days later on July 24, 1974. The network sighed joyous relief in making the announcement, with an NBC vice president telling *TV Guide*, "It adds up to a very happy ending for our great host hunt." Certainly, Hartz was happy, particularly with his $250,000 a year salary.

Ironically, Hartz was a protégé of the late Frank McGee. He was a native of Oklahoma, which McGee also claimed to be.* He had also delivered the eulogy at McGee's funeral. When asked her opinion of her new cohost, Walters said, "Jim doesn't mind sharing the stage with me and he isn't offended when I try to help him." It was more a back-handed slap at McGee than a compliment to Hartz.

Hartz officially began as *Today* cohost on July 29, 1974, in what he hoped would be a long and fruitful association. Yet, even as he settled into his chair on the set, there were forces at work that would dramat-ically change both his expectations for the future and early morning television.

---

*McGee was actually born in Monroe, Louisiana, but was never particularly proud of his roots in the Pelican State.

THE RACE

*J*im Hartz was a likeable slug who charmed those around him with his ability to stay calm and focused regardless of the tension on the set. Moldable in any circumstance, Hartz had what one reviewer called "nerves like overcooked spaghetti." He was equally mellow whether discussing the news or interviewing guests, and viewers wondered if there was a stifled yawn just beneath his mild-mannered reporter exterior.

Hartz was objective about his languid nature. He once remarked that while there were plenty of newspeople with hyperactive egos and personalities, "a lot of time people confuse emotion with progress. It came to me a long time ago that that's not the most efficient way to operate."

After the angst that marked the reign of Hartz's predecessor, it reasonably followed that the peace he brought to the *Today* set was welcome by the cast and crew. Unfortunately, viewers, who were used to expecting the unexpected on the program, began to feel that *Today* had lost its drive and energy.

"The happiness that everyone involved in the program was feeling was actually translated on the air as complacency," said one longtime *Today* producer. "We moved through our days mechanically at a time that was about to become a competitive race."

Soon after Hartz's debut, ABC announced its final plans to give *Today* its first real taste of time-slot competition by programming its first early morning news/entertainment series. The network titled the entry *A.M. America* and spent thousands of dollars to carefully research exactly who was watching *Today*—and more importantly, who was not.

The program was designed under the watch of ABC's vice president of morning programming, Dennis Doty, who would later win accolades for his telefeatures (including the NBC-TV AIDS drama *An Early Frost*). Doty had contracted Frank N. Magid, a news research consultant in Marion, Iowa, to conduct a series of surveys of potential *A.M. America* viewers. What Magid uncovered excited the ABC network. His surveys pointed to a largely untapped audience of 18–49 year olds who were not currently tuning in to early morning television, not because they were unavailable, but rather because they were unimpressed by what they saw.

Having observed *The CBS Morning News* crash and burn in its attempt to unseat *Today*, ABC executives knew that hard news was not the direction its new series needed to take. If attacking *Today* at the front door didn't work, perhaps it was wise to enter through the back. *A.M. America* would entertain, or more precisely, present information in an entertaining way. "We want to inform, stimulate, and sometimes flat out amuse the viewer," Doty said. "We're going to provide information with snap, style, and personality."

To front the new program, ABC followed NBC's lead and gave the nod to Bill Beutel, the *Eyewitness News* anchor from its New York affiliate, WABC. Beutel, at 43, was reasonably young, very witty, prone to puns, and eager to launch the new program. As his cohost, Stephanie Edwards, a red-haired, L.A.-based actress and sometime trombone player (she once performed on *The Merv Griffin Show*), was added to the line-up, along with news anchor Peter Jennings.

By veteran newsmen's standards, Jennings was a baby, having cut his teeth during his assignment in the Middle East, which included reporting on the terrorist attack during the 1972 Winter Olympics in Munich. After years overseas gaining experience, however, the native Canadian begged ABC management for an opportunity to return to Washington, D.C., and found it in anchoring the news on the new *A.M. America*. As things turned out, it might have been less dangerous to stay in Beirut.

A.M. America debuted on January 6, 1975, and was, in a word, bright. The hosts were enthusiastic to the point of effervescence, the topics were breezy with a youthful slant, and even the set, designed in tones of orange and yellow plastic, seemed to shout "get up."

Viewers learned that the day marked the birthdays of Joan of Arc, Loretta Young, and Danny Thomas. Beutel did a feature on flowers and vegetable seeds, Edwards read a story about a man who was shot in the neck and then broke his leg while chasing his attacker, and Jennings reported from Washington on the price of gold. Jennings later interviewed former Secretary of Health Elliot L. Richardson, as the on-screen graphics identified him as "Elliot Richardson—AMerican," in what was the first of the show's overuse of the play on the letters *A.M.*

The hosts sat on stools in front of podiums, backed by a huge sunburst clock that threatened to eat them alive at any moment. Edwards might have actually welcomed the opportunity, for when she was introducing the show's first celebrity interviewee, Dustin Hoffman, she called him a "man of many faces—once he looked like this." On the screen flashed a set of color bars.

Eager for media exposure, former New York Mayor John Lindsey joined the cast as a part-time regular. Introduced as "one of the country's avid students of the British parliamentary system," he interviewed the British home secretary. He was thankfully brief.

Despite the arrival of *A.M. America,* viewers of *Today* and *The CBS Morning News* remained loyal. Ratings at both shows remained basically consistent—nearly four million viewers for *Today* and just over 1.2 million for *Morning News.* Although *A.M. America* did not initially beat either program, it seemed, nevertheless, to bring new viewers to the early morning time slot—an encouraging sign for all three networks. As the months passed, however, none of the networks was pleased.

Given the money and research it had devoted to *A.M. America,* ABC failed to generate the volume of audience attention it had expected. CBS had hoped that Jim Hartz's arrival at NBC would give a boost to Hughes Rudd on *The CBS Morning News*—a wish that never was granted. And *Today* found the chemistry between Walters, Hartz, and Shalit now *too* relaxed and friendly.

In an effort to add spice to its personality stew, *Today* hired its first African-American regular, former major-league player Bill White, who was then a member of the New York Yankees' broadcasting team. Executive producer Stuart Schulberg hired White for a twice-a-week trial run to anchor many of the same segments that Garagiola had done previously. In the meantime, Shalit was concentrating on movie reviews and celebrity interviews, providing media critics with ample material. "Shalit looks like he was born sitting," one said. Another suggested he was a marionette in another life.

Newsman Frank Blair, finding himself increasingly dependent on alcohol and bored with his position on the program after twenty-one years, announced his intention to resign from *Today*. He had hoped that he would be assigned to another position within the network's news organization. Instead, the network maintained that since *Today* was the only program he was contracted to do for NBC, his resignation from that show was in essence a resignation from the network. NBC executives wasted little time in announcing as his replacement newsman Lew Wood, who took over the *Today* news post on March 17, 1975.

The following May, Stephanie Edwards became the first casualty of the new *A.M. America* show in an attempt by senior producer Jules Power to ventilate the series's suffocating ratings. By the fall, ABC had informed the remainder of the *A.M. America* crew to pack their bags as well. The network had decided to scrap the program and try once more to chart new territory. "The program hasn't worked," ABC president Fred Pierce said. "We've got to take another shot at the apple. We've arbitrarily set a deadline of October 27 to force the issue and make it happen." Pierce hired veteran TV producer Bob Shanks *(Tonight)* to oversee the new project as vice president in charge of primetime specials and of *Good Morning America,* their retitled early A.M. entry.

ABC Entertainment president Fred Silverman, whose support

was vital to the survival of the series, was so unimpressed by the initial weeks of rehearsal for *Good Morning America* that he delayed the premiere of the program. When it finally did debut on November 3, 1975, the show was televised for its first week on tape, with only the news portions inserted live. Actor David Hartman, who had previously starred in NBC's hour-long drama *Lucas Tanner*, toplined the program as host, with actress Nancy Dussault, whose credits included the Broadway shows *The Mikado* and *The Sound of Music*, riding shotgun as the token female sidekick.

Hartman had been born in Pawtucket, Rhode Island, the son of a Methodist minister–turned–advertising executive who moved his family to Pelham, New York, when David was a short, fat, five year old. Those who knew him as a child remember a pleasant, unmotivated boy who showed little in the way of enthusiasm for anything other than baseball until his teen years, when he "sprouted like a corn stalk." Hartman would grow over a foot in a three-and-a-half-year period, eventually stretching to 6 feet, 5 inches in height by the time he went off to Duke University, where he lettered in baseball and worked part-time as an announcer at a radio station.

After a three-year tour in the air force, Hartman enrolled in the American Academy of Dramatic Arts in Manhattan and worked part-time at NBC as a tour guide and page. A national tour with the Harry Belafonte Singers followed, as did a role as Randolph the singing waiter in the original Broadway cast of *Hello Dolly!* It was only after relocation to Hollywood that Hartman entered the world of television, first through bit parts and then as a series regular on *The New Doctors*. He portrayed Dr. Paul Hunter, a medical researcher, and the actor immersed himself in the role, not only visiting medical facilities around the United States, but speaking, now as an authority, at medical conventions. "He had a sense of control of his destiny—and ours," observed his late costar E. G. Marshall.

This ability to control accompanied Hartman in his starring role in *Lucas Tanner*, the NBC series that followed *The New Doctors* in 1974, the same year Hartman married TV producer Maureen Downey. He once told an interviewer that he thought he would "be like Tanner" had he decided to become a schoolteacher. His call to *Good Morning Amer-ica* came the following year, and Hartman used much of Tanner's folksy openness to craft his persona as a communicator.

Bob Shanks suggested that the retooled *A.M. America* would still deliver news, but "with a comforting point of view." Claiming that TV viewers were being bombarded with reality that could "drive them into shock and anxiety," Shanks pledged that *Good Morning America* would lace its news with human interest "without scaring people to death." Mel Ferber, who had produced the pilot for CBS's *60 Minutes* and ABC's coverage of the 1972 Democratic National Convention, was tapped as the program's executive producer. It was a job that was orig-inally offered to Bob Precht, who was gaining fame as producer of CBS's *The Ed Sullivan Show,* a post he decided to keep.

With renewed energy and a seemingly bottomless pocketbook, ABC executives hired Broadway and film composer Marvin Hamlisch to compose the show's catchy theme song and populated the two hours with an equal number of correspondents and departments: columnist Jack Anderson reporting "Inside Washington"; quidnunc Rona Barrett supplying gossip via "Hollywood Worldwide"; comic–turned–film reviewer Jonathan Winters as "Critic on the Loose"; Erma Bombeck as "Housewife at Large" delivering comical tips for the homemaker; Dr. Tim Johnson, redubbed "Family Doctor," prescribing medical advice; *Cosmopolitan* editor Helen Gurley Brown offering "Men/Women" advice; plus such entries as "Talk Back" (man on the street), "People in the News" (human interest), and "Face Off" (journalists and politicians in mock debate). Reporter Geraldo Rivera, who had made his name locally in New York for his investigative pieces, was busy unearthing injustice, and from Washington, Steve Bell and Margaret Osmer shared the news-reading responsibilities.

What ABC had created, America's TV critics were hard-pressed to interpret—from its homey set, which *The New York Times* TV editor John O'Connor called "gracious country living, at a decorating level far beyond the means of average Americans," to its many departments, which *The Hollywood Reporter* labeled "busy, busy, b-u-s-y." *Good Morning America* was designed to be easy to watch, but it popped off the screen as simple-minded.

There were funny moments—Bombeck stated that "if God had meant you to scrub johns, he'd have clogged your sinuses"—but not enough of them for the show to be called comical. There was a stab at issues—Frank Mankiewicz and Victor Gold shouting at one another over the question, Should the federal government bail out New York City? Unfortunately, since Gold spoke over most of Mankiewicz's comments, the question remained unanswered. The end result seemed to be what *The New York Times* called "a curious content jumble."

TV Guide's critic Cleveland Amory, who for a short time himself had toiled on the *Today* show in a segment on society, said of *Good Morning America:* "We have a feeling that ABC's idea of morning programming is to throw darts at the screen and see if any of them stick." He attacked gossip columnist Rona Barrett, pointing to the fact that she appeared on the right-hand portion of the screen "as if about to steal second base" and sounding as if "she had been programmed by a correspondence-course student on an inexpensive computer."

Amory reminded readers that Hartman had once played a schoolteacher, Lucas Tanner, "but that doesn't mean he always knows his subject." He admitted, however, that Hartman did manage to "say 'Have a good day' as if he really meant it." Amory saved his most telling comment for Ms. Gurley Brown, who was asked by Dussault "the best way to make a man feel good." With an opening like that, Brown's answer was an amazing, "Ask him what he had for lunch. Men love to say what they had for lunch." Such banter left Amory lamenting, "With a tip like that early in the morning, you're ready to lick the world."

In analyzing *Good Morning America*'s initial months on the air, *Today*'s producer Stuart Schulberg proffered, "They could use Barbara Walters." Schulberg didn't realize how prophetic his comment would become.

Walters's stock at NBC had risen to the point at which she was now arguably the most famous woman on network TV. Not only was she seen for two hours every morning, she was ruling the broadcast. It was now Walters who asked the first questions on interviews. It was Walters who signed on and off most of *Today*'s broadcasts.

Walters had convinced the network to allow her to have her own ninety-minute daytime special, which would be shot on location in Europe. Hoping to regenerate much of the royal fever that had swept the country during the coronation of Queen Elizabeth II and the marriage of her daughter Princess Anne, the program was titled "Barbara Walters Visits the Royal Lovers." Equally important to Walters was the fact that her name appeared first in the program's title.

At a cost of $250,000, the show—presumably about the Duke and Duchess of Orléans and Queen Margrethe and Prince Kenrik of Denmark—was in reality more a showcase for Walters: Walters dashing madly along a French boulevard looking at dresses in windows, twirling in front of mirrors, gushing "the money, the brocade" while touring Marie Antoinette's bedroom, dining at Maxim's as a violinist serenaded her every bite. It was an indulgence that even the royals found nauseating.

Mary Murphy in the *Los Angeles Times* labeled the special "Barbara in Wonderland," adding, "Walters is the most powerful newswoman in America, yet send her to Europe to interview royalty and she becomes a cooing schoolgirl."

The special served several important purposes, despite its failure to generate ratings. It set the stage for future Barbara Walters personality specials, and it gave her a taste of life outside the confines of the *Today* show. Walters's career had always been important in her life—now, it *became* her life.

In early 1976, Walters sued for divorce from her husband, Lee Guber, and pressed her agents into demanding a new contract that guaranteed a salary of $1 million a year, plus a quartet of primetime specials. While NBC executives were not unreceptive to her demands, they weren't in a rush to renegotiate a new deal. Walters's old contract did not expire until the end of July, and given her loyalty in the past, there seemed little likelihood that she would shop her talent elsewhere.

Walters, however, had just been presented the Broadcaster of the Year Award by the International Television and Radio Society, as well as an Emmy Award by the Academy of Television Arts and Sciences, and had been included in *Time* magazine's list of the most influential people in the country. For the first time in her life, she had power, and she proceeded to tell her agents to use it. Their first stop: ABC.

Agent Lee Stevens's boss at the William Morris agency was Lou Weiss, who headed its TV department. It was Weiss who first broached the idea of Walters's defection to ABC while playing tennis with ABC president Fred Pierce on his home court in Westchester, New York. Weiss's demands were essentially the same ones Stevens had presented to NBC, with one addition: he wanted Walters to co-anchor the *ABC Evening News*, whose current anchor was Harry Reasoner.

Weiss, known for his ability to push through deals where others had failed, was prepared to support his proposal. He had little need. Pierce immediately saw the value in adding Walters to his News Division. In addition to helping the ratings of the third-place *ABC Evening News*, he was eager to deal the *Today* show a deadly blow. With Walters no longer on the show, ABC's *Good Morning America* might finally be able to shake loose from the ratings basement. Pierce shared his idea with ABC News president William Sheehan, who also saw dollar signs and ratings fireworks. The only task that remained was convincing anchor Harry Reasoner.

A veteran newscaster, Reasoner was steely haired and tight-mouthed, often delivering his reports through what one reviewer called "clenched teeth." Orphaned as a teenager, Reasoner wrote a book in his early twenties titled *Tell Me about Women*. Even in 1976, he claimed to know little, despite a long marriage and five daughters. One thing Reasoner *did* know: women didn't belong behind a desk delivering the news, and particularly not on what he considered to be *his* broadcast.

As Reasoner was busy attempting to dissuade ABC executives from offering Barbara Walters a job in its News Division, NBC's heads continued to bide their time, renegotiating Walters's contract but not consenting to her demands. And when *The New York Times* leaked the news that ABC was about to offer the *Today* cohost a million dollars a year to co-anchor its evening news broadcast, NBC did what Barbara Walters hadn't anticipated: they balked, removing any pending offer for a new contract and wishing her luck at her new network.

On April 22, 1976, headlines across America screamed MILLION

DOLLAR BABY, as Walters instantly became known—the highest-paid newswoman in the world. For all the public clamor over the money, it was the sense of moving to a news broadcast that meant the most to Walters. It gave her a legitimacy she felt she previously lacked, but at the same time it caused her to lose sleep and suffer from self-doubt. Now that she got everything she had demanded, Walters had no clue whether she could actually deliver the goods.

Walters's last *Today* broadcast was on June 4, 1976. Although she would continue to be paid until the end of her contract in July, the network's executives didn't want the star to gain any additional publicity for ABC through her continued appearances on *Today*. In the finale, no tears were shed and no dedications were made. It was business as usual, with the exception of the playing of "Auld Lang Syne" as the words "Bon Voyage Barbara" flashed across the screen. Barbara Walters left the *Today* studio for the last time, and wisely never looked back. Had she done so, she would have found the door slammed and locked.

Walters's departure initially buoyed Jim Hartz into a false sense of complacency. The *Today* cohost had been supportive of Walters's decision to leave NBC, even though he privately felt she was making a mistake. As the show's remaining host, Hartz anticipated that his own star would rise and that he would become involved in the selection process for a female replacement.

There would be no decision-making involvement for Hartz, however, since he was also being replaced. Unhappy with the lethargic image that Hartz projected on the air, NBC executives used Walters's exit as a convenient excuse to change *Today*'s pace and look. Unbeknownst to Hartz, NBC News chief Richard Salant had approached Tom Brokaw and already was in serious contract negotiations with the White House correspondent.

By the time *TV Guide* discovered that Brokaw was showing renewed interest in the *Today* spot, Hartz had been quietly informed that he would be utilized as a "roving correspondent" on the program. Although this was a surprise to Hartz, it was not an unpleasant one, since he had always found reporting from the field to be the most exciting part of his job. Now, he would have little choice.

Once again, Brokaw was insisting that he would not do commercials. When NBC broke with tradition and agreed to his demands, it re-gessoed the canvas on which all future early morning entertainment/news series would be based. From the look of what was happening on-air, it came not a moment too soon.

During July and August 1976, the *Today* show clearly was in transition. Lloyd Dobyns had been brought in to temporarily replace Hartz, who began reporting from the field. Meanwhile, a veritable parade of auditions was going on for Walters's coveted spot. Of the 217 applications for the position, network executives had selected the top five candidates. In addition to Betty Furness, who had stepped in to substitute immediately upon Walters's departure but was judged to be too old for the role, newswomen Cassie Mackin (from Washington, D.C.), Jane Pauley (Chicago), Betty Rollin (New York), Linda Ellerbee (Washington, D.C.), and Kelly Lange (Los Angeles)—in that order—were each given a two-day run in the cohost chair.

By August, Lange and Pauley were the leading candidates for the job. Lange was a popular anchor at KNBC-TV, NBC's local affiliate in Los Angeles, and carried with her years of journalistic experience. She was blonde, attractive, and efficient, and had previously substituted for Tom Snyder on the network's *Tomorrow* show with enormous success.

Pauley had the long brown hair of a beauty queen, had been with Chicago's WMAQ-TV for a year, and at 25 was only one year older than *Today* itself. With the demographics of the program taking a beating from the younger skewing *Good Morning America,* youth won out over experience and, in late September, Pauley became the newest female to grace *Today,* scarcely a month after Brokaw himself began on the program.

News reader Lew Wood had previously been demoted to weatherman and was replaced by Floyd Kalber, leaving Gene Shalit as the only familiar face on the program. Even longtime executive producer Stuart Schulberg resigned, using the massive changeover as a convenient exit cue. Schulberg was suffering from chronic anxiety and high blood pressure, both of which dramatically improved during his first week free of *Today*. In his place came Princeton-educated Paul Friedman, who, at just 31 years old, was hired to give the show some youthful vigor. Friedman remembered that period as "traumatic," while a stagehand called it "a shakedown cruise in the face of a typhoon."

As the once-proud standard-bearer of NBC News struggled with its image, its upstart rival, *Good Morning America,* was making slow and steady inroads into the rarified early morning airtime. Now second in the ratings, having pulled ahead of *The CBS Morning News* the previous February, *GMA* had settled into a comfortable format that found its niche around the folksy, toothy David Hartman.

Soon after Friedman came on board and not long after Jane Pauley debuted on October 11, 1976, the *Today* show hit an all-time record low in viewership—a 3.7 rating and 24 share. The same week, *Good Morning America* posted a 2.4 rating and 17 share, with *The CBS Morning News* a not-so-distant third at a 1.9 rating and 15 share (for the 7:00–8:00 A.M. hour).

"For the first time in the life of *Today,* we were in a three-way race," Friedman said—and it was one that *Today* found itself uncertain of winning. What made *Good Morning America*'s accomplishment that much more amazing was the fact that it was being televised on only 177 stations, compared with *Today*'s 221 affiliates.

Jane Pauley began her *Today* show run as if she had been yanked from the womb of the Barbara Walters's school of broadcasting. She played at being composed on the air, but was noticeably nervous and uncertain. Realizing perhaps that she was somewhat underprepared for the assignment, Pauley nervously chain-smoked Kool cigarettes— some thirty a day—in an effort to make it through each show.

She didn't particularly mind that she was not officially the series's cohost. That title disappeared with Walters. Pauley was merely "talent" (albeit expensive talent—her annual salary was $100,000). Brokaw, on the other hand, was the host; much like David Hartman on *GMA,* the show developed around his own particular style.

Brokaw was born in Webster, a small town in the northeast corner of South Dakota. His family ran the Brokaw Hotel, an off-the-
beaten-path bed and breakfast in the town of Bristol, some sixteen
miles away. Bristol was a town of only 419 people, and the potential for
prosperity was so limited that by the time Brokaw was a teenager, the
family had moved from Bristol to towns with names like Igloo, Pick-
stown, and, finally, Yankton, on the Missouri River. It was in Yankton,
just off Interstate 29, that Brokaw gained entry into broadcasting, at the
250-watt radio station WYNT. It was also in Yankton—population
12,703—that he met and married his high school sweetheart, Meredith
Auld.

Brokaw attended and dropped out of both the University of Iowa
and the University of South Dakota before finally returning to the latter to get his degree. He began his television career in his senior year at
the NBC affiliate KTIV in Sioux City, moving next to KMTV, Omaha,
where he delivered the local morning news, including the five-minute
breakaways from *Today*. The year was 1963, a year filled with assassina-
tions and protests; the salary was $100 a week.

While at KMTV, Brokaw had taken his wife to visit the New York
World's Fair and the *Today* show. Looking in at the show from the
street-level studio, the Brokaws had held up a hand-painted sign that
read, WATCH *TODAY* IN OMAHA WITH TOM BROKAW AT 7:25 AND 8:25.
Now, thirteen years later, he was actually plotting the course of the
broadcast.

After stints in Atlanta, Los Angeles, and Washington, D.C.,
Brokaw was considered a likeable and effective news journalist, one
who benefited from his small-town ethics and local values. In effect,
those same qualities proved to be *Good Morning America*'s calling card
into the homes of new viewers, who found that show's country warmth
and wholesome features appealing, and who helped celebrate its first
anniversary as though they were attending an old-fashioned block
party, with everyone invited to stay a while.

But what Tom Brokaw's *Today* delivered was news, much of it
from Washington, D.C., all of it relevant. There was little in the way of
frivolity on *Today*, save for an occasional Brokaw pun that Pauley

strained to catch. If there was camaraderie on the set, it was the exception rather than the rule, as Friedman attempted to loosen up his hosts
to allow for natural give-and-take and a more sophisticated tone.

In an effort to accomplish spontaneity, the writers stopped script-
ing every line. Instead, they began to function more as researchers, providing facts on subjects that the hosts could then weave into a natural
commentary. Brokaw was used to improvising on the spot, but Pauley
was put at a disadvantage. Having had only a few years of broadcast
experience—first in Indianapolis at the CBS affiliate WISH-TV and
then at Chicago's NBC outlet, WMAQ-TV, where ironically she co-
anchored the evening news with Floyd Kalber—Pauley was learning on
the air. Unfortunately, she wasn't learning quite fast enough to keep up
with the changes surrounding her.

There was a certain strained quality to the broadcast that not even
Gene Shalit's electric-shock hair and off-center reviews could liberate.
Even the set seemed to be working against the regulars. Deskless,
Brokaw was "forced to cross his ankles like a nineteenth-century debutante" while Pauley wore dresses "that all but touch the floor," according to *TV Guide,* which actually ran a contest inviting readers to suggest
what the hosts should do with their legs.

Today celebrated its twenty-fifth anniversary with an on-air
reunion party that was an oddity of souvenirs, as old-timers mixed
with newcomers young enough to be their children. Dave Garroway
was back, but not at his best. Informed by Jane Pauley that she was just
learning how to walk when *Today* premiered, Garroway reacted as if he
had just smelled an errant burp, and looked away. Frank Blair and Jack
Lescoulie had already had a few shots from the bar next to the celebra-
tory food spread and looked like they longed to have more. Tom
Brokaw resembled a prep school student next to Garroway, who ended
the show by stabbing the two-layer birthday cake with a long knife
through its core—fun stuff if you like pain.

On *Good Morning America,* home of warmth and fluff, things
were only slightly less intense. Nancy Dussault's role on the telecast was
becoming increasingly restricted as David Hartman flexed his popular-

ity around the set and in production meetings. While Dussault was never thought of as an equal partner on the set's living room, by late 1976, she had been relegated to interviewing animal acts and handling "women's issues." When she balked at the treatment, ABC's management sided with Hartman and began a search to replace her.

Vice president Bob Shanks drafted a list of several candidates from within the network's news organization who would best complement Hartman. According to an interdepartmental memo, they were looking for someone who was "attractive, inquisitive, and eager," which seemed to leave the search for candidates wide open. In reality, what ABC needed to find was a young woman with news experience who could accommodate the increasingly dictatorial Hartman.

One candidate interviewed for the job was Joan Lunden. A recent transplant from Sacramento's NBC affiliate KCRA-TV, Lunden had worked for a little over a year in the News Division at ABC's New York affiliate, WABC, when she received a call from ABC vice president Bob Shanks about interviewing for Dussault's position.

Lunden had entered the news world with precious little experience, but she made up for lost time as a field reporter covering drug busts, murder investigations, court trials, and politics in an eager, if not always flawless, style. Blonde, attractive, and overtly inquisitive, the naturally bright Lunden seemed a perfect choice to replace Dussault on the *GMA* sofa.

After several meetings, including one with Hartman himself, Lunden was naively floating with enthusiasm over the prospect of moving into network television. One evening, however, as she was washing her hands in the ladies' room at WABC's *Eyewitness News* after a broadcast, she overheard two men talking from the men's room next door.

"Hey, you ought to see this new girl named Sandy Hill they hired to do *GMA*. Wait till you see the legs on this broad," said the loud, laughing voice through the wall.

It was thus that Lunden learned that she had lost out to another woman. Hill was a newswoman from Los Angeles who, like Lunden, was "attractive, inquisitive, and eager." Apparently, her long legs didn't hurt either. She joined the *GMA* family in April 1977, and from her on-air appearance next to the 6-foot, 5-inch Hartman, she was appropriately proportioned for the role.

Things seemed to be looking up as well on the *Today* set as the show traveled to London in June to cover the twenty-fifth anniversary of Queen Elizabeth II's ascension to the throne. With Brokaw heading the coverage of the event from a London TV studio, camera crews managed to capture the best views of the queen and her prince riding in a golden carriage from Buckingham Palace to Saint Paul's Cathedral. Jane Pauley was positioned in a British pub called the Princess Louise, where she attempted to corner those watching the festivities on television and generate some reaction.

One woman enjoying the celebration over a pint of lager told *Today*'s viewers that she thought the monarchy was a waste of money. "I think Prince Charles, if he were a man at all, would say he doesn't want to be king," she said, slurring her words. Pauley smiled, trying not to look too amused. Back in the studio, the editor of England's *The New Statesman* said he agreed, adding that he thought that the queen should open up Buckingham Palace to tourists "as the White House is open." Now it was Brokaw's turn to smile meekly.

Subsequent ratings for the broadcast proved that Americans appreciated the royals without such reservation,. The special five-hour broadcast, which had begun in the United States at 5:00 A.M., easily won its timeslot and buoyed Friedman, who had had little over which to celebrate up until that point. Rumors had continued to fly that NBC executives remained unconvinced of Pauley's abilities and that Brokaw was destined to replace John Chancellor on *NBC Nightly News*, which was suffering from its own ratings problems.

One unrumored change was the replacement of weatherman Lew Wood with meteorologist Bob Ryan, who combined broadcasting experience with weather credentials. Plans were also initiated for a new set that would match the stronger tone and more sophisticated image that the show was attempting to deliver. Even the theme song, which had been played on the show for years, was ordered updated, although not entirely at NBC's instigation.

In late 1978, the song "This Is *Today*," written by Ray Ellis, was the subject of a copyright infringement suit. The federal court decided that the song was too close to the popular tune "Day by Day" from Stephen Schwartz's Broadway musical *Godspell* and ordered it changed. Once again it was Ellis who got the nod.

Ellis incorporated the three-note NBC chimes into the song and debuted his new theme on January 8, 1979, the same day that *Today*'s new set was unveiled. Upon seeing the design, one critic lamented, "If NBC thinks that a panoramic blowup of Manhattan pasted on a backdrop is going to cure the ills it has with its *Today* show, perhaps it's time for us all to stay in bed." Producer Paul Friedman excitedly predicted that the new "comfortable area for conversation"—basically two easy chairs facing one another—was going to allow for more intimate dialogue.

In April 1979, *Today*'s executive producer Paul Friedman was given his walking papers and was replaced by Joe Bartelme. One of Bartelme's first moves was to import a hot-shot producer from Los Angeles named Steve Friedman (no relation to Paul). Ironically, Friedman had been *Today*'s field producer on the West Coast and was known for his brash, cocky attitude and can-do style. And it was Friedman who hit upon one of the major problems that was keeping the *Today* show marching in place rather than advancing in the ratings.

The show was still mired in its traditional broadcast format, which dictated that the second hour of the show in the East was still being televised as the first hour of the program in the Midwest and West. If a breaking news story was being discussed on the program between 7:00 and 8:00 A.M. Eastern Time, it couldn't be discussed again in the second hour. To do so would mean that those in the West would get the end of the story before the beginning. Friedman knew it was an untenable situation. Unfortunately, he seemed to be the only one.

Despite the fact that *Good Morning America* was broadcast straight through from beginning to end in all time zones, the engineers at NBC said it wasn't possible for them to duplicate the feat. As Friedman would later say, "I grabbed this engineer by the tie, brought him close to my face and said, 'You don't understand. I want you to record the *Today* show like you record a football game. That's how I want it done.' Then I pushed him back into his chair."

Friedman's message finally got through and the *Today* show eventually began to be shown in sequence throughout the country for the first time. Yet, it seemed that everything the program tried failed to stop *Good Morning America*'s march toward victory. By the end of January 1980, and for months to come, *GMA* actually surpassed the *Today* show in viewership. The series that for years had had no competition was now being beaten at its own game, and by what NBC News considered to be "entertainers." *Good Morning America* did not lead its rival by much—usually by only tenths of a rating point. But in television, as in other sports of prey, there is only one winner. Placed in the uncomfortable position as runner-up, *Today* began to scramble for salvation.

Good Morning America had made inroads into Americans' early morning viewing habits by excelling in exactly those areas in which *Today* was the weakest. Because it was new, *GMA* had no heritage on which to draw. Nothing it did could break tradition, since it had no tradition. Each day represented a new frontier, and men, women, and children alike began to tune in to the program with a sense of joining in the adventure.

This wasn't much of a leap, of course, since the show represented something as comfortable as an easy chair. Whereas *Today* attempted to give viewers Mies van der Rohe, *GMA* offered a La-Z-Boy Lounger. From the fireplace on the set to the paintings on the walls, this was home. If not *our* home, at least a place in which many Americans felt *at home*.

David Hartman, whom Steve Friedman nicknamed "Mr. Potato Head," was a bit goofy, a bit dopey, and very appealing to women. He didn't frighten viewers with his intelligence, or even try to impress them with his integrity. He was like a pair of worn slippers that each morning awaited at the foot of the bed—nothing special to look at, but a perfect early morning fit.

For all his easygoing exterior, however, Hartman was quite the egotist off the air. As *Good Morning America* began its ratings climb, Hartman's ego swelled with the numbers. As the official host and central figure, he took full credit for the success of the program. The fact that Sandy Hill was by his side was a bonus but, as far as Hartman could see, irrelevant to the show's popularity.

Hartman made little effort to conceal his pride in his accomplishment, and even less at letting Hill know that he considered her little more than window dressing. In January 1980, Hill left to cover the Olympic Games in Lake Placid and was replaced by Joan Lunden. Hill took advantage of her absence from the set to contemplate her future and decided that *Good Morning America* was not going to be part of it. At the same moment that she was alerting network executives to her decision, Joan Lunden was receiving news of her own: she was going to have a baby.

For Lunden, the news was a mixed blessing. Although she was delighted to be expecting her first child, the timing of her pregnancy could not have been more traumatic. Lunden had waited years for the opportunity to be Hartman's official female counterpart, and now that it looked like she might actually be offered the job, she wondered how her pregnancy might affect the network's decision.

Woody Fraser, who previously had produced *The Mike Douglas Show* and the NBC daytime series *America Alive!* and who had taken over the executive-producer reins of *Good Morning America,* was instrumental in bringing Lunden to the program, first to do insert spots on new consumer products, and subsequently as a guest host filling in for Hill. Unaware of her pregnancy, he was now pushing hard for her appointment as Hartman's full-time sidekick. Ironically, the news that Lunden was expecting became the deciding factor in landing her the position. The addition of motherhood to the warm-home-and-hearth illusion that the series projected was certain to generate ratings.

The network's executives wasted little time in promoting Lunden. If Hartman was the new king of daytime, Lunden was his lady-in-waiting. Magazine articles in *Redbook, TV Guide, Women's Day, Time,* and *Newsweek* made much of the fact that viewers across America were tracking the progress of Lunden's pregnancy from its earliest months. By the time she left the program on maternity leave at the end of June, just days before her daughter Jamie was born on July 4, 1980, Lunden had gained fifty-five pounds.

During the last few months of her pregnancy, Lunden appeared happy and glowing on-air; her skills were developing even as her size increased with each passing week. Behind her flashy smile and look of contentment, however, Lunden was suffering in dreaded fear, unable to shake a clairvoyant warning that a handwriting analyst/priest had shared with her when he made a guest appearance on the program. Privately, he had alerted Lunden that he sensed something was amiss with the pregnancy, and despite continual reassurance from her gynecologist, Lunden was now living in dread. It was a fear that was alleviated completely only with the birth of a healthy baby girl.

Lunden's pregnancy pushed *GMA* into an undisputed ratings lead over *Today*. Desperate to turn the tide, NBC dropped the show's executive producer, Joe Bartelme, replacing him with Steve Friedman in May 1980. Aware that his mandate was to destroy the competition at any cost, Friedman developed a plan that left no doubt that the competition between the two programs had shifted from a race to all-out war.

In analyzing the reason for his rival's success, NBC president Fred Silverman attributed much of David Hartman's appeal to his abilities as an actor. *GMA* was created when Silverman was president of ABC Entertainment,* so his input came from a unique perspective. Silverman observed how, rather than approaching topics in the manner of an informed newsman, Hartman became the viewers' ears and mouthpiece, asking the kind of questions that they themselves might pose.

Hoping to capitalize on this "everyman" aspect, Silverman made an offer to actress Mariette Hartley, giving her a shot at Jane Pauley's position on *Today* when Pauley took a planned vacation—an event of special proportions related to Pauley's on-air announcement that she

---

*Fred Silverman was president of ABC from 1975 to 1978, when he joined NBC as its president and CEO. He was ousted from that position on June 30, 1981.

was marrying political cartoonist Garry Trudeau. With her head full of romance and the excitement of a long-anticipated honeymoon, Pauley was none-the-wiser when she signed off for a three-week hiatus.

Although Hartley was then in the full flush of fame, thanks to several successful and popular commercials for Polaroid cameras in which she was paired with James Garner, she arrived on the set of *Today* on June 9, 1980, both ill prepared and ill informed. She would later attest to the fact that Silverman had actually offered her a seven-year contract replacing Pauley as cohost of the foundering program. Despite Silverman's denial, then as now, Hartley claimed in a *Parade* magazine interview that "Fred Silverman told me he would change my life," adding, "The *Today* show is dying and Silverman wanted some pizzazz, some loosening up."

Given her mandate as Hartley saw it, it was hardly surprising that on her first day on the air, she hurled one-liners and smart-aleck comments to a startled Tom Brokaw.

"Good morning all. I'm Tom Brokaw," he began the show. "Let me introduce you to Mariette Hartley, if I may. Jane Pauley is off on three weeks' vacation—"

"Vacation?" Hartley interrupted, smiling. "She's getting married. That's hardly a vacation. . . ."

Tom Brokaw paused as if slapped by a wet fish in a synagogue, then valiantly carried on. "Anyway . . . Mariette, it's nice to have you with us, without your Polaroid along."

"Do you know this desk is just about as uncomfortable as I always thought it would be?" she bantered. "Now, if I can just get my red lights and my words straight, we'll be okay."

Had Hartley's vamping in clever tongue-in-cheek style happened on Johnny Carson's *Tonight* show, it would have been thought of as clever and witty. But to Tom Brokaw, it was an affront to his dignity and position as a broadcast journalist, and he took every opportunity to make Hartley aware of that.

"I felt like I was in the enemy camp," Hartley told *Parade*. "Silverman put me on the show, and then he disappeared. He went to Hawaii. There was very little support. I wrote him a telegram—'Wish you were here, 'cause nobody else is.'"

Ironically, Hartley had not been tutored in the art of reading a TelePrompTer and, squinting into the brightly lit set, found it difficult to follow the copy as it scrolled in front of her eyes. The network's executives were well aware of what had happened when CBS put the unprepared Sally Quinn in the host seat and allowed her to die slowly on the air, so it was especially inconceivable that they would allow history to repeat itself.

Hartley had to read copy, follow time cues, watch for her key camera, and listen to the dialogue in her earpiece—all while appearing to have a great time on a set that was populated with people eager to see her fail. It was little wonder that she later referred to the program as "the *Titanic.*"

Undaunted, Hartley managed to get in a few licks among the news giants. On the air one morning, Brokaw acknowledged his surprise at how articulate Sidney Poitier had been during the host's interview with the Oscar-nominated actor. Film critic Gene Shalit responded by saying that he thought it curious how the "second tier of actors" always seemed to be the most articulate. Hartley, taking the term "second tier" to suggest something less than box-office premium, sprang to the actor's defense—and her own as well—equating watching Poitier to "watching a burning coal." When Shalit complimented her interpretation, Hartley slammed back, "Yes, we second-tier actresses once in a while can be articulate, too. Want to see the third tear?" she asked Shalit, pretending to wipe one from her eye.

It was a dramatic outburst that left Brokaw obviously outraged. A crew man on the stage that day commented that Brokaw "was about as naturally funny as torn panty hose. He just didn't get it, and he didn't try to get it."

Steve Friedman would later come to Brokaw's defense, attributing the behavior of those on the set to loyalty to Pauley, who had worked with the show at this point for four years and was nearly "one of the boys." In reality, Pauley, who didn't even hear about the Hartley debacle until she returned, was nearing the end of her initial contract with *Today.*

There was much speculation that Pauley's time on the program was indeed limited, since her on-air skills had not dramatically

increased during her tenure. Her re-signing to a new contract had less
to do with her skills than with the network's reluctance to rock the boat
any further.

Pauley would vacillate between being succinct, intuitive, and
probing during interviews to blanking out completely, as if forgetting
where she was and to whom she was speaking. As chants of "Earth to
Jane" echoed from the control room, Pauley sometimes resumed control of the interview, but often she did not. One never knew—least of
all Pauley herself, who was unable to control her performance from one
day to the next.

Soon after returning from her honeymoon, Pauley was visibly
jolted by a segment about Cap d'Agde, a town along the French Riviera
where dressing *en déshabillé* is considered part of the culture. While
every attempt was made to cover most bare breasts during a video of
supermarket shoppers, there was an abundance of bare buttocks that
left little to anyone's imagination. As Friedman later commented, "It's
pretty hard to run something about a nude town without showing
some nudity."

To Jane Pauley, the segment was out of place on the program.
"This was morning television," Pauley said. "I must say it caused my
heart to palpitate a bit, but then I'm probably a little queasier than most
of America." One can only imagine what Mariette Hartley would have
done with such material.

Joan Lunden returned from maternity leave in September 1980, as
Good Morning America continued to nip at *Today*'s throat and fre-
quently bested it in the ratings race. The woman who had brought
pregnancy to early morning television now brought her eight-week-old
baby to the set, breast-feeding her during commercial breaks. On her
first day back on the job, Lunden had gotten up early, showered,
changed Jamie, zipped her into her bunting, and headed into Manhattan. Unfortunately, along the way her limousine broke down, leaving
Lunden to hitchhike to the nearest taxi stand and catch a cab. All in a
day's work for the brand new mother.

For its part, CBS remained an also-ran, confused and unfocused, despite its latest effort at turning news into information. Canceling the last remnants of *The CBS Morning News*, the network had recently created an early morning series with a revolving title—on Mondays, it was labeled "Monday Morning," Tuesdays, "Tuesday Morning," etc.—with newsman Bob Schieffer as anchor and Charles Kuralt on the road. Attempting to bend toward entertainment as best as it could, the antediluvian series began featuring a magazine format that was heavily reliant on the news of the day. However, its attempts at rejuvenation fell flat, mostly due to the network's inability to bring an entertainment producer in to handle the assignment. Still stuck in its pledge to present hard news, the network regurgitated *The CBS Morning News*, placing Charles Kuralt in the anchor seat that had supported Bob Schieffer.

While ABC and NBC continued to jostle for the undisputed ratings crown, the pressure was building in the executive suites to produce television's equivalent of the atomic bomb and simply blow away the competition. To NBC, that answer appeared to be a direct raid on the enemy camp, and an offer that one *Good Morning America* regular could not refuse.

CHAPTER SIX

THE RAID

*R*ona Barrett was one of *Good Morning America*'s most popular regulars. The queen of Hollywood insiders, who the *Washington Post* once said had "all the warmth of a self-service gas station at 2:00 A.M.," appeared twice daily, filing stories on Tinseltown and those who made it glow. The self-styled "Miss Rona," who previously had a series of magazines bearing her name—their titles accompanied by the words "gossip" or "Hollywood"—also had written a best-selling novel, *Lovomaniacs,* and had recorded an LP, "Miss Rona Sings Hollywood's Greatest Hits."

Barrett became famous by uncovering facts about those even more famous than she and revealing them to America before the studios, press agents, networks, and the stars themselves wanted those facts known. She was the best at what she did, but for Miss Rona, what she did wasn't enough. What others labeled gossip, Barrett saw as legitimate news. She did not traffic in rumors; she dealt only with fact, and she wanted her next step at ABC to land her a series of celebrity specials that would prove the point.

ABC, however, saw things differently. Rather than hold out the carrot of primetime to Barrett, the network pointed to its new "Million Dollar Baby," Barbara Walters. It was Walters who would do the celebrity specials—Walters, who had learned her trade in news, not entertainment. Wounded by the put-down and eager to prove her worth, Barrett began to air her displeasure to anyone who would listen. One of those listening the hardest was the newly installed president of NBC Entertainment, Brandon Tartikoff. At the expiration of Barrett's three-year contract with *Good Morning America*, Tartikoff offered her an opportunity to raise not only her earning power, but her television exposure as well.

NBC's *Tomorrow* show, which had previously aired as an hour entry following the *Tonight* show and was hosted by Tom Snyder, was expanding to a ninety-minute format under a new title, *Tomorrow Coast to Coast*. Tartikoff was excited by the prospect of offering the opportunity to cohost the program to Barrett, who would be positioned in Los Angeles, while Snyder continued to broadcast from New York. Additionally, he offered Barrett a spot on the *Today* show. Since *Tomorrow* was an NBC Entertainment production and *Today* an NBC News program, Tartikoff could substantially increase Barrett's take-home pay, which totaled $500,000 (plus the cost of her staff), by spreading the payments between both corporate entities.

Barrett eagerly jumped at the opportunity, as much to snub her former network as to help her new one, all the while anticipating following Barbara Walters's footsteps into the News Division. When ABC executives heard of her plans, they dropped her from the air before her contract's official expiration date of October 23. Barrett wasted no time in turning her talents to *Tomorrow*.

NBC's Tom Snyder, who perceived himself a newsman, felt less than enthusiastic about being coupled, even remotely, with Miss Rona. He also was still feeling the pangs of ego deflation at having been saddled with a costar when previously the *Tomorrow* show was *his*. Consequently, the reception he gave her was sub-zero. Yet, even Snyder reluctantly admitted that Barrett had enormous fan appeal, and that viewers had a seemingly endless lust for the kind of keyhole journalism in which she specialized.

Fate, however, would deal Barrett a cruel blow after her first major celebrity interview for *Tomorrow Coast to Coast*, a fascinating and in-depth conversation with Mary Tyler Moore, who was eagerly discussing her upcoming film *Ordinary People*. Moore played a mother whose own selfishness is masked by the perfection of her *Better Homes and Gardens* home. As the film opens, that mask is ripped off in the face of the accidental death of her older son and the attempted suicide of her younger son.

Directed by Robert Redford in an Oscar-nominated performance, Moore appeared justifiably proud of her portrayal in the Barrett interview. Soon after granting the interview, however, Moore's own
son tragically committed suicide. The analogies to the film escaped no
one, and it became obvious that the Barrett interview could not be
aired out of respect for the actress.

Snyder used the episode as fodder for the arsenal he was building
against Miss Rona. The on-air dialogue between the two was obviously
strained, and as the year ended, only increased in its hostility. Having
experienced the reaction she received from Snyder on *Tomorrow,* Barrett was braced for what was to come from Brokaw on *Today.*

When Barrett began to appear Tuesdays through Fridays on
Today in January 1981, Brokaw refused to introduce her. He had
assumed the mantel of one being groomed for *NBC Nightly News* and
let it be known that he did not want to be associated with Barrett in any
way. As *Good Morning America* was receiving kudos for its warmth,
Brokaw was becoming more formal. He had apparently forgotten that
he once held the title for having turned the most revolutions while riding inside a clothes dryer at the local laundromat in Deadwood, South
Dakota.

Fortunately, Jane Pauley had no reservations about introducing
Rona Barrett, who began her *Today* run amid a high-profile campaign
from NBC's publicity department. Barrett had come to *Today* insisting
on certain conditions that she had negotiated while on *Good Morning
America.* In addition to having the network pay for her seven-member
staff, she insisted that she be photographed from only one side, with the
camera using a soft-focus technique. Compared to the rest of the show,
Barrett's segments always appeared to have been shot by a slightly
drunk cameraman who couldn't quite get his focus to snap into place.

With precious few friends among the cast and crew, Barrett began
to feel like a pawn in some larger game. While Brokaw spoke out against
her with regularity and Jane Pauley remained her neutral, noncommit-
tal self, only weatherman Willard Scott openly supported the newcomer in New York's *Today* offices.

Scott himself knew what it was like to be an outsider. He had
arrived on the show in March 1980 as a replacement for weatherman

Bob Ryan. The outgoing and friendly onetime comic had begun his career as the original Ronald McDonald of the successful burger chain. He had modeled the character after Bozo the Clown, a character he had once portrayed.

Scott had made his way to *Today* through NBC's Washington, D.C., affiliate, WRC-TV, where he was on staff as an announcer when the weatherman position opened up at the station. Since Scott was available and already paid for, it made economic, if not common, sense to use the bald, rotund performer in the position. Hardly a meteorologist like *Good Morning America*'s John Coleman, he learned as he went, filling in with trivia and warmth what he lacked in knowledge about tropical lows and cumulus clouds.

Scott's comical style and ability to make conversation about any-thing—from a frog-throwing contest to a Toe Jam Festival—made him an easy target for critics. In fact, in his first few months on the show, the weatherman, who had been a favorite in Washington, D.C., was nearly universally panned by both reviewers and viewers alike. *Today*'s executive producer, Steve Friedman, remembered that "not even my father liked him." Even Scott himself wondered if the *Today* show move was a "serious mistake."

Initially, Scott didn't move to New York to join the other regulars on the set, preferring instead to stay in Washington, D.C., where he could "sleep in my own bed with my dogs" and broadcast from a local studio. It was another thing he had in common with Barrett, who shot her segments from Hollywood. But, unlike Scott, who gained acceptance over time, Barrett continued to generate ill will with Brokaw and the crew.

After six months of what she considered abuse on *Tomorrow Coast to Coast*, Barrett left the program, leaving her *Today* spots as her only broadcast outlet. Unable to justify her high salary, which now was being paid only by NBC News, the network made an attempt to pare it down to $150,000, plus a token amount for her staff. Barrett instantaneously refused to even consider a reduction, labeling the move "sexual discrimination" and purporting that if her name were Ronald Barrett such a salary cut would never even be attempted.

Mary Tyler Moore's ex-husband, Grant Tinker, who had replaced Fred Silverman as head of NBC, chased Barrett down at the beauty salon and attempted to convince her to remain on the program. Barrett would not budge, despite the loss of income and position. She held her ground, as did NBC (which officially claimed that the network "couldn't afford" her demands), and joined the ever-enlarging group of women who once worked on *Today*.

For its part, ABC had replaced Barrett with a new entertainment editor, Joel Siegel. A toned-down Gene Shalit look-alike, Siegel brought varied experience to his witty film reviews and entertainment pieces. He had previously been a joke writer for Senator Robert Kennedy, a radio commentator, and a book reviewer for the *Los Angeles Times*, as well as an inventor of ice cream flavors for Baskin-Robbins.

In an effort to stay competitive with the increasingly popular *GMA*, the *Today* show added several new on-air talents of its own, including Los Angeles sportscaster Bryant Gumbel and Phil Donahue, who reported on lifestyle issues from Chicago. Gumbel had previously worked with Steve Friedman, and the two men formed a renewed mutual admiration society in New York.

Gumbel's arrival on *Today* was a fortuitous one. Both ABC and CBS were making overtures to Brokaw to leave NBC when his current contract expired at the end of the year, and Brokaw was doing little to quiet the rumors that he would change networks to topline an evening news telecast. NBC was eager to keep Brokaw at all costs and began to look for available options.

Brokaw was uncomfortable with the idea of doing a show that viewers still looked upon as entertainment, not news. More important, he knew that John Chancellor was stepping down as head of *NBC Nightly News* in the coming months and wanted to be free to keep his name at the top of the list of potential replacements.

Unfortunately, NBC executives already had contracted with veteran newsman Roger Mudd to replace Chancellor if and when he vacated the news-anchor position. By September 1981, it no longer was a question of "if," and the "when" was quickly being determined as well. Knowing that Brokaw was NBC's top choice, Mudd made a politically correct move by meeting with the *Today* host and subsequently advising NBC News executives that he had no problem in waiving the exclusivity clause in his contract and sharing *Nightly News* duties with Brokaw.

For Mudd it was a wise move, since by this point Brokaw's stock had risen so high due to the interest from the competition that NBC executives were hellbent on ensuring that they didn't lose him. If that meant paying off Mudd, so be it. In large part due to his accurate analysis of the situation, Mudd managed to keep his on-air job and save face with the network. For its part, NBC joined what it considered the two hottest newsmen in the business for what would soon be called *NBC Nightly News with Tom Brokaw and Roger Mudd.* One problem was solved, but an even larger one was created.

Replacing Brokaw on the *Today* show was a difficult challenge for a number of reasons. In every other occurrence when the host position became vacant, *Today* was the timeslot leader. Such was no longer the case. NBC not only needed to fill the slot, it needed to fill Brokaw's job with someone who would build *Today*'s ratings back to the show's former place in the sun. Jessica Savitch and Chris Wallace were the first names proposed as replacements, but Steve Friedman had another idea. If *Today* was to stay competitive, it had to be dragged into the fast-paced world of live TV, kicking and screaming if need be. For Friedman, the key was moving *with* the news, not reacting *to* it. And nobody knew about following a play-by-play better than Bryant Gumbel.

Gumbel was one of those rare talents who seemed to be able to memorize facts and dialogue easily and remain unfazed by the unexpected—all without any formal training in broadcasting. He had graduated from Bates College in Maine, where he majored in Russian history and played some intramural sports. After graduation, he worked as a traveling salesman of corrugated containers for the Westvaco Corporation, and then spent a year in New York writing for *Black Sports* magazine, where he became the editor before leaving to join KNBC-TV in Los Angeles as a weekend sportscaster. His voice, while slightly high pitched for television work, was nevertheless well schooled and his pronunciation was flawless, thanks to a parochial upbringing dictated by his father, a probate judge in Cook County, Illinois.

As Friedman remembers it, Gumbel was hired based on "the most flawless audition I've ever seen," a tribute to his ability to stay focused under pressure. That was in 1972. In subsequent years, Gumbel perfected his style, improved his contacts, and moved up within the NBC Sports Division. He arrived in New York prepared for anything, except perhaps the opportunity to host the *Today* show.

When Friedman first approached Gumbel with the idea, the sportscaster was flattered but overwhelmed by the prospect. For Gumbel, however, nothing stays insurmountable for long, and so it was with the potential that the *Today* show position presented. Some say it took only a matter of minutes, others several days. Regardless, Gumbel became convinced that he was capable of doing a first-rate job for NBC, and it only remained for Friedman to sell the concept to the network.

Although NBC chief Grant Tinker was a Gumbel fan and supporter, NBC News president Bill Small was not. Small preferred to keep the position within his News Division, specifically with Chris Wallace, Mike Wallace's son and a rising star at NBC News. In an effort to placate Small without losing Gumbel, Friedman made what he later described as his "biggest mistake at my time at *Today*."

After a power powwow at 30 Rockefeller Plaza, it was decided that for the first time in its history, the *Today* show would have a trio of co-anchors. Bryant Gumbel was hired to join Jane Pauley in New York, while Chris Wallace would anchor *Today* from Washington, D.C. The concept was designed to allow each to handle what he or she did best. The problem was figuring out exactly what that talent was. "Hodgepodge Lodge" is how Friedman described it.

Once he was permitted to leave NBC Sports (the Sports Division did not want to lose Gumbel before his contract expired at the end of 1981), Gumbel had little trouble adjusting to life outside the locker room. Brokaw, who was anxious to leave *Today*, signed off on December 18. In keeping with his dignified, pompous newsman persona, he ended his nearly half-dozen years on the series in nonhumorous fashion, with the exception of his introduction.

"Good morning all. I'm Tom Brokaw, here with Jane Pauley and Gene Shalit ... ," he began.

"This is not *Today*," Pauley interrupted. "This is *the* day."

"The day you get rid of me, *finally*," Brokaw continued. "I was just explaining that Mrs. Brokaw showed very good judgment this morning. She woke up and said, 'On this occasion I ought to go down and fix you some fresh orange juice and some coffee,' and with that she promptly rolled over and went back to sleep, in keeping with the last five and a half years."

The two hours that followed included an interview with President Ronald Reagan, who wished Brokaw "Good luck in the new work schedule." Willard Scott, ever the humorist, sang a tribute, backed by the entire University of Maryland choir:

> You're leaving *Today*,
> And we've got the blues,
> But we'll see you at night
> On NBC News.

After a taped tribute and a surprise visit from skiing buddy Robert Redford, Brokaw recapped his tenure with a farewell speech that provided more insight into the *Today* anchor position than the man delivering the message:

> This is one of the most privileged seats in broadcasting, whoever occupies it. The occupant is guaranteed a close-up look at the passage of life, large and small, good times and bad. What makes it especially appealing, I think, is its active nature. In five years, I've been able to examine questions, ponder the issues and personalities of our time. It's a privilege and I am grateful.
>
> I'm grateful, too, for the continuing interest and support of all of you. More than any other news program of which I'm aware, there's a personal bond between here and out there, and I have learned from all of you as well.
>
> I'll miss being here for a lot of reasons. The people

with me in front of the camera and those behind the camera are first among them. Gene and Jane and Willard truly are my friends as well as my colleagues, and for those of you who don't see the people behind the cameras, I am simply in awe of them. Think of what they accomplish every week: live television, two hours a day, five days a week, fifty-two weeks a year. And always on time—or almost always.

As for me, after a couple of months of other reporting assignments, I'm off to *Nightly News* with Roger Mudd and John Chancellor doing commentary. In the meantime, the next time someone comes up to me and says, "What time do you have to get up in the morning anyway?" I can answer with a smile and say, "Just in time to hear my good friend, Bryant Gumbel, say, 'Good morning, this is *Today* on NBC.'"

As Brokaw was signing off on NBC, CBS was rearranging its own early morning line-up to take advantage of what the network hoped would be a period of viewer indecision. In one bold stroke, it cut *Captain Kangaroo* from one hour to thirty minutes and moved it from 8:00–9:00 A.M. to the 7:00 A.M. timeslot. From 7:30 to 9:00 A.M., it offered yet another version of *The CBS Morning News* that joined Diane Sawyer with Charles Kuralt. While not exactly a new show, it was revitalized with the addition of a female cohost.

The daughter of a respected judge, Diane Sawyer grew up in Louisville, Kentucky, shy, smart, and beautiful. Once called a "Hallmark teen" for her all-American childhood, she played the organ, loved basketball, joined the Seneca High cheerleading squad, and edited her high school newspaper. As America's Junior Miss in 1963, she traveled around the country, tiara and sash properly in place, conquering her fears and chancing to meet inspirational writer Catherine Marshall, a lifelong mentor.

By the time Sawyer moved to Washington, D.C., she was a Wellesley graduate and a seasoned weather girl, albeit one with vision problems who could not tell the difference between the East and West coasts. She did, however, find her way around Washington, where she worked in the White House as an assistant to the deputy press secretary before landing several positions within the Nixon administration. After helping the former president write his memoirs in San Clemente, Sawyer joined CBS News as a floor correspondent at the 1980 Democratic Convention. Two years later, her political savvy and probing style won her a place on the dawn patrol next to Kuralt on *The CBS Morning News,* where she remained typically cool and confident despite pressure to overtake *Today* in the ratings.

When Bryant Gumbel took over *Today*'s New York anchor chair, the show was limping along in second place. Even its most loyal fans had checked out the competition on ABC, after a series of guest hosts during the month of December added to the program's woes. Yet Gumbel, who was not used to losing in any contest—sports or otherwise—was confident that with his arrival, *Today*'s flaccid ratings would be dramatically improved.

During the first weeks of Gumbel's tenure, the show's ratings did rise above its ABC competition, but dramatically fell back once viewers' curiosities had been satiated. Part of the problem was the lack of special guests—the star quality that brings both prestige and interest to any early morning series.

Executive producer Steve Friedman, who had placed an ever-increasing priority on booking stars on the program, created a talent department headed by onetime *People* magazine staffer Judy Kessler. *Good Morning America* already had its talent wing up and running under the thumb of top talent booker Ellin Sanger. The two women competed manicured nail to manicured nail in an effort to win the hottest names for their individual programs, each relying on their wits and a Rolodex full of home telephone numbers to make the impossible happen.

Along with Gumbel's arrival, however, there was an immediate dearth of celebrity guests. Since no one really knew how well the sportscaster's skills would translate from the playing field to studio interviews, few wanted to test the water and take the first dip. During Gumbel's debut week, no stars appeared. It was not until ten days into his run that the studio found itself a home to stars, and only then for a very special occasion—*Today*'s thirtieth-anniversary celebration.

On January 14, 1982,* NBC threw an on-air party marking the birth of early morning television three decades earlier. *Today* segment producer Karen Curry was assigned the task of assembling as many of the series's stars as she could. Dave Garroway led the parade of notables. Back as well were Garroway's sidekicks Jack Lescoulie and Frank Blair along with Betty Furness, Estelle Parsons, Lee Meriwether, Betsy Palmer, Helen O'Connell, and Florence Henderson.

John Chancellor, Tom Brokaw, Barbara Walters, and Hugh Downs also dropped by with reflections and memories, joining Curry's collection of arranged film clips. So, too, did Joe Garagiola, Jim Hartz, Edwin Newman, and Sylvester "Pat" Weaver. Notably absent was J. Fred Muggs, who was happily entertaining vacationers at Busch Gardens in Tampa, Florida, still under the watchful eye of trainer Roy Waldron.

It was a show as much about the future as the past, since those who had come before had laid a very carefully constructed foundation for the years ahead. More than anything else, the collection of talent impressed viewers with the legacy that had been placed, with no amount of undue ceremony, in Bryant Gumbel's care. Despite the fact that Chris Wallace was contractually Gumbel's equal on the program, there was an obvious distinction that placed Wallace, along with Jane Pauley, into a supportive role. Steve Friedman labeled the trio the Mod Squad, after the seventies hit TV series featuring a black Afroed youth

---

*The day before the thirtieth anniversary show, an Air Florida 737 took off from Washington, D.C.'s National Airport and slammed into the 14th Street Bridge, killing seventy-eight people, including several on the bridge. While the other early morning programs covered the tragedy extensively, booking survivors on their broadcasts, *Today* kept its original special program intact and celebrated with a party.

who joins forces with a WASPesque dropout and a blonde female runaway to become undercover cops. Yet, the Gumbel-Wallace-Pauley team was anything but synchronized in the first months of the new show.

In an effort to bring stability to the program, Friedman now moved to keep segments and features consistent, to build viewer familiarity, and to increase ratings, while CBS, eager to capitalize on *Today*'s vulnerability, made its own moves. Ending months of industry rumor, the network added Charles Kuralt to the now-long list of *The CBS Morning News* hosts suddenly "reassigned within the department," and announced the addition of former CBS news correspondent Bill Kurtis to the early morning broadcast.

Van Gordon Sauter, who had previously been president of CBS Sports and was known in the industry for making decisive moves, became the new head of the CBS News Division. As 1982 began, Sauter expanded *The CBS Morning News* to two hours for the first time in its history, in the process canceling *Captain Kangaroo* after a twenty-seven-year run. By March, he had convinced Kurtis, then the most popular newsman in Chicago, to leave the Windy City for Manhattan and take a stab at the network's morning show. The newly retitled *The CBS Morning News with Bill Kurtis and Diane Sawyer* debuted on March 15, 1982. If the title lacked originality, at least it kept pace with the program, which, despite the new faces, seemed awfully familiar. Perhaps it was because in its rush to compete with *Good Morning America*, CBS hired away that show's executive producer, George Merlis. Lean, thorough, and intense, Merlis had worked his way through the ranks at *GMA* after serving as a producer on ABC's *Weekend News*.

Given the mandate to beat his former program at its own game, Merlis immediately began to take much of the strait out of the lace of the *Morning News* program, splattering it with entertaining segments similar to those on *Good Morning America*. His first hire was Pat Collins, who herself had briefly replaced Rona Barrett on *GMA*. Collins was brought aboard to do Hollywood pieces and celebrity gossip. Sportscaster Jim Kelly was contracted to handle a regular sports spot, and Steve Deshler took a position on the weather board. Merlis choreographed his anchors to move through the set, over to the weather map when the forecasts were due, then to the sports desk to check on the latest scoreboard—all the while making pleasant conversation.

The critics had a field day ripping apart the show's stumbling efforts. Tom Shales, writing in *The Washington Post,* asked: "What goes *chirp-chirp thud, chirp-chirp thud?* An 800-pound canary on *The CBS Morning News.*" In the *Los Angeles Times,* television critic Howard Rosenberg noted what he labeled "the cloud of interaction." He said it hung heavy over *The CBS Morning News,* adding, "Deshler cannot initiate a weathercast on his own. First, Kurtis or Sawyer must hike over to the weather board to engage him in chitchat."

Gone was Kuralt's theme music. In its place was a new up-tempo piece from Joe *(The Muppet Show)* Raposo that sounded like something out of *Star Wars.* The score was somehow appropriate, for as it appeared on the screen electronic starbursts exploded with the kind of pretend enthusiasm that one gives to visits of in-laws from a foreign land.

In one way, CBS was lucky. Since viewers were only beginning to discover the program, the show had precious on-air time to work out traffic flow and pacing. The constant movement on the set proved confusing for both hosts and guests. During an interview with Diane Sawyer, former Secretary of State Cyrus Vance, apparently thinking the show was not on the air, asked the anchor to get him a cup of coffee. Unfazed, Sawyer responded, "Perhaps a little later," and continued the interview. It would take months, but slowly *The CBS Morning News* would hold a core audience of fans.

By June, *Good Morning America* had attracted 27 percent of the morning viewing audience, compared to 23 percent for *Today* and 14 for *The CBS Morning News.* The real drama unfolded in the direction in which the numbers were moving. While ABC's ratings remained consistent, CBS was climbing and NBC was dropping. The network that counted on the $50 million in income generated by the *Today* show to sweeten its bottom line was clearly worried. By July, worry turned to panic as *Today* fell to within one-half a rating point of *The CBS Morning News.*

Viewers had finally discovered CBS, and many of them would develop into long-term fans. Kurtis and Sawyer had an easy rapport that was as professional as it was natural. While lacking the folksy warmth of Hartman and Lunden, they had authority. Whereas their counterparts at ABC and NBC were required to keep segments short and snappy, George Merlis allowed his anchors the luxury of time when the segments warranted lengthy examination.

Seeking a way out of its predicament, NBC commissioned a survey to discover why it was losing viewers. At the same time, it attempted to attract the increasing number of early morning viewers by launching *Early Today,* a news hour that preceded the *Today* show. In a stroke of lunacy, NBC pushed Gumbel and Pauley into anchoring the new show, increasing the burden it was placing on the already stressed cohosts.

Gumbel and Pauley weren't the only ones having trouble facing each new day. In Los Angeles, Dave Garroway had visions of regenerating his stalled career with an afternoon show geared to viewers over 40. He had originally pitched the idea to Fred Silverman soon after Silverman had taken over the helm at NBC. Silverman knew better than most that advertisers and therefore network affiliates were anxious to attract viewers in the 18–49 age bracket. A Garroway-hosted production for graying viewers hardly fit into the framework. With respect for Garroway's contribution to the medium and the veteran broadcaster's ego, Silverman told Garroway that he was "ahead of his time" and that although the concept was a good one, Garroway should come back and see Silverman in a couple of years, after he had had a chance to put NBC back on target.

By 1982, however, Silverman was gone from the network, taking with him Garroway's hope for a series. Depressed, forgotten, and despondent, Garroway looked out across his lawn in Swarthmore, Pennsylvania, the upscale suburban Philadelphia community he called home, and found that the world had passed him by. With only his classic cars and memories to remind him of his glory days, Garroway lost his reason to live. On July 21, 1982—failing to capture the peace that he lamented as he signed off each broadcast, palm to camera, in a hope for the future—he committed suicide by putting a gun to his head.

Garroway's sudden death seemed to hush a certain energy, not only on *Today* but on all the morning news shows. It was as if the village elder had passed on, taking with him to the grave some special magic.

Although Garroway's demise was noted in passing by newspapers and newsmagazines, unfortunately his suicide was more newsworthy than the passing itself. In death, as in life, Garroway had escaped being understood, most likely because he was never able to understand himself. The "Great Communicator" was dead at age 69. The curse had won.

CHAPTER SEVEN

THE GUMBEL GAMBLE

*D*uring *Early Today*'s first month, it became evident to even the most casual observer that Bryant Gumbel and Jane Pauley were wearing themselves thin, physically and emotionally. NBC News brought news anchor Connie Chung from Los Angeles to New York to take over the show, now renamed *NBC News at Sunrise.* Although the move was needed and welcome, it had the effect of adding grist to the madly turning rumor mill concerning the *Today* show.

Chung was a longtime buddy of NBC's chairman, Grant Tinker, and it was less than a stretch for some observers to predict that she was being groomed to take over *Today. TV Guide* and other magazines ran articles about the ongoing paranoia on the *Today* set, contributing further fuel to the predictions that a change was being contemplated within the network's executive suites.

When executive producer Steve Friedman finally made a move to alter the on-air assortment of host and assignments, it was more punt than touchdown. Claiming that "three doesn't go into two," Friedman admitted that his concept of a trio of anchors wasn't working and pointed to Wallace as the odd man out. Reassigned to cover the White House, Wallace actually was pleased with the rearrangement of duties. He had the most prestigious assignment in Washington, D.C., and he didn't have to wake up before the sun. John Palmer, who had been covering presidential politics, was brought into the studio to read the news each morning on *Today,* guaranteeing him a higher salary and daily airtime. Palmer, too, was excited by the musical chairs.

The same could not be said for Jane Pauley. In ridding the program of its three anchors, Friedman returned to the tried-and-true
arrangement of a male host with a female sidekick. Pauley saw the
move as a demotion and her disappointment evidenced itself on-air in
the form of a distracted and often amateurish performance.

A production assistant on the set at the time said, "It was something to watch. Jane's eyes would just glaze over and she'd space out,
losing her concentration and the pace of the program. Bryant
Gumbel was faced with the task of handling two hours of live television, never knowing in which direction Jane was about to vacillate
next."

By September, the *Today* show had dropped a total of 15 percent
in the ratings, compared with *The CBS Morning News*'s gain of 23 percent. It seemed as if it were only a matter of time before *Today* would
fall into third place. New York advertising executive Michael Wexler
seemed to vocalize what viewers were thinking: "The *Today* show is
tired and people are tired of the *Today* show."

What NBC needed was a minor miracle. What it got was another
jolt from *Good Morning America*. Just in time for the November ratings
sweeps period, David Hartman made an announcement: "If you've
noticed that Joan has put on a few pounds, it's because she's pregnant,
and we all want to congratulate her." Predictably, the audience did just
that, sending letters and gifts as they hung on to every detail of the
pregnancy.

One weekend in March 1983, Lunden went into labor (again) and
was rushed once more to the hospital. Hartman announced on the air
the following Monday that Joan's absence was caused by the imminent
arrival of her newest baby. Apparently, however, no one told the baby,
since the labor contractions stopped and Lunden returned home.
Viewers and mother-to-be waited as days went by uneventfully. Finally,
a week after Hartman's original announcement, Lunden went into
labor and was raced to the hospital by her husband, producer Michael
Krauss.

Unfortunately, New York was in the first stages of a transit strike
and the highways heading into the city were blocked. Krauss crossed

the medial strip and started to drive against the light flow of traffic leaving Manhattan, hoping to attract the attention of a policeman. Krauss got that, and more. When pulled over by a patrol car, Krauss pointed to Lunden retching with contractions in the passenger seat and asked for an escort to Lenox Hospital. Even with sirens blaring and lights flashing, pushing through the gridlock of New York proved painfully slow. Finally, at 10:04 A.M., Lunden, Krauss, and a slightly frazzled cop arrived at the emergency room entrance of Lenox Hospital. At 10:40 A.M., Lindsay Krauss was born. The following morning, *Good Morning America* was there, with cameras in the hospital room to show viewers the latest addition to the *GMA* family. Despite having given birth less than twenty-four hours earlier, Lunden looked typically flawless. And baby Lindsay made her show business debut.

The joke making the rounds of the *Today* office was that the only way to break *GMA*'s stranglehold on the ratings was to get Jane Pauley pregnant. Something about fighting fire with fire. Although no one actually told Pauley the joke, she must have gotten the vibe cosmically, for in the June 26, 1983, issue of New York's *Daily News*, gossip columnist Liz Smith alerted those on the *Today* show as well as the rest of the universe that Jane Pauley, Miss I-Don't-Like-Seeing-Nudity, was with child. What Smith didn't know, and Jane wasn't telling, was that she was having not one baby, but *two*. Twins.

Hoping that the news would have the same effect on *Today*'s ratings as Lunden's two pregnancies had on *GMA*'s, Steve Friedman anxiously anticipated that viewers would flock back to NBC's early morning programming. The tension that had been building in the offices of *Today* eased perceptively. Friedman and Gumbel took to playing games of catch as production assistants dodged baseballs, and each week saw reassurances that *next* week would be *the* week that *Today* returned to its leadership position.

If ever NBC needed proof that the viewers of *Good Morning America* and those of *Today* were not interchangeable, they received it during Pauley's pregnancy. As things developed, *Today*'s ratings actually *dropped.* In fact, on the very week in October when Pauley left on maternity leave, the *Today* show fell into *last* place for the first time in its history. Pauley had announced to viewers that she would be "home sleeping late, watching TV and twiddling my thumbs," and viewers apparently took her words as their exit cue to change channels. *The CBS Morning News* beat the *Today* show, and *Good Morning America* beat them both.

Industry pundits were busy writing off Gumbel as the reason for the dip in *Today's* ratings, but Gumbel himself was his own worst critic. He ripped apart his performance on every show, attempting to detect flaws in his presentation, interview style, and interaction with the other *Today* regulars. Others joined him in the rush to place blame.

Gumbel had risen to the position of *Today's* latter-day version of the "Great Communicator," with nary a rustle about the fact that he was black. What critics found offensive was his attitude of superiority, which most observers reasoned was a cover for his insecurity and which Gumbel, himself, explained was due to racism. Gumbel felt that viewers and reviewers held him to a different standard, dismissing the fact that his on-air demeanor was brash, interruptive, and difficult for most viewers to take in large doses, especially the first thing in the morning.

To his credit, however, Gumbel began to soften his sports-talk delivery and exercise patience, if not humility. The change in his on-air persona was most noticeable when he was teamed with Connie Chung, who was substituting for Pauley. Chung was all-business, articulate, and highly intelligent. Unlike Pauley's nondescript Midwest deportment, Chung was hard-edged and precise.

The youngest daughter of a Chinese diplomat who elected to remain in America after the 1949 Chinese revolution, Chung went to high school with the likes of Goldie Hawn and Watergate news hound Carl Bernstein. Remarking to *People* magazine that she was always a quiet child, she suddenly matured and became "like my father's son. I've carried on the family name in a different way."

Chung was selected because she was a no-nonsense interviewer and a highly skilled reporter and she gave Bryant Gumbel a serious challenge. Rather than trying to "fit in," Chung wanted to stand out—and she did. On one broadcast, when a speech by President Reagan finished early, Gumbel wanted Chung to help him fill time with commentary. Chung refused, saying she hadn't been paying attention to the speech and would only make a fool of herself. Gumbel, who later admitted that he also wasn't paying attention, was left to go it alone. He never forgave Chung for what he deemed as unprofessional behavior, and the two remained one level above enemies.

Those who predicted that Pauley would never return to the *Today* show had to recant their words when, in February 1984, she not only returned to the program, but returned a different woman. More relaxed, self-assured, and possessed with a wisdom with which motherhood seemed to bless her, Pauley radiated confidence.

Moved by the change he saw in his sub-host, Gumbel began to relinquish interviews and segments to her. Pauley had suffered a miscarriage in 1981, only a week after Tom Brokaw announced the news of her first pregnancy on the air. Some of the crew, however, were aware that she had also suffered a miscarriage the following year, and had kept the news private. It made the successful birth of her twins that much more of a miracle, and the change that transformed Pauley reflected the relevance of that truth.

Although the NBC executive suite was applauding the performance of its cast, it nevertheless had taken the precaution of hiring the Frank N. Magid research group away from ABC. Aware that Magid had produced results in his evaluation of *Good Morning America*, NBC put the survey titan on the scent of specific problem areas within the *Today* show. As Magid set forth to plan and execute a statistically significant study of the program, the show began on its own to etch slowly upward in the ratings. Although *Today* was consistently beating *The CBS Morning News*, it still wanted to attract *Good Morning America*'s viewers—and its advertising dollars.

Once it received word from the Magid organization that the key to viewer enthusiasm was location shoots, the early morning program went into a "remote frenzy," traveling to places across the country and around the globe. First stop: the wide-open range.

In August 1984, all three competing morning shows turned their attention to the city of Dallas, where the Republican National Committee was holding its political convention. The Texan theme and *Today*'s new family feeling made it appear quite natural to find Gumbel, Pauley, and weatherman Willard Scott floating on a raft in the middle of a "shark-infested" City Hall Plaza pool, eating watermelon and trying to stay cool in weather that Scott deemed "hotter than hellfire."

As Scott tackled trick ropers, armadillos, Texan cuisine, boot makers, and purveyors of fine cowboy hats, both Gumbel and Pauley loosened up a bit. The combination only helped the show's image. By comparison, *Good Morning America* seemed positively dry and straightforward, while Bill Kurtis on *The CBS Morning News* seemed a lone cowpoke, lost without his sidekick Sawyer, who was in Texas covering the Republican Convention and was then scheduled to join the regulars on *60 Minutes.*

The following month, while its competition remained in Manhattan, *Today* traveled to Russia, in what would prove to be the bellwether performance of Gumbel's career. For an entire week beginning September 6, 1984, the series broadcast live from various locations within the Soviet Union. A tremendous gamble, both financially and politically, the effort was complicated by the intense scrutiny from Soviet officials.

Gumbel left the United States with a coterie of producers, writers, cameramen, and technicians, but without the confirmation of a single appointment within the Russian government. Eventually, he did interview Soviet Deputy Minister of Foreign Trade Aleksi Manzhulo, the Russian cosmonaut Svetlana Savitskaya, two stepchildren of writer/physicist Andrei Sakharov, and Soviet Central Committee member Vitaly Kobyshysh. The show also traveled into a Russian home, speaking with the family and giving viewers a sense of what life within the Union of Soviet Socialist Republics was actually like.

Yet, Gumbel's true challenge came when he gained access to Chief Deputy Foreign Minister Georgi M. Korniyenko. While drawing on his background in Russian history to discuss the differences between Russian and American policies, Gumbel broached the subject of a possible summit between Foreign Minister Andrei Gromyko and President Ronald Reagan. During the course of the week, Gumbel was actually able to confirm that such a meeting had been arranged.

Gumbel also scored well with the new head of the Soviet army, Marshall Sergei F. Akhromeyev. Only a few weeks before the *Today* crew arrived in the Soviet Union, there had been a major shake-up within the Soviet military command. Gumbel's interview with Akhromeyev was America's first opportunity to explore what impact the resulting changes might bring. Gumbel was prepared, insightful, and able to spear the issues with a refreshing directness.

At that moment, for all intents and purposes, Gumbel was no longer the smart-aleck sportscaster who carried a chip on his shoulder large enough to cause dislocation. He had grown into a journalist of the most professional order—quietly and purposefully.

Gumbel returned to the United States with much less of the attitude that had caused him problems both on and off the set. To observers of the transformation, it was as if he finally realized that he didn't need to hide behind a pompous persona or his race. "He had a reality check," said a writer on the show. "He somehow knew he had grown into his destiny. There was no need to tell us. You could feel it when he was on the air."

Viewers picked up on the change as well, leaping back into the *Today* camp over the crumpled carcass of the once-proud *CBS Morning News*. Without Diane Sawyer's energy, Bill Kurtis had turned back into a formal newsman, that is to say competent and boring. CBS's early morning ratings plunged and the SOS went out to find Kurtis a new partner.

Initially, the top names on the list were Meredith Vieira and Jane Wallace from the News Division. Both, however, were rejected as lacking Sawyer's warmth. CBS decided to take a left turn into the world of sports with Phyllis George. So what if she wasn't exactly Bryant Gumbel, with his ability to think on his feet and enter male locker rooms?

George, who was Miss America of 1971, had joined CBS the following year as the network's first female sportscaster and had a successful run as cohost of *NFL Today*. She also had handled the pablum of hosting *Candid Camera* and the CBS series *People* and *Challenge of the Sexes*. It was easy, then, to see how the network would view George as the right combination of personality and talent to hit the mark in early morning TV.

On January 14, 1985, after a three-week trial run, George made her debut on *The CBS Morning News*. Bill Kurtis told TV critic Tom Shales that George's addition to the show brought "class" to the program.

Despite a $2 million makeover of the set, graphics, and theme song, the new *Morning News* was a repainted version of the old. Less homey than *Good Morning America*, the updated set looked more like the lobby of a Ritz-Carlton hotel. Executive producer Jon Katz promised that the show would grow into a "fast-paced electronic news magazine," which, when one thought about it, wasn't a whole lot different than Pat Weaver's initial conception of the *Today* show.

The last time CBS News had dared to venture beyond known territory, it had brought America Sally Quinn. Yet, any association between George and Quinn was quickly discouraged. Quinn, who was untried, earned $50,000 a year. George, thanks to the efforts of her manager, Ed Hookstratten, was hired at $750,000 for her first year, with annual increases taking her well over the million-dollar mark.

At the time, Hookstratten also represented Gumbel, whose own contract with NBC had expired the previous month and was the subject of ongoing negotiations. When Gumbel finally did re-sign, he had topped the million-dollar mark himself, but didn't approach the early morning salary leader, David Hartman.

At $1.5 million, Hartman was making more money than any other anchor on television, except for Tom Brokaw, whose salary had pinnacled at $1.75 million a year. Hartman had ridden the popularity of *Good Morning America* like a rodeo king, clinging onto the back of the bucking upstart program until he had tamed it into something savvy and inviting. As Hartman's salary grew, so, too, did his control of the program. But unfortunately for ABC, the very thing that had made *GMA* attractive to new viewers was now slowly beginning to turn them off.

Being folksy in a "golly-gee" way had worked well for Hartman. His Ichabod Crane looks and toothy grin seemed to beam into America's bedrooms straight from the farm. Hartman's instincts appeared infallible, and ABC encouraged his input into the program. The network labeled him a star, and Hartman gladly wore the crown. In contrast, not only was Joan Lunden not royalty, she didn't even have a title on the show. Publicity releases at the time referred to Hartman as the "host" of *Good Morning America,* who "was joined in the studio each morning by Joan Lunden," as if she were dropping by to deliver coffee and Danish.

As the ratings game tightened, leader *Good Morning America* was clearly losing ground. The effort of the early morning programs to outfox one another became more a war than a skirmish. *The CBS Morning News's* executive producer Jon Katz labeled it a "dogfight," adding, "We wrestle around on the cliffs a lot."

NBC's contribution to the slugfest was its emphasis on travel. Given *Today's* success in Moscow, the network announced plans to take the show to Rome during Holy Week, 1985. Yet even before the series had departed the familiar surroundings of the studio, *Today* drew even with *Good Morning America,* tying the show in the ratings one week and effectively ending its long solo run at the top of the Nielsen chart. Recharged with the victory and out for blood, *Today* launched itself into its Rome remote with renewed dedication.

Good Morning America's executive producer, Phyllis McGrady, was convinced that the key to recapturing and maintaining *GMA's* lead was to increase its share of male viewers, most of whom were loyal to the competition. During the spring of 1985, that meant baseball, specifically the spring training camp of the Detroit Tigers in Lakeland, Florida. To counter *Today's* lead, the network sent Hartman to baseball camp.

As a college student, Hartman was considered a major-league prospect at first base, and had been making trips to watch spring training for over fifteen years. "There's very little in life I enjoy more than playing baseball," he said. When *GMA* returned to the top position the following week, McGrady presumed she had touched on the answer.

Yet, it was NBC who, by the end of March, popped the corks of champagne bottles—Italian champagne, no less. As the *Today* show pulled into Rome, the series received word that it had generated a 5.3 ratings and 22 share to win the week ending March 22. *Good Morning America* earned a 5.1 rating and 21 share for that time period. *The CBS Morning News* trailed with a 3.6 rating, 15 share.* While not ignoring the numbers, ABC did allow that David Hartman was on vacation (he was replaced for the week by Frank Gifford). At that point, *Good Morning America* had been number one for 167 weeks.

On March 27, 1985, during his regular public audience, the Pope acknowledged *Today*'s presence by saying, "I am particularly pleased to welcome the group from the American television network NBC that will be broadcasting directly to the United States from the Vatican during Holy Week. It is my hope that your work will bear much spiritual fruit during this holy season when Christians all over the world celebrate the death and resurrection of Jesus Christ. Through you I send warm and cordial greetings to all the people of America."

Valuing the connection between religion and its ratings, NBC announced that it had been "honored" by the Vatican with the right to tape inside the Pope's private chapel—the Pauline Chapel. "This will be a network television exclusive," NBC News president Lawrence Grossman promised in a press release. Additionally, the press was informed that the Pope would greet the *Today* staffers (including Bryant Gumbel and Jane Pauley) and "is expected to exchange informal remarks with the entire crew." While NBC strutted around, peacock proud of its "exclusive," the press had a field day with what it labeled the "showbiz mass."

"Never mind the mass," countered Raymond Coffey of the *Chicago Tribune*. "The Pope is going to chat with—actually chat with—the really big stars, Pauley and Gumbel. Will he ask for their

---

* *Today* was seen in 4,499,700 homes, compared with 4,329,900 for *Good Morning America* and 3,056,400 for *The CBS Morning News*.

autographs?" he wondered. "What they're going to ask him, I can't imagine," he continued, "since as far as I know the Pope is not currently on tour pushing a new book."

Although the concept of a papal visit on an early morning talk show left many dumbfounded, to *Today* it was nothing short of inspiration. The credit for the supposed coup went to Tim Russert, who was Grossman's assistant and as such a vice president of NBC News. Russert, a Catholic from Philadelphia, had written to Archbishop John Foley, also of Philadelphia and the head of the Pope's panel on social communication. Foley saw the broadcast as a way for the Vatican to do some public relations at a time when the Church's image was in need of repair.

While hardly guaranteeing *Today* an interview with the Pope, or even an "informal chat" as the press release stated, what Foley did manage was permission to shoot inside the Pauline Chapel and allow Gumbel, Pauley, and weatherman Willard Scott to wear microphones as they attended the mass.

"Never before have American television cameras been inside this private chapel for the Pope," Pauley whispered as the Boys Choir of the Philadelphia Archdiocese chanted in the background.

The chapel, which was constructed in the fifteenth century, holds the last two paintings done by Michelangelo, *The Crucifixion of St. Peter* and *The Conversion of St. Paul.* During the mass, Gumbel, who was raised a Catholic, was overcome by the spirituality of the moment. It did not, however, prevent him from handing the Pontiff a floral wreath.

"Holy Father, on behalf of NBC News—from Warsaw," Gumbel choked forth.

The perplexed Pope asked, "From Warsaw? You brought that from Warsaw?" in amazement that anyone would go to Poland for flowers.

"We brought them from Warsaw—NBC News," Gumbel sputtered, as if sneaking in a plug. The Pope also was handed an NBC News cap, which somehow seemed appropriate to those in attendance.

When the Pontiff reached Willard Scott, also standing in the receiving line, he asked the weatherman if he was from Philadelphia.

"No, I'm a Baptist," Scott answered. The Pope laughed nervously as if he understood Scott's humor, and moved right along, muttering a prayer of salvation under his breath. "That Pope, he's my kinda guy," Scott later said.

As if there were anyone left in the viewing audience who missed the point, Willard Scott, broadcasting from the Colosseum, got to the bottom line of the location shoot: "Friends! Romans! Countrymen! I come to bury David Hartman, not to praise him."

Back in New York at *Good Morning America,* executive producer Phyllis McGrady labeled Scott's tongue-in-cheek lambasting "in the poorest taste." Inside word suggested that Shakespeare wasn't very impressed either. Meanwhile, *The CBS Morning News,* which had planned to be on location during the same week as well in Israel, canceled the trip after two CBS cameramen were killed by Israeli gunfire in Lebanon.

For all the success of the *Today* shoot, it wasn't without its negative side. Location producer Karen Curry, who had worked tirelessly in putting together the pieces of the remote assignment, remembered that at the end of the week, a group photo of the Rome team on the broadcast stage was being planned. As executive producer Steve Friedman, supervising producer Marty Ryan, producer Cliff Kappler, Bryant Gumbel, and Karen Curry were moving onto the stage, Gumbel is said to have commented, "Just the guys, Karen," while motioning her off the platform. It was typical of the "old boys club" mentality that had been encouraged at *Today* since Garroway's days and against which Barbara Walters had struggled for years.

For the most part, however, the *Today* team was jubilant at its success in returning to the ratings race and winning the top spot. On one of their last evenings in Rome, the cast and crew had a wrap party in a disco, where, under a mirrored ball, Jane Pauley actually kissed Steve Friedman's ring and said, "We've done it." Homage to hard work and little rest.

With barely time to unpack his suitcases, Gumbel was on the road again the following month, this time to Vietnam for live reports from Ho Chi Minh City marking the tenth anniversary of the U.S. pullout.

On this occasion, however, *Today* was competing with news reader Steve Bell, who was covering the event for *Good Morning America.*

Bell, who had covered the war for four years, was effusive with memories of his time in Vietnam. "I can almost hear, smell, and see the unique presence that was Vietnam," he said, and his reports reflected the history he carried with him since his departure in 1974. Gumbel, who, due to multiple breaks in a wrist, had never served in the military, gave lip-service to NBC's coverage of the anniversary, without the soul or compassion that Bell laced into each of his live reports.

The following week, David Hartman reported live from Bonn, Germany, where President Ronald Reagan was attending an economic summit. Days later, Bill Kurtis was in London with Phyllis George to commemorate the fortieth anniversary of the end of World War II. In a feeding frenzy of location mania, the gloves were off, and the most coveted guests were courted with all the intricacy of ancient mating rituals. Sometimes it worked; more often than not, it didn't.

The CBS Morning News was eager to get royals—any and all royals—on its London broadcast. However, the location trip to England was programmed only three weeks before airtime. "Buckingham Palace were quite charming. They didn't laugh when they told us that the royal schedule is prepared a year—not a month—in advance," said executive producer Jon Katz. Instead of a royal visit, Phyllis George did her Princess Diana impersonation on one program from London. Americans were not amused. Apparently, neither was Buckingham Palace.

During the May ratings sweep period, fate played into the hands of the morning telecasts via a highly publicized rape case and its aftermath. Cathleen Crowell Webb claimed to have been raped in 1977 by a man named Gary Dotson, who was subsequently convicted of the crime despite his claims of innocence. After serving six years in prison, Dotson learned that Webb had recanted her story and that his 25–30-year sentence was commuted.

Jane Pauley, who had interviewed Webb on *Today* when she first changed her story, was slated to do a segment on May 16, 1985, in which

Webb would meet face-to-face with the man she had sent to prison. *Good Morning America* had other plans.

Armed with information from Webb's attorney that she was flying in on May 12 to do the *Today* show, and eager to scoop the competition, *Good Morning America* staked out the United Airlines terminal at John F. Kennedy Airport. *Today* writer Phil Griffin had been dispatched to JFK to meet Webb's plane and was told to hide her in a hotel until Dotson was formally released from prison and flown to New York.

When Griffin met the plane, *Good Morning America*'s camera crew was on the scene, as were camera crews from several tabloid programs—all attempting to tape the arrival of the woman, her husband, and their attorney. The camera crews followed as Griffin hustled the trio into his waiting limo. A cloak-and-dagger chase through the boroughs of Queens and Manhattan ensued and continued for the next several hours. From expressways to side streets, the limo driver attempted to lose the pack of cars in hot pursuit.

"We went from the far left lane to a right turnoff and lost two cars," Griffin remembered, "but we still had four other cars behind us. You would have thought we were hooked by magnets."

It was only after speeding through Chinatown, Little Italy, and Battery Park, and then pulling up to the South Street Seaport, unloading his passengers, and speeding away, that the NBC driver finally lost the competition. Unsure what to do, the cars continued to follow the limo as Griffin and his captives disappeared among the shoppers.

Only after he had Webb and her entourage safely ensconced in an Upper East Side hotel did Griffin relax, and only then for a moment. There was still Dotson to worry about. This time, *Today* took no chances, actually chartering a plane to bring the man into Teterboro, a private airport in New Jersey.

Dotson and Webb formally met in the hotel before the program, and shortly thereafter made their *Today* appearance. No sooner had their segment finished than *Good Morning America* took the pair and their respective attorneys uptown via limousine to the ABC studio. After ABC was finished with Dotson and Webb, *The CBS Morning News* got its turn. It was one of the rare times that all three programs shared a guest on the same day. Although *Today* got its "exclusive" by airing its interview first, it was *The CBS Morning News* that received most of the attention, thanks to Phyllis George.

By the time Dotson and Webb reached the *Morning News* studios, they had recounted their individual stories twice. There was Gary Dotson, who might or might not be a rapist, sitting next to Cathy Webb, who proclaimed to be a born-again Christian and was an admitted liar. Dotson claimed to be unable to remember what he had said to Webb— the woman responsible for his six-year imprisonment—when they first met, despite the fact that the meeting had taken place only hours earlier. Webb, whose memory of the rape itself was now questionable, couldn't remember what she said either.

Presented with this odd mix, George gushed enthusiastically to Dotson, "I read this morning that you've had forty-one television offers to put this into a movie. Is that right? Do you feel like a celebrity?" Dotson, appropriately subdued and looking like he needed some sleep, responded that he had gotten some offers. "To star in your own movie?" George pushed.

"No," the monosyllabic Dotson replied.

Soon afterward, George asked the pair to shake hands and make up, as if they had just quarreled over who gets to ride in the back seat. Blushing, they did. Unable to turn off her Southern hospitality, the onetime sportscaster, onetime beauty queen, and onetime first lady of the state of Kentucky asked them to hug. The onetime accused rapist and the onetime victim stared at one another and refused.

The switchboards at CBS's headquarters in New York and Los Angeles were overloaded with viewers protesting George's gaffe. Executive producer Jon Katz, who was hospitalized at the time with pneumonia, could do little but cough in pain. Bill Kurtis couldn't even do that, for he had to say something, *anything,* to close the program.

After the show and for the weeks that followed, Kurtis took every opportunity to publicly indicate his displeasure with George, the series itself, and his involvement with both. He formally requested to escape his contract and return to Chicago. CBS did not want to lose Kurtis, but in order to keep what remained of its early morning viewership, the network agreed, asking for time to make an on-air transition.

Despite her flaws, George continued to receive the network's unequivocal support. Rather than tone down her role, CBS suggested that viewers see *more* of the cohost, as if daring the smiling hostess to transgress with flair once more. The fact that the program remained under the auspices of CBS News began to seem the biggest enigma of all. There was precious little of the legacy of Edward R. Murrow, or even Walter Cronkite, as *The CBS Morning News* entered the summer of 1985.

In late May the *Today* show romanced the rail, continuing its itch to roam. Boarding the "*Today* Express," a special Amtrak train, in Houston, Gumbel and Pauley traveled a whistle-stop tour of the Midwest. They broadcasted on successive days from New Orleans, Memphis, Indianapolis, and Cincinnati—all stronghold cities for *Good Morning America,* not coincidentally. The cost to NBC was a staggering $800,000 (about the same as it cost to take the show to Rome).

As NBC committed itself to returning *Today* to its past glory, even if it meant losing money on the show for the first time in thirty years, ABC's *Good Morning America* was almost lulled into a sense of its own immortality. Despite NBC's all-out effort to regain the ratings leadership, ABC confidently predicted that its fans were made of more "loyal stuff" and wouldn't be tempted by trains or any other "ratings stunts," as Phyllis McGrady labeled them.

No stunt or preplanned event could have mesmerized viewers as completely as did history itself when on June 14, 1985, a TWA flight from Athens to Rome was hijacked by members of the Islamic Jihad group and forced to land in Beirut. The terrorists, realizing the power of television, invited an ABC cameraman and a reporter from a French news agency aboard the plane, where an interview was conducted at gunpoint with the pilot, Captain John Testrake. The plane was then forced to fly to Algiers, where a few hostages were released before flying back to Beirut. Once there, negotiations began with Nabih Berri, a Shiite negotiator and the leader of the Amal militia.

Over the weekend, all three early morning programs latched on to the developing story. *Today* sent Karen Curry and her assistant, Amy

Krivitzky, to Paris to try and lock up interviews with the released hostages and their families. *Good Morning America* sent a team of producers to Frankfurt, where the United States government was centering its negotiation efforts. As *The CBS Morning News* began to make its own contacts within Lebanon, executive producer Jon Katz elected to replace the entire CBS news show line-up on both Monday and Tuesday with exclusive hostage coverage, explaining, "I'd feel very uncomfortable and think it would be in very poor taste to put on movie stars at a time like this."

Unfortunately, Bill Kurtis, who had finally been granted his early release from his *Morning News* duties, hosted his final show the Friday preceding the hostage crisis. In another bit of interesting timing, Phyllis George was also off the set, arranging the funeral of her father-in-law. Substitute co-anchor Terrence Smith was on duty when he was informed that *Morning News*'s planning editor Peter McCabe had outscooped the competition by arranging an exclusive interview with Nabih Berri.

ABC's talent booker Ellin Sanger also managed to catch up with Berri over the telephone several days later—the same day ABC correspondent Pierre Salinger linked up with the wife of hostage Allyn Conwell (an oil man from Texas) in Cyprus, where she had flown in order to rendezvous with her husband upon his release. Berri was patched across to David Hartman on the *GMA* set to be interviewed about his demands for the release of Shiite prisoners being held in Israel. During the half-hour news break that followed, Berri offered to allow *GMA* to speak with a hostage. Knowing that Mrs. Conwell was standing by in Cyprus for her interview with Salinger, Sanger asked Berri to allow Allyn Conwell to come to the phone. Through Sanger's determination—and the magic of television—Conwell and his wife were reunited over the phone for a few precious seconds. "Won't you please release my husband, Mr. Nabih Berri?" Conwell's wife pleaded. It made for remarkable morning television in anyone's book.

The *Today* show, unhappy at being outflanked by the competition, rolled into action in Frankfurt. Two weeks after the terrorist takeover of the TWA flight, the remaining hostages were released from

Damascus and were flown into Frankfurt to be debriefed. NBC decided to fly the families of two of the hostages into Germany for a reunion with their relatives on the *Today* show, including Mrs. Conwell, who had been brought in by charter from Corfu.

Allison Davis, *Today*'s first black writer, who was on vacation in Europe, was rerouted to Frankfurt to coordinate the operation. Davis met the arriving family members at the airport and safely shuttled them to their hotel. However, their arrival was quickly discovered by the competition, each of which wanted its own airtime with the families. Davis refused to divulge the location of the hotel. The resulting brouhaha produced headlines in the American media suggesting that the *Today* show was holding the hostages' families hostage. *The New York Times* ran the story on its front page and spared no hyperbole.

Mr. and Mrs. Allyn Conwell finally appeared together on the *Today* show just before Independence Day. Even with this victory, the morning-show hostage skirmish wasn't quite over. As a result of Ellin Sanger's perseverance, ABC ended up with an exclusive interview with the pilot. The morning that Captain Testrake was brought into the *Good Morning America* studios for his segment, NBC's *Today* writers were lying in wait. As Sanger escorted Testrake and a TWA press attaché to the World Trade Center's Windows on the World for breakfast following the show, *Today*'s talent booker Marianne Haggerty was in hot pursuit, unwilling to admit defeat until a screaming match with the TWA representative led the show to finally allow the hostage crisis to pass into history.

Without a news disaster to supply fresh faces, the *Today* show turned to a "Star of Tomorrow" segment, whose first act was Way Moves, a new-wave rock group from Chicago. Executive producer Steve Friedman defended these on-air performances as appropriate for the NBC News show, "the equivalent to light summer reading," he said. While affirming that there was no contest, and there were no prizes, when asked if the winner got two hours on *Good Morning America*, Friedman countered, "No, but the loser gets two weeks."

The following September, *The CBS Morning News*'s Phyllis George went on vacation and quietly resigned while at home in Kentucky. The official reason: she wanted to spend more time with her family. A CBS executive announced that although "it wasn't a mistake to hire Phyllis," things really hadn't panned out as expected with the anchor about whom critic Howard Rosenberg wrote: "She was swell-looking and sweet-sounding, but unprepared to stay afloat on even a lightweight newscast, a nonswimmer washed overboard without even water wings."

CBS replaced George with Maria Shriver, a Los Angeles reporter then engaged to actor/bodybuilder Arnold Schwarzenegger. Forrest Sawyer, who had moved from Atlanta several months earlier to anchor the *CBS Early Morning News*, was given Bill Kurtis's job, and Faith Daniels was brought in to read the news. Shriver, the daughter of Eunice Kennedy and Sargent Shriver, and Senator Ted Kennedy's niece, was not a beauty queen, but had enough hair to look like one. Sawyer (no relation to Diane Sawyer) was at least articulate and, unlike Kurtis, didn't frown.

However, even the pair's best efforts didn't stop TV critic Tom Shales from writing in the *The Washington Post* that the *Morning News* looked like "a local news show with expensive plants on the set." Marc Gunther wrote in *The Detroit News:* "Now that Phyllis George has gone home to Kentucky and Bill Kurtis is back in Chicago, the kiddie corps has taken over *The CBS Morning News*."

By October, with Sawyer and Shriver still in place, Jon Katz was asked to take a hike and Johnathan Rodgers was hired to fill his post as executive producer. Rodgers, who came to *Morning News* from the weekend edition of *Evening News*, needed to reprogram his internal clock but little else for the job.

Even as CBS held its corporate breath and hoped for the best, as fate would have it ABC was the network about to learn a hard lesson about ratings, anchors, and the fickle viewer at the breakfast table.

CHAPTER EIGHT

THE SHAKE-UP

*S*uccess has many parents. *Good Morning America*'s David Hartman had long overlooked that fact and had taken enormous singular pride in bringing the ABC series from its infancy to leadership in the early morning ratings race. As the series's success grew, Hartman demanded and was granted more control, until he had approval in the selection not only of his costars, but also of the guests, scripts, even the order of the series's rundown. After ten years, Hartman considered *Good Morning America* his property, and his $2-million-a-year salary suggested that ABC agreed with him.

In March 1985, the announced merger of Capital Cities/ABC Inc. for $3.5 billion made headlines around the world, and made many at ABC wonder about their future with the network. Hartman was one of them. By the time the merger actually took place and the keys to the washrooms were exchanged, on January 3, 1986, Hartman had gotten the message that his star was dimming around Capital Cities. The company was conservative, in both outlook and pay, and the concept of any single individual commanding $2 million per year was difficult to accept.

Had the series been the clear-and-away ratings champ of early morning television, Hartman may have had a case for his continued control. But in fact, as 1986 began, and NBC's *Today* mounted its relentless crusade for first place, *GMA* was lagging and its popularity among 18–49-year-old women was down. Hartman had been trained for battle, but he saw in Capital Cities a company more interested in profit than war.

To Hartman, *Good Morning America* was a better program than *Today* because it opened up topics of interest to the average American. "I don't have to show how smart I am," he once said. Indeed, Hartman became the viewers' surrogate, asking the kind of naive questions that Bryant Gumbel on *Today* would deem too simple-minded. "We have a capacity on television to present information, sure, but the trick is to do it in an interesting way," he said to the *Christian Science Monitor*.

By 1986, the interest in the way in which Hartman presented information was declining, yet Hartman saw it as a temporary trend. And he defended his imperious manner by pointing to the $70 million that *Good Morning America* made in 1985 for ABC. "If the charge is made that I'm imperious or demanding, I will say, 'Yeah, I am,'" he told *Los Angeles Times* writer Jay Sharbutt. "But it's in the interest of doing things right. What you don't see and read about is that I am one of an army of staff members who share that feeling for the most part."

Unfortunately for Hartman, ABC Television's new president, John Sias, who came to the position through Capital Cities, did not get that impression. What he heard was that Hartman was domineering and suffocating in his attempt to push his creative control on all those associated with *GMA*. As Sias mocked Hartman's offish behavior and the size of his salary, ABC Entertainment president Brandon Stoddard admitted that he was taking "a serious look at *Good Morning America*."

While NBC placed its faith in the future of *Today* and allocated $1.3 million to send the show on location to South America, ABC pulled the plug on expenses at *GMA*, holding it to a budget that constricted the show's ability to promote itself. "Cap Cities was being cheap and killing us," said a production assistant who was fired during the summer of 1986. "They trimmed us wherever they could in the name of efficiency. And they did it despite David Hartman's protests."

As *GMA* continued to moan, the *Today* show celebrated in Rio de Janeiro at Carnaval. All the show's equipment that was shipped by plane to Rio was confiscated by customs officials until officials were bribed under the table. Additionally, the Brazilian government collected 10 percent of the production staff's pay, levied as a form of on-site tax and payable in advance.

While *GMA* was televising safety-for-seniors tips and *The CBS Morning News* interviewed Geraldine Ferraro about how women get elected to office, *Today*'s crew in Rio was offering exciting fare. Segment producer Lisa Freed and a two-man crew were spending five days with the Kayapo Indians, and Bryant Gumbel, Willard Scott, and Jane Pauley were experiencing Brazil's nightlife. American schoolteachers from São Paulo's Chapel American School held up signs saying hello to their mothers and asking for M&M's, and soccer legend Pelé showed off his kicking talents and his legs. There was little question as to which early morning program American viewers were watching, or why. "We were having fun, and it showed," commented a segment producer who spent two days in a Argentinian hospital for food poisoning. Over at ABC, David Hartman felt just as sick.

If *Good Morning America*'s drop in the ratings had an effect on Hartman's influence, the opposite was happening to *Today*'s executive producer Steve Friedman, who was invigorated by the results of his nonstop, round-the-clock push for supremacy. The man who once kicked his foot through a TV monitor to get the network to replace it and routinely ripped telephones out of the wall was fueled by the adrenaline rush of beating the competition with increasing regularity. His outbursts became so intense that Jane Pauley had taken to removing her earpiece to maintain her calm, Midwest decorum.

Back in the studio, during one of his segments of on-air birthday wishes to centenarians, Willard Scott made news of his own when his wig caught fire while attempting to help 100-year-old Alfred Burin blow out the candles on his birthday cake. "It melted the glue on my hairpiece," Scott later laughed. "Seriously, we had to go touch up my hair."

The same week, *Good Morning America* seemed to be hot itself, beating *Today* for the first time in fourteen weeks. Unfortunately for David Hartman, he was off that week, replaced by actor Wayne Rogers. The third-ranked *CBS Morning News* lost its short-lived executive producer, Johnathan Rodgers, who was sent to Chicago as vice president of the network's affiliate WBBM-TV. Rodgers was replaced by onetime *Good Morning America* executive producer Susan Winston, who was hired with the lofty title Director of Morning News Planning and said she intended to "turn things around" within three months.

In May, *Today* went on the road again, or more precisely the high seas. Using as its base the SS *Norway,* at the time the largest cruise ship afloat, the show's cast and crew went steaming along the coasts of Florida, Georgia, and the Carolinas. Pauley, very pregnant once again, was permitted to bring husband Garry Trudeau, and admitted to feeling queasy. Gumbel, who was not pregnant but ate for two anyway, jumped to the show's defense when a critic suggested that it was all glitter and no substance. "I do get offended when people suggest that it is a ratings gimmick or that it's a quick fix. Television, especially a program like ours, should not only inform you, but also entertain you." Scott, after spending most of his on-air time kibitzing with some of the 1,800 passengers on board, announced, "They're giving me the signal. Back to Bryant Gumbel. No, to your local station." Raising his arm and putting his elbow in his left fist, he laughingly added, "That's a television signal, folks. Not an Indian salute." The SS *Norway* remote cost NBC $1.75 million.

Good Morning America dismissed *Today*'s success as little more than "stunting" and, insisting it wasn't "panicking," pumped up its on-air team by hiring Ron Reagan, the president's son, as a roving correspondent. In addition, the network hired talent coordinator Steve Lewis of *Nightline* to the staff.

Unfortunately, one of Lewis's first bookings was a man named Joe Bones, who claimed to represent the Fat Squad, a group of people from New York who were available for hire to supervise those trying to stick to their diets. The *Philadelphia Inquirer* ran a story about the group, as had *The Washington Post.* CNN, in its piece with Joe Bones, introduced him with: "At least he says that's his name for this week."

By the time Bones appeared on *Good Morning America,* the *New York Post* had already been tipped that the group was a hoax created in the fertile imagination of artist Joe Skagg, who claimed he was making a social comment on the "hypocrisy, gullibility, and vulnerability" of the media. The *Post*'s agreement not to print the truth until after *GMA* aired its piece didn't help the network's embarrassment when the truth was revealed.

"Yesterday morning, here on *Good Morning America*," Hartman announced the day following the *Post* revelation, "we were had. In spades. We talked with a man who called himself Joe Bones. You may have seen the interview. He told us about his Fat Squad that supposedly would go into people's homes for a fee and help them lose weight by physically keeping them away from the food in the refrigerator. Well, Joe Bones is not his real name, the Fat Squad is a hoax, we were had, as were many other respected newspapers and broadcasters, and we apologize."

By July, exactly three months after Susan Winston took over *The CBS Morning News* as executive producer and promised changes, the final curtain fell on the run of Maria Shriver and Forrest Sawyer. They were replaced in the game of trapdoor-under-the-anchor seat by Faith Daniels and Bruce Morton—at least temporarily. CBS News's Van Gordon Sauter was the man wielding the pink slips to not only the anchors, but the entire series cast as well, announcing that *The CBS Morning News* would be history by January.

A new show, which would "eliminate the traditional boundaries" between news and entertainment—as an interoffice memo from Sauter explained—was planned, but not by CBS News. The timeslot was turned over to a "new division" at the CBS Broadcast Group. Gone in the same breath was Susan Winston, who disagreed with the move, which she termed "improper," and quit as a result. The network's Atlanta affiliate, WAGA-TV, got so upset with the ongoing turmoil at *The CBS Morning News* that it dropped the program altogether and replaced it with syndicated programming, including *Hour Magazine* with Gary Collins.

Things were no less dramatic at *Good Morning America*, which had tried to compete with *Today*'s location shoots by scheduling one of its own—sailing into New York Harbor from Bermuda on the Cunard flagship, *Queen Elizabeth II*. ABC made much of the fact that *its* broadcast was from a moving ship, while NBC's was from the docked SS *Norway*, but the distinction was lost on viewers.

There were on-air changes at the ABC show as well. Weatherman Dave Murray exited and was replaced by WABC-TV's sportscaster Spencer Christian, who had several points in his favor. He was black (now seemingly a big selling point on early morning television), he knew weather (before doing sports, he was WABC-TV's weatherman), and he was droll. His wit and use of puns made him a charming catalyst for on-air conversation; although most of them fell flat on Hartman, at least they were tossed.

Far more striking was the announcement in August that Joan Lunden had successfully renegotiated her contract and was named cohost of *Good Morning America* for the first time. Hartman was quoted as saying he was pleased by "Joan's growth." Presumably, he meant professionally. Privately, he was livid at what he saw as a deliberate move by the network to limit his position and demanded contract concessions of his own. The network gave every outward indication that it was eager to renew Hartman's contract, but those behind the scenes tell a completely different story.

"Hartman was finished as soon as Cap Cities bought ABC," an attorney in ABC's Business Affairs Division maintains. "They wanted to get out from underneath his thumb without making it seem like they were firing him." When Associated Press broke the story of Hartman's exit from the show on September 26, 1986, it was anything but subtle. GOOD MORNING DROPS HARTMAN AS ITS ANCHOR read the headline in the *Chicago Tribune*. "Sources said ABC's new Capital Cities management has insisted that Hartman relinquish his production control," the article contended.

Hartman's official response was, "Eleven years is enough and I want to spend more time with my family." Although ABC did not pick up on the "family" explanation, it nevertheless announced that Hartman would continue to provide specials to the network. ABC vice president Phil Beuth suggested, "We will miss him and so will millions of Americans who looked to him and *Good Morning America* every day for assurance that all was well with their world and their lives." Presumably, those assurances would now come from Lunden, who seemed to be smiling more and told *People* magazine, "My chair on the set feels a little different now."

GMA executive producer Phyllis McGrady had announced several months earlier that she would leave the series in September to produce Barbara Walters's primetime personality interview specials. Veteran producer Jack Reilly got the nod to replace McGrady and joined Beuth in attempting to recharge a show that had become borderline complacent.

Adding to the changes on the set, the network brought on Chantal Westerman as an entertainment reporter and accepted the resignation of Erma Bombeck, who cited her own busy writing schedule. "We're hoping to appeal to a younger audience," Beuth commented on the changes.

David Hartman began taking Fridays off, allowing auditions for hopefuls to fill his seat. He also flew to Africa to do a five-part series on the continent, stopping off along the way in Libya for an exclusive interview with leader Moammar Gadhafi. Gadhafi, who controlled the conversation, claimed that Secretary of State George Shultz was a Jew and a Zionist,* and that President Reagan should be impeached. Hartman's interview, the first that Gadhafi had granted any American journalist since the United States attacked Libya the previous April, helped to solidify his reputation as a legitimate newsman—a welcome response to the potshots the actor–turned–broadcast journalist was receiving from the news organizations.

As Hartman announced his departure from *Good Morning America,* Jane Pauley was welcomed back on the *Today* set. After covering the wedding of Britain's Prince Andrew and Sarah Ferguson, Pauley had gone on maternity leave and was replaced on the air by Gloria Steinem, who had scored several major star bookings for the series, including Cher and Robert Redford. Yet, when Pauley returned, even the prideful

*Shultz was a practicing Episcopalian.

Bryant Gumbel had to admit that he missed her. If Pauley had matured during her first round with motherhood, this second plunge gave her a sense of humor. "She actually learned how to tell a joke," said Friedman, with a look of amazement. "At least I think it was a joke."

The biggest laughs at *Today*, however, were saved for CBS, which announced that it had decided to hire Mariette Hartley to anchor its newest morning show, tentatively titled *The Breakfast Club*. "It was as if a time capsule had exploded and out popped Mariette," said a researcher on *Today*. "Didn't anyone at CBS tune in during her three weeks here in 1980?"

As it happened, not only had CBS been watching, but so had Bob Shanks, the vice president originally responsible for *Good Morning America* at ABC. In September, Shanks had defected from ABC to join CBS as the executive in charge of the second half of CBS's planned three-hour show that was slated to replace *Morning News*. The first ninety minutes, running between 6:00 and 7:30 A.M., would be produced by CBS News, while the remaining hour and a half, which awkwardly bridged the 7:30–9:00 A.M. time period, would be geared toward "infotainment." Shanks felt that Hartley had the right mix of irreverent humor and intelligence to sell America on the program. As co-anchor, Shanks had selected Rolland Smith, a popular anchor with the network's New York affiliate, WCBS, and hired comedian Bob Saget as announcer and sidekick. A comic and deejay, Mark McEwen, was signed as weatherman.

For its part, *Good Morning America* was conducting on-air tryouts for Hartman's replacement with actor David Birney (then married to *Family Ties* star Meredith Baxter Birney) and ABC's Washington correspondent Charles Gibson. It also received word in December that Steve Bell, co-anchor of the show's news segments, was leaving to take a job at NBC's KYW-TV in Philadelphia. Yes, there were changes all around, but at least ABC had a show and people knew what to expect. The same could not be said for CBS.

The 90-minute *The Morning Program* (no longer titled *The Breakfast Club*) debuted on CBS on January 13, 1987. It wasn't a Friday, but it might as well have been. Rolland Smith and Mariette Hartley were viewed as the Ozzie and Harriet of news/entertainment, and the critics fired additional attacks at the program with unfettered enthusiasm. "Some TV shows seem to call less for a review than for an exorcism," Tom Shales wrote in *The Washington Post*. "Such is the case with *The Morning Program*. . . . Watching it was like waking up and finding the house overrun with last night's party guests, most of them stewed to the gills and gabby as all get-out. . . . Think about it: Does television really need a program for viewers who find the *Today* show on NBC and *Good Morning America* on ABC too intellectually demanding? . . . If there are heights of inanity, this show scaled them, and if there are depths, it plumbed them." Slap.

"Nowhere is it written in the scriptures: 'Let There Be TV Lookalikes in the Morning,'" claimed Howard Rosenberg in the *Los Angeles Times*. "So it's all right that CBS finally opted for Something Else. Unfortunately, Something Else turned out to be This." Rosenberg didn't spare anyone on the program, including Bob Shanks. "Executive producer Bob Shanks, one of TV's brighter minds, has inexplicably drawn the worst elements from *Today* and *Good Morning America* and repackaged them as *The Morning Program*. He's trimmed the meat and retained the fat, then girdled the roly-poly leftovers into ninety minutes of thick belly." Slap the other cheek.

CBS chalked up the reviews in much the same way as it regarded the ratings. They were a starting position, according to Bob Shanks, more a point of reference than a measuring stick for the future. While 2,697,000 viewers turned on *The Morning Program* (representing a 3 percent jump from pre-Hartley weeks), there was little to cheer about when compared with *Today*'s numbers—4.8 million—or *Good Morning America*'s 3.7.

Hartley and team welcomed such guests as Roseanne Barr (a full year and a half before *Roseanne* debuted on ABC), Martin Sheen, newly elected Congressman Joseph Kennedy II, and Sophia Loren (on tape). The show had a studio audience that laughed and applauded as if forced to be alive at the early hour and a working fireplace that was, well, working. So, too, was Hartley, who strained to carry the show mostly on her own.

As CBS worked out the kinks on-air, ABC's David Hartman was winding down his run as early morning TV patriarch. His last broadcast, on Friday, February 20, 1987, was a tribute to the fallen host. He had managed to survive on the job for eleven years—a run that, in any other industry, would hardly qualify for honorable mention. On early morning television, he was saluted with a two-hour testimonial with all the earmarks of *This Is Your Life* as well as the predictable accolades.

Nancy Reagan said goodbye. So too did former presidents Gerald Ford and Jimmy Carter, while George Bush gave a vice presidential authority to his "So long, David." Hartman maintained the "golly-gee-whiz" look that had served him well as *Good Morning America*'s folksy centerpiece. Joan Lunden, despite a new contract specifying her title as cohost, was strictly second fiddle, exactly as she had been during most of Hartman's reign. Lunden would later call their pairing "a nice relationship," adding, "I never took any of his big stories, and he never made me kiss his big ring."

Earlier in the month, it had been decided that Charles Gibson would replace Hartman, but not much was made of that upcoming transition on this final broadcast for the man many of the crew had nicknamed "David Heartless." If Hartman was disliked for his fanatical need to control, he was also respected for his incredible ability to relate and explore, explain and interpret.

"Until I see you again," he said as the show drew to its close, "make it (pause) a really good day *today.*"

Charles Gibson slid into the host chair the following Monday. The show continued the celebration—the goodbye party was now a hello party, and the mood on the set was equally upbeat and laudatory. It was evident from the interplay between Lunden and Gibson that these personalities were soul mates of sorts. Whereas Lunden was merely tolerated by Hartman, she was clearly respected by Gibson.

As *Today* continued to explode in the ratings, it put out its own welcome mat—this time to the younger brother of Princess Diana, the Viscount Althorp. Downplaying the Viscount's royal lineage, executive producer Steve Friedman said, "He's really a regular guy. You'd think he was just like the rest of us bums." Not so, and Friedman knew it more than most. While hoping that the 23-year-old Althorp would develop into a viable talent on the air, Friedman limited—but heavily promoted—his participation on the set.

Friedman didn't realize at the time that the Viscount would be his last *Today* hire. Surprising most of the NBC staff—and all of the television industry—he announced in June that he would be leaving the program he had commanded for seven years and passing the scepter to his supervising producer, Marty Ryan. Ryan, who had once been a news anchor at the NBC affiliate in Columbia, Missouri, had been at *Today* for ten years. His style was more laid back, more sophisticated than his predecessor's hell-on-wheels fanatical behavior. In fact many, including those with whom he worked the closest, questioned if this gentleman could run a show that was used to being whipped instead of stroked.

While *Today* was at the top of its game, its competition was coping with on-air changes and attempting to stabilize. *Good Morning America* had dropped slightly in the ratings with the arrival of Charles Gibson, while CBS's early morning entry had tumbled to its lowest rating in the fourteen years that ratings were tallied for the timeslot.

Rumors abounded that CBS was dropping *The Morning Program* as well as the ninety-minute *CBS Morning News* that preceded it. Meanwhile, the mood at ABC's *Good Morning America* was hardly more secure. Joan Lunden, pregnant with her third baby, announced that she had signed a development deal with Paramount Pictures Television for an hour-long talk/variety series titled *Daytime,* and would be leaving within a year. Kathleen Sullivan, who had substituted for Lunden in September 1987 during her first maternity leave, was working without a contract, stalling her negotiations for what insiders viewed as a crack at Lunden's spot.

Sullivan was also being courted by ex–*Today* show executive Steve Friedman, who was developing the video version of *USA Today* for Grant Tinker's production company, GTG Entertainment. When the smoke cleared and negotiations ended, Sullivan opted for neither ABC nor GTG. At the beginning of October, just as Lunden was due back on the air after the birth of another baby girl, Sullivan announced that she was moving to CBS to be the newest anchor for its new morning show to be titled *CBS This Morning*.

The trap door that seemed to swallow anchors at CBS had opened up again. Into that black hole of merciful salvation had fallen Mariette Hartley and Rolland Smith. By November 30, Sullivan was sitting on a new set at her new network with a new co-anchor—CBS news correspondent Harry Smith.* "The feeling around here is sort of like kids in a candy store," Smith said, obviously unaware of the enormous task ahead. The new president of CBS News, Howard Stringer, had made it clear that the network was going to give this latest incarnation of CBS's early morning program every opportunity to succeed.

Rather than being heralded as the second coming of Cleopatra into Rome—which the network had done with its other morning entries—*CBS This Morning* quietly lobbed onto the screen. Executive producer David Corvo emphasized the show's distinction: "We have a different personality. We have a different perspective." What it didn't have was a different design. Like *Good Morning America* and *Today* before it, *CBS This Morning* originated from a set that resembled a living room in a comfortable country estate.

Mark McEwen continued on the program as weatherman. Joining him on the set were newcomers Jim Lampley on sports, economist Ken Prewitt, medical advisor Dr. Robert Arnot, consumer reporter Erin Moriarty, and film-director-turned-critic Peter Bogdanovich.

Television critics, tiring of CBS's refusal to nurture any of its early morning efforts, labeled the new program "yesterday's cornflakes" and "a clone in progress." Howard Rosenberg of the *Los Angeles Times* reflected the ho-hum sentiments of many when he wrote: "One wishes that CBS would either try something so outrageous in this time period that it can't be defined, or abandon this mimicry and return to what it did long ago—provide a straight, solid, credible newscast that would appeal to a small minority and let ratings come what may."

---

*Smith was hired after CBS's first choice, Canadian broadcaster Peter Mansbridge, turned it down.

Rosenberg also couldn't resist taking a shot at Sullivan while he was at it. "As it now stands," he wrote, "[Sullivan] may be early morning TV's first news coquette (Phyllis George was more the prom queen type), a sort of anchor bunny on a mission of seduction."

In *USA Today,* critic Monica Collins thought "beige." According to Collins, "*CBS This Morning* is as beige as toasted white bread. Its infamous predecessor, the riotous *Morning Program,* was a frosted Pop Tart; this umpteenth CBS attempt to lure viewers in the morning is as dry as bland can be."

On the *Today* show, suitcases were packed once more as cast and crew traveled to China in a joint effort with other NBC News shows, garnering praise from critics and viewers alike. Buoyed by leading the competition by a comfortable margin, *Today* found itself relaxing on the air in a fashion that would have been unheard of only a few years earlier.

Jane Pauley had begun to use what critics labeled "a side-ways glance and a raised eyebrow" to keep Bryant Gumbel's ego in check. The anchor had slipped back into old habits of arrogance and grandiosity that marbled both presentation and posture. Willard Scott, meanwhile, was acting wilder with each passing week. Some thought he had hit the height of camp and buffoonery when he dolled himself up in makeup and fruit to deliver the weather in drag as a Carmen Miranda look-alike. Yet, Scott was only beginning. The more he clowned, the more fans felt his genuine warmth and heart, which balanced Gumbel's brash efficiency nicely and kept *Today* at the top of its form.

Scott's popularity disturbed Gumbel, who once asked stagehands not to laugh so loudly at the weatherman's on-air segments. "We have one very irresponsible person in the studio who lacks demeanor. It's one thing to laugh, another to guffaw," Gumbel said in his own defense. In August 1988, however, nobody was laughing in St. Marys, Georgia. A woman named Jackie Lynnwood had checked into the Kingsland Ramada Inn on Boone Street just off route I-95, claiming to be doing advance work for Scott and newsman John Palmer. After a ten-day stay, and much excitement throughout St. Marys, Lynnwood had disappeared, with two T-shirts intended as gifts for Scott and Palmer from the Kingsland Tour and Travel Association. NBC denied any knowledge of the woman.

That same month, Gumbel left little doubt about his own popularity by signing a $7 million, three-year contract with NBC. Gumbel celebrated in his office with a cigar the size of a corn cob, refusing to comment on the amount of his deal. "However much I may find it distasteful, I am aware that most people are fascinated by numbers," Gumbel managed between puffs to explain to the press. "What do I think about the numbers that people who do what I do command? They're certainly disproportionate for our worth to society, if the truth be known. But I think they *are* proportionate to our worth to our employers." Large ego; mouth to match.

Gumbel was about to leave town to cover the Summer Olympic Games in Seoul, South Korea, for three weeks, and wasn't particularly excited. The last time he was set to go to an Olympic Games was in 1980, when NBC was televising them from Moscow. However, the United States had decided to boycott the games in response to the Soviet invasion of Afghanistan, and NBC dropped its telecast. This time, Gumbel suggested he was saving his excitement for his return. As for the critics, Gumbel said, "If Michael the Archangel hosted these games, he'd be lucky to satisfy 50 percent of the people."

Today had planned to go off the air—for the first time in its thirty-five-year history—while Gumbel was in South Korea to allow the staff some needed rest and the network additional time in which to show the Olympics and gain increased ad revenues. Prior to the Olympics, however, the show was broadcast for a week from Seoul, during which executive producer Marty Ryan asked Gumbel to critique the series and prepare his critical evaluation in the form of a memo. Gumbel eagerly accepted the task, anxious to privately vocalize what he saw as the program's critical problems.

While Gumbel was riding the crest of his popularity—proud of his accomplishments and his life—Rick Reilly, a writer for *Sports Illus-*

trated, was quietly working on a cover story that would break while Gumbel was broadcasting from Seoul. Titled "The Mourning Anchor," the piece shattered any illusion that Gumbel had crafted of a perfect life. Rather, the story painted a picture of a man who had few friends and who was overwhelmed by the memory of his father, a man he called "his only hero." It said that Gumbel carried the eulogy he had delivered at his father's funeral around with him at all times, and quoted a portion of it, including, "Goodbye, Daddy. We love you so very much. God has taken from us and unto himself the finest man we'll ever know." The story also quoted his mother, Rhea, lamenting the fact that her only fault was that she was his mother, not his father. She was quoted as reading from a letter she had written to her son, in which she said, "O.K., so I'm not a big shot. I'm not a big person in the social life, not a cultural leader. But I brought you into this life, not him." His mother spoke of his younger sister's wedding. Gumbel's older brother attended. Bryant "was at Fergie's wedding in London."

The story recalled Chicago in the summer at 96 degrees. Rhea sat in her apartment on the seventh floor of an older building with all the windows open. She couldn't afford an air conditioner and was afraid to ask Bryant to buy one for her. "It would hurt me like a knife if he said no," Rhea Gumbel figured. "Besides, if he wanted to do something for me, he'd go ahead and do it on his own, wouldn't he?"

The question lay there, open ended, a festering wound that weighed not only on Rhea Gumbel's mind, but on Bryant's as well. Reading the piece, which was faxed to him in Seoul, Gumbel is said to have refuted the accuracy of the information to his friends, while never referring to the article publicly. Like most criticism, he ignored it. Unlike most criticism, this one cut with savage impact.

Gumbel's coverage of the Olympics was well received. Critics pointed to his flawless recitation of facts and records, distances and speeds—all without stumbling or stammering or even mispronouncing an athlete's name, as far as anyone noticed. When he returned to New York and the *Today* set, Gumbel was welcomed back as a victorious knight returning from the Crusades, stronger and more powerful because of his success. He absorbed the praise with spongelike enthusiasm, wanting for little except more of the same.

With Marty Ryan now in charge of the program, Gumbel was in an excellent position to demand and receive. More pliable than Steve Friedman, Ryan would stop at nothing to keep *Today* on top, and that meant keeping Gumbel happy at all costs—a price that would turn out to be dangerously high, and whose repercussions would shake the *Today* show to its very foundation.

CHAPTER NINE

THE MEMO

*M*arty Ryan could not help but be amazed at Bryant Gumbel's candor. Although he had asked the anchor to be forthright and outspoken in his critical assessment of the problems and strengths of the *Today* show, the executive producer found the tone of Gumbel's memo in August 1988 to border on hostility. He had given Gumbel a list of topics to be specifically addressed. Included in the guide were all the contributors on the program with the notable exception of his cohost, Jane Pauley. (It wasn't that Ryan wanted to spare Pauley's feelings, for he already was aware of how Gumbel viewed Pauley's shortcomings.) Yet, as Ryan read the resulting memo, he discovered that Gumbel had not only covered each of his points, but had also expanded into other areas that the newsman had found lacking, taking the opportunity to attack as much as criticize.

Although the *Today* show was riding the crest of its popularity and enjoying a slim lead over ABC's *Good Morning America* and a healthy viewership advantage over CBS's *This Morning,* Ryan had felt that the long-running NBC series was getting complacent. He anticipated that as Gumbel left New York for the Summer Olympics in Seoul, South Korea, he would have a unique opportunity to examine the show from a different perspective. As it turned out, Gumbel was a willing critic. Despite a schedule that called for him to anchor over eighty primetime hours of Olympics coverage, he still found the time to view the *Today* show over Armed Forces Television.

Gumbel subsequently wrote down his impressions of the program in a four-page memo that was delivered to Ryan electronically over the NBC computer system. Highly confidential and equally inflammatory, the memorandum moved point by point through Ryan's checklist. On-screen talent, behind-the-scenes crew—all were judged through Gumbel's precise vision of perfection.

He began his memo: "Marty—First off, let me say that I think your idea to go over these things with the staff's terrific . . . long over-due. I also think your list is very comprehensive. I'll add any new sub-jects on the back and . . . for now let me put my two cents in on each of your items. I hope you understand that this note will be for your eyes ONLY. In trying to be honest and helpful, I don't want to gain more enemies than I've already got."

Gumbel had complete faith in Ryan's pledge to keep his com-ments private. In fact, the very existence of the critique remained con-fidential until February 1989, when NBC changed its computer system. In what was officially viewed as a system upgrade by those in charge and as an irritation by those who weren't, the bottom line was that the old BASYS system was out and the new SISCOM system was in.

Although NBC would later attempt to deny any security breach, sources within the network confirmed that during the conversion process from one system to the other, confidential memos from most of the network's divisions were briefly accessible by any employee who wanted to look. And when they looked—and found—the Gumbel memo, they not only got an eyeful, but quickly circulated copies of the hostile critique within NBC's New York offices at 30 Rockefeller Plaza. The following day in the mail, the venerable *Harper's Magazine* received a hard copy of the confidential missive in the mail and imme-diately attempted to verify its authenticity—a verification that was not forthcoming. When *Today*'s literary booker Emily Boxer received the call for substantiation from *Harper's*, her uninformed yet instinctive response was a flat denial. Boxer's opinion was that the portions of the memo that were read to her were too inflammatory to have been writ-ten by Gumbel. Although *Harper's* respected Boxer's word as gospel, the producer herself went directly to the source and confronted Gum-bel face-to-face.

Much to Boxer's astonishment, Gumbel admitted that the memo was authentic. Not only was he unashamed of its contents, he offered to allow Boxer to read the entire note. However, preferring to stay "uninvolved," Boxer turned down Gumbel's offer and kept the information about the existence of the memo to herself. She did not know that whoever had sent the memo to *Harper's* had also given it to NBC's late-night TV talk show host David Letterman and to *Newsday,* the highly respected New York tabloid. Despite a long-standing feud between the two media stars, Letterman returned the embarrassing leak to Gumbel's office. *Newsday* did not.

With shades of intrigue recalling the involvement of Watergate's Deep Throat, *Newsday* veteran reporter Kevin Goldman was alerted by an anonymous caller to the existence of the memo over the phone and was told to meet his secret informant at a clandestine rendezvous on February 24, 1989. While the scoop would hardly have the political ramifications of Watergate, for Goldman it was just as exciting. Like those at *Harper's,* the *Newsday* journalist was unconvinced of the validity of the memo and spent the weekend attempting to track down either author Gumbel or recipient Ryan to verify its authenticity.

Having flown to Los Angeles to begin a preplanned, week-long vacation, Bryant Gumbel could not be reached easily. Goldman had better luck with Marty Ryan, who was both accessible and cooperative. Seeing no reason to hide the existence of a memo that he personally had read and destroyed months earlier, Ryan adopted a "so-what" attitude, labeling the entire piece "old news."

Armed with a backhanded confirmation, Goldman next telephoned then-NBC News president Michael Gartner, a newspaper journalist who only recently had moved over to the network. Gartner not only denied any knowledge of its existence, he also refused Goldman's offer to read the memo. "Yesterday's news," he mumbled under his breath.

What began as an exercise in dismissal quickly turned into one of containment as it became clear that Goldman was intent on printing selected portions of the private communiqué. With Gumbel out of reach, and Ryan indifferent, NBC's press department raced into action in a last-ditch effort to keep *Newsday* from leaking the memo's contents.

The public relations personnel first attempted to bargain with

Goldman, offering certain exclusive stories in exchange for his silence. When that tactic proved ineffective, the press department tried guilt, appealing to the veteran reporter's sense of honor and stressing all the hurt that exposing the Gumbel memo would cause. Replying that any guilt should be Gumbel's, not his, Goldman began writing a front-page story for the tabloid's Tuesday edition.

While Bryant Gumbel played a sun-blanched game of golf in Rancho Mirage, California, the network assembled an emergency team at 30 Rockefeller Plaza. Michael Gartner called upon Betty Hudson, senior vice president of publicity; her assistant Peggy Hubble; vice president Tim Russert; and an outside publicity consultant to develop a plan to limit the damage to both personnel and the *Today* show.

Within hours, the team decided that Gumbel should issue a statement indicating that the memo was a private communication between producer and host whose contents were addressed months ago. It was clean, simple, and easy. It also would not happen.

Gumbel had just walked off the Thunderbird golf course when he received the phone call from Gartner alerting him to the situation. Edgy and uncertain about the effect the critique's publication would have on *Today*'s staff and cast, Gartner was well aware of the power of the press and thought his plan was a good one. He even suggested that Gumbel call Willard Scott and other members of the *Today* team to soften the imminent blow.

If Gartner had been in his position at NBC News longer and had had a deeper association with Gumbel, he would have known better than to make that request. To Gumbel, there was nothing sacred about the truth, and he considered his critique of the program, its content, and personnel to be both accurate and fair. Forget the personalities and egos involved; Gumbel was eager to correct what he saw as weaknesses in the production. In his opinion, the memo's publication could only hasten its implementation.

Gumbel had no intention of making a statement about a memo that he believed stood on its own merit. Furthermore, he did not even feel the need to warn those mentioned in the memo that it was about to be published. "It's no big deal," he assured Gartner, who hung up the telephone and wondered if perhaps Gumbel might be right.

Gartner got his answer the following morning, when *Newsday*'s headlines screamed GUMBEL GRUMBLES: *TODAY* SHOW STAR RIPS STAFF IN MEMO TO BOSS, and ran head shots of Gumbel, *Today* show weatherman Willard Scott, and movie reviewer Gene Shalit. Under Scott's picture ran the quote, "He holds the show hostage to his assortment of whims, wishes, birthdays, and bad taste." Captioning Shalit's picture: "His reviews are often late and his interviews aren't very good."

Labeling the memo "candid" and "blistering," Goldman revealed selected sections while theorizing about internal strife between Gumbel and Ryan. Yet, even Goldman appeared unprepared to reveal the memo in its entirety, gingerly editing out many of Gumbel's most outrageous statements while centering on those pertaining to Scott, Shalit, and medical consultant Art Ulene.

The unabridged text of the actual memo follows, complete with profanity, grammatical errors, and misspellings.

> Consumer News: However much we may poo-poo consumer shit, folks do care about it, so the question is how and with whom do we do it. [Consumer reporter David] Horowitz is a walking cliche, but unless you have research to indicate otherwise, I've got to believe he's known and effective. The same for [consumer reporter] Betty [Furness]. I like her and some of her stuff is good . . . but lots of it isn't and she's VERY local. Bottom line: I'd suggest we keep Horowitz, but NOT take any and everything he does. The same for Betty. While I'd not advise a 3rd consumer type, I'd like to see if either of the 2 we've got could do pieces that we would assign. If they couldn't, maybe we should find a fresh body to replace one of theirs.

> Medical: I think on the whole we're being well served by [medical correspondent Art] Ulene . . . but his "health week", "women's month", children's year shit is both boring

and repetitive. (I know they're sponsored, but more often than not they suck. I'd like to see us kepp [*sic*] Art, but nuke his series.) In addition I'd like to see him spice up his weekly medical news with some tapes. Beyond that I'd like to see us keep our eyes/ears open and bring in specialists when warranted much more oftenh [*sic*] than we already do.

Music: Day in and day out, I think [music correspondent] Rona [Elliot] is solid. Beyond that in hert [*sic*] industry her reputation is good and she seems to be a personb [*sic*] who can effectively fill the show's rock needs for years to come. On the whole I think 90% of our music stuff is good . . . but we should avoid sending Rona ANYWHERE outside the states to get someone who'll surely come thru New York. Beyond that we should avoid putting on too many folks no one ever heard of, as we sometimes do. Our viewers may care about Whitney Houston and Elton John; but I doubt they give a shit about Icehouse or Simple [*sic*] Red. That's not to say we shouldn't do folks who aren't big names; but we should make sure they're different or have a new angle involved before we put on a newcomer.

Shalit role: This one's difficult because I like Gene and more than anyone I guess think [*sic*] he's very important to the show. But his reviews are often late a[nd] his interviews aren't very good. I suspect we can live with a few of the latt[er] but we should limit them much more than we have to date. As to his reviews, t[he] answer may lie in assignments. If we told him that by such and such dates we wanted reviews of such and such films, he could set his screening schedule and give us the reviews WE want, ON TIME. I don't think this problem's insoluble but it should be dealt with tactfully and directly and not as if it's on a trial basis.

After 8: I think moving AFTER 8 up higher has helped a great deal. But I don't have a better idea on how to get around our first break. I's [*sic*] counter-productive to go to a break before A-8, but it's be [*sic*] worse to split the segme[nt] or save ALL the breaks till the end of that half-hour. Seems we should consi[der] any and all reasonable options. Beyond that, in keeping with our new format for this, we should program the A-8 folo [*sic*] spot with flexibility in mind . . . mo[re] authors would be perfect.

The former sportscaster next turned his attention to an area in which he felt particularly attuned.

Sports: Although it doesn't bother me, I do find it odd that we do medicine, science, economics, etc with regularity . . . but not sports. Give that some thought. I think [Paul] Brubaker COULD be much more productive and valuable than he is but he more than anyone needs to feel special. His duties should be spelled out, he should be exzclusively [*sic*] sports and he should have his back patted for it once in a while . . . so he knows what your expectations are.

Contributors: You and I have discussed these enuf, so you know my feelings about whose [*sic*] good and whose [*sic*] not. Among the main cutables: Christy Ferrer, Betty Rollin (has she EVER produced a person you reallyt [*sic*] wanted to know?), and Bob Berkowitz . . . (is he still with us?)

Talent Dept: Here too I think we've talked of this so much I doubt I can say anything you don't already know. [Talent coordinator Jeffrey] Culbreth is terrible . . . a lazy broad whop [*sic*] uses bad judgement. Surely there are better, hungrier people to be found. Bottom line: Culbreth doesn't help us in an area that is vitally important to the show.

Trips: I think our trips, whikle [*sic*] they've become common, are nonetheless still important to the image and prestige of the program. What we need is to work harder to DO something on our trips beyond just parking our butts in some foreign land. WHERE to go is a tougher question. Japan is an obvious choice, but it would be terribly expensive. Africa remains untapped and I think newsworthy and do-able. I would strongly urge you NOT to do another military series . . . but for the Willards of the world, once was plenty.

Staff: This is an area with which you're clearly more familiar than I am. But it seems clear that we have too few writers, and I suspect, too many of themleaning [*sic*] oin [*sic*] researchers because they're plentiful. Seems both problems could be addressed by having fewer reseaerchers [*sic*] and more writers . . . no?

I don't know if it's possible to have too many celebs. I guess you could make the audience sick of them but I don't see us realistically at that point. I do know that too many of them have nothing to say. That's partly the[ir] fault and partly ours. Seems we should be guided by a couple of prinmciples [*sic*]; among them that multi-parters be granted only VERY rarely and that we put on celebs ONLY when they've something to say . . . not just cause they're in town (i.e. Bill Maher, Johnny Mathis). In addition we should try to find and use tapes that might illicit [*sic*] a response, as opposed to "here's a clip." Having said all this we should still remember that not having 'names' is a surefire way to go broke.

Hollywood News: This one's interesting. Fact is people continue to be fascinated by the glitter of Tinseltown and the movie industry. Whikle [*sic*] Jim Brown is obviously well connected, he doesn't do the kind of multi-item stories that folks buy *PEOPLE* for or watch *E.T.* for. While I don't think we need [*sic*] compete with those vehicles we should noe [*sic*] ignore what makes them popular either. Whether it's in addition to, or instead of Jim Brown, it seems we need a 2nd body doing Hollywood News, almost like Ulene does medical news. This new reporter need not deal with rumors

of whose [*sic*] fucking whom, but could legitimately fill a
segment with items of whose personal movie stock is up or
down . . . whose [*sic*] having what difficulties working on
which film . . . whose [*sic*] hot in comedy clubs, etc. A young
aggressive type with a sense-of-humor and a good sense of
film/tape would be perfect here . . . and could prove a perfect spot to compliment the 8A half-hour bridging the
newly configured After 8.

Gumbel next directed his attention to the literary division and
Emily Boxer, the producer who received the initial call regarding the
memo.

Books: Let me preface this section by expressing my
faith in Emily Boxer. We have no one who works harder or
is better connected, or more effective than Emily. She gets
EVERY big book that comes out, and part of the price we
pay that is puttibng [*sic*] on some authors who aren't so
great. My suggestions then are two-fold. First we should try
to limit the number of dullards we put on . . . as much as
possible without weakening those relationships. Emily cul-
tivates effectivbely [*sic*]. Second, in those cases where the
author isn't a name, we should look for fresh approaches . . .
maybe VTR of them at work . . . VTR of their subject matter (if it's non-fiction) . . . addas [*sic*] of controversial or critical reviews, etc. etc. Whatever approach we take to this I
suggest we tread carefully. This is an area where we ROUT
the competition and by so doiung [*sic*] we have gained a
great reputation as a "smart folks" show among the learned
people who populate the world of serioyus [*sic*] literature.
Even in times whene [*sic*] ratings are off . . . as they were and
will untimately [*sic*] be again . . . this reputation never
wavers and is invaluable . . . let's not piss it away to get rid of
the one or two boring author [*sic*] we have a month.
Producers: This one's as much of a personality question

as it is one of personnel . . . so let me give some observations only. While I have a world of affection for . . . and confidence in [senior producer] Cliff [Kappler] . . . we need to get more out of him. He needs to be more 'in charge' than he is. He does NOT do nearly asd [*sic*] much as you did when you had his job, and his oft-expressed cynicism, while hilartious [*sic*] by my standards is I fear often counter-producticve [*sic*]. [Supervising producers] Coby [Atlas] and Michael [Pressman] are, I think, solid and professional . . . both can give you a lot of effort and good results . . . but they do not work on planning as effectively as they could . . . to moftewn [*sic*] it seems they look at their weeks away from the back deck as weeks off. As for [news producer Ron] Stienman [*sic*], he is not only expendable but shoukld [*sic*] be jetti-soned for your good and the good of the office . . . he's poi-son. [Producer Janet] Pierce [*sic*] and [producer Cindy] Smaules [*sic*] are ffective [*sic*] if not spectacular . . . I do think both work very hard. Despite so many producers we still have no one either working with the writers, checking their progress or improving their scripts. This has been a major, major problem since I've been here . . . and it's no better today than it's ever been.

In the area of graphics, Gumbel admitted, "I know absolutely ZIP about graphics," before going on to add, "only that ours suck." On the subject of news, Gumbel was no less restrained.

This continues to be one of our weakest links for a lot of reasons. . . . the department doea [*sic*] us no favors . . . it's not terribly well-written . . . [Newsman] John [Palmer] doesn't make it a, [*sic*] lot better and it looks like evry [*sic*] other newscast anywhwre [sic] and evrywhere [*sic*]. Seems we should make our morning newscasts try to reflect the fact that they are often the first newscasts people see on any given day . . . more looking ahead and less looking back wiould [*sic*] seem warranted. What bothers me most about Johnm's [*sic*] newscasta [*sic*] are that when there's a ton of news, they're five minutes long and when there's nothing going on their're [*sic*] 4;59! [*sic*] ... they bear no relationship to the neeeds [*sic*] of any particular day and so I think they exhibit a sameness that the audience observes and rejects. Bottom line: I'd like to see a more ACTIVE newscast ... fewer tapes, more LIVE reports ... beyond that I'd like to see our newscasts better reflect the needs of that day. . . . sometimes 3 minutes, sometime [*sic*] 6.

Gumbel had been typically blunt in his assessment of the show and its personnel. He had taken potshots at every item on Ryan's list for evaluation and hit many subjects on target. Yet, Gumbel wasn't finished. He had several pet peeves to launder, and while the line was up, he tossed them out to hang in the wind.

Now, having given you my 2 cents (unsolicited) on all your topics, let me add some stuff:

Politics: While it's tough to fault the job our Washington people do . . . I think their first response too often is to round up the usual suspects and once two people are booked the job is done. I'd like to see us bringing on different people . . . and get away from the idea that we ALWAYS need 2 people to comment in order to be fair. Having one expert to justify his positions could be jst [*sic*] as effective. The thing we don't do often enuf [*sic*] is instructional, educational background pieces. Oft-times we ignore a chance to do them as a perfect tie-in to a 7:15 spot. If for example [Defense Secretary Frank] Carlucci's booked . . . why not put him at 7;15 [*sic*] and run a 3:30 close-up spot that details what the Pentagon scandal is all about? If [Israeli Prime Minister Yitzhak] Rabin is booked for 7;15 [*sic*] why not run a 4 minute close-up that puts west bank events in chronological order? Too often

it seems we ASSUME people got in on a ciontinuing [*sic*]
story at the beginning. Most don't and so have trouble
being interested in something they don't truly understand. Offereing [*sic*] instructional or educational background pieces would I think help the show and show a
greater degree of concern for our audience . . . I suspect it
would do the show's public and critical image a world of
good.

Having made a valid point regarding the show's political reporting, Gumbel next suggested expanding its entertainment arena into
video cassettes.

Movie cassettes: Somehow, someway . . . either thru
Shalit or Hollywood news or something we've got to have
something that addresses the public's huge ongoing
appetite for video cassettes. People are renting them by the
millions . . . why aren't we telling them what's being released
when or reviewing these tapes. Would it be too much to
expect Sahlit [*sic*] to each week have a critix [*sic*] corner that
deals only with cassettes to be released that week. He could
put 8–10 films in his segment and do a couple of one-
liners about each over footage from eachg [*sic*] film. Think
about it.

Turning from salient advice to personal vendetta, Gumbel saved
his most hostile unsolicited assessment for fellow *Today* show family
member Willard Scott. Remarkable for its candor, Gumbel's attack on
Scott cut deep and jagged.

Willard: This one's a big problem but something has
got to be done. Each and every dasy [*sic*] he holds the show
hostage to his assortment of whims, wishes, birthdays and
bad taste. We can't do business like that and you know it. If
you're looking for a pleasant way around this one there is

none . . . and if you can't bring yourself to do what's unpleasant then maybe you need to ask yourself what kind of job you're doing. This guy is killing us and no one is even trying to rein him in. Some suggestions: nuke [Scott's assistant] Morrison Cruise . . . if Willard had no one giving him that shit every day, he'd be too lazy to organize it himnself [*sic*] . . . if you keep Morrison you should demand to see a listing of the crap he wants to put on by noon of the previous day . . . that way you'd have a chance to limit the stuff he's got, and nuke the stuff that's stupid or too commercial . . . you should also limit him to one birthday per weather report. However it's done Maerty [*sic*] you have GOT to exhibit some control over this guy. He's got your shgow [*sic*] by the balls and is doing what he damn well pleases . . . you don't limit him or edit him, and so he drags us all down. In addition to any or all of the above I'd like to see us take a further step and elimiante [*sic*] him from the first half hour altogether. That half-hour is hard and all he does is take up 3 valuable minutes (when we're lucky). Palm,er [*sic*] could easily give the weather headlines and get us quickly into the top stories of the day. We'll lose no one by eliminating him in the 1st half hour, we already do that with Shalit. Yes, Willard will be pissed . . . so what . . . what's he going to do, walk away? He's got a contract that pays him more than anyone in their rite [*sic*] mind should . . . he can;'t [*sic*] leave this job and couldn't get a better one. Until or unless you bring this buy [*sic*] into line, you're going to continue to have major problems that render anything said in this nmote [*sic*] useless.

Gumbel's irritation at Scott found much of its foundation in the anchor's inability to control the weatherman's behavior. It was also the basis for his frustration with executive producer Ryan himself.

Marty Ryan: You're my last topic . . . but my concern

primary in this memo. I suspect a second reading would rerveal [*sic*] a sameness to the problems and solutions. They concern lack of guidance and a lack of willingness to stand on folks and make sure they do what's necessary. Nice guys may not finish last, but it's hard for them to stay in first. Somehow or other, you're going to have to find it within yourself to do some unpleasant things . . . to crack down on Willard . . . to tell Betty what to do . . . to let Gene know what you want and when . . . to get rid of Stienman [*sic*] . . . to make sure writers do what they're told . . . none of those things are pleasant but they've got to be done. At our fateful dinner long ago, you told me you thought yopu [*sic*] could be a great executive producer. Well, you can't be a great executive producer and a great guy to boot. You've got to look hard at yourself and either do what's necessary or admit you're not up to it . . . you can't have it both ways. I'll be gla;ad [*sic*] to give you all the support you need . . . and I'll even be happy to play the heavy when needed, but for the good of yourself and your show, you've got to show people that you've got the balls to make some hard choices. . . . I'm not sure they think you can. Anywho . . . I've ramblned [*sic*] on enuf . . . I hope you've read all this in the spirit in which it was given . . . yours seemed a serious request so I took it as such. I just hope this all remains confidentia [*sic*] because it's meant only to help you . . . not hurt others.

When the Gumbel memo became public on the morning of February 28, 1989, the slap was heard around the country. Stars and staff alike licked their wounds and attempted to outwardly contain their reaction. NBC News president Michael Gartner faced the crisis by directing his attention to the breach in security. Rather than attempting to rein in the scandal with the press, Gartner issued an internal memo to "all network news bureaus and staff." The missive did not discuss Gumbel's opinions or his flagrant insults. Rather, it attempted to use the Gumbel memo to reinforce policy within the department:

1. The memo is ancient history. Five months old. It was written, I'm told, when Bryant was in Seoul doing the Olympics. 2. The memo apparently was stolen out of Gumbel's computer file and then was given by an NBC employee to Kevin Goldman of *Newsday*. . . .

The troubling aspect of all this is that someone at NBC would take this memo—a piece of private correspondence—and then give it to a reporter. That, quite simply, is theft. It won't be tolerated. Anyone who steals will be fired. Period.

This morning, I have spoken with Marty and Bryant and Jane and Willard and Gene and John and others, reaffirming my own pleasure with the success of the show and reinforcing my belief in open and candid discussions in an effort to make us ever better. I'm always ready for such discussions with anyone . . . frank, face-to-face discussions are a hell of a lot better for all of us than half-baked anonymous cheap shots.

Acknowledging that the *Today* show was enjoying a comfortable lead in the ratings, a position it had held since the fall television season began, Gartner laid the show's success squarely on "a cast of producers and anchors and correspondents and writers—an entire team—that is unmatched in television." Presumably that included the producer who was "poison," the talent coordinator who was "a lazy broad," the weatherman who had "the show by the balls" and the executive producer who had to take "a hard look" at himself.

"Everyone connected with the show wants to make sure that it continues to excel," Gartner's memo contended, "so we always are probing, questioning, suggesting, prodding. Bryant's memo was part of that process and was written in response to a request from Marty. It is a continuous, healthy procedure. We encourage dissent, discussion, disagreement."

Although he opened up the issue with the staff, not even Gartner could have anticipated the extent of the dissent that Gumbel's memo and his reaction to it would generate. Before the debacle was put to rest, major changes would take place among the on-air and behind-the-scenes staff of not only the *Today* show, but also its competition at ABC and CBS.

CHAPTER TEN

THE NIGHTMARE

*H*ad any other business leader written an internal memo about the effectiveness of personnel within his company, it would have been totally ignored by the press. But because Gumbel was the author—and the stars of *Today* his subjects—the memo became front-page news across the country. Big news.

Helping to fan the flames of outrage was Willard Scott, admittedly the most criticized of the cast and the most sensitive of the group. As *USA Today* was polling viewers as to whether Scott helped or hurt the *Today* show, the weatherman was only saying of Gumbel, "He's not a happy man. I don't want an apology. I'd just like to see him happy."

The following day, *USA Today's* front-page headline declared GREAT SCOTT, YOU'RE LOVED. The newspaper's poll revealed that 27,500 readers thought Scott was a valuable addition to *Today*. Only 854 thought he detracted from the broadcast.

As Gumbel continued on his vacation, and Scott continued on the show, the issue of the memo did not disappear; rather, it seemed to gain in intensity with each passing hour. Two days after the publication of the memo, Scott commented, "I'm absolutely distraught." The next day, he said about Gumbel, "He's not a son of a bitch," quickly adding, "Quite frankly, I don't care one way or the other about him."

Jane Pauley, who was spared Gumbel's sword, issued a statement. "Somebody did an evil thing. It hurt a lot of people," she said, attempting to shift the blame from the writer to the exposer.

Gumbel was due back on the *Today* set on Monday, March 6, the same day that both Scott and Gene Shalit, another of Gumbel's targets, were slated to begin their vacations. While America waited to see how *Today*'s anchor would handle his predicament, at least one member of Congress—Virginia democrat Frank Wolf—decided to set the record straight. "Scott touches America's heart and focuses on her goodness," he entered into the House record.

Before heading to Florida for his vacation, Scott took a moment to appear on the syndicated *Entertainment Tonight*, where he said that he was ready to quit *Today* if the "problem" wasn't worked out. "If it's not real and if there isn't an honest, genuine reconciliation, I don't think I belong there," he said. "My whole act hangs on working the neighborhood, doing the T-shirts, and plugging the birthdays. I wasn't aware that he was unhappy with that. I'm a real person and I've always been genuine on the air. And I'm not going to sit there and hug and kiss if it's not real."

When Gumbel returned to the set the following Monday, he opened the show with the line, "Good to be back after what should have been a quiet vacation. The fact that it wasn't is something we'll get into a little bit later."

Jane Pauley responded, "You were never far from our thoughts."

After John Palmer read the news, Gumbel faced the camera and the music. "Jane, Willard, Gene, and I are very grateful," Gumbel said. "We do appreciate your concern, and despite what you may have heard or read in recent days, we are together and hopefully we're going to be with you for many years. Now that may come as bad news for those who have tried to capitalize on our differences, but rest assured that our *Today* family is intact and still smiling, albeit through some pain. We'll still be here long after the recent headlines are forgotten. Enough said." Well, not quite. Gumbel tried to telephone Scott in Fort Meyers, Florida, where the weatherman had gone to celebrate his fifty-fifth birthday. A technical snafu made the phone pickup impossible, and Gumbel and Pauley were left to awkwardly ad-lib for the last two minutes of the broadcast. "That does it for us on what has been a very unusual Monday, in many ways best forgotten," Gumbel closed.

On Tuesday, Gumbel attempted the call again, this time more successfully. After some brief banter, in which Scott said the previous connection didn't work because he had hung up on the host, Scott attempted to turn the tables on Gumbel. He told Gumbel to raise his right hand. Gumbel raised his left. He told Gumbel to repeat the following: "I, Bryant Gumbel, promise to never write a memo and leave it in the computer again." Gumbel refused to budge from his position, lowering his hand and saying only, "I can't write longhand and my penmanship is bad."

If this was peace, it was a strange version of it. The following week, when Scott returned to the *Today* studio, the air on the set was heavy with the same phoniness that Scott said he would never tolerate. On the way into the studio, Scott had been ambushed by the crew from *Entertainment Tonight* and said that he couldn't wait until he saw Gumbel. "I want to give him a big kiss. That usually drives him crazy." As the two sat side by side, Scott waited patiently until the camera was pointed directly his way and, in what passed as Scott's form of restraint, kissed the anchor on the cheek.

Unfazed, Gumbel asked, "How you doin'?"

Scott, obviously unsatisfied with Gumbel's lack of reaction, tried a different approach. "I'll live," he answered. "It's the worst vacation I've ever had."

"Well, welcome to the club," Gumbel responded to crew laughter.

Holding out a checked hat, Scott changed directions and began to talk about Purina. "They make all sorts of food for animals," he said to Gumbel. "Goat food, rabbit. They make horse food. They make it for the *complete* horse, so *you* wouldn't be interested," he added in purposeful reference to a horse's ass.

Viewers never saw if and how Gumbel reacted, since at that very moment the camera turned to Lelah Eastburn of Venice, Florida, who was celebrating her hundredth birthday. After walking to the weather map and talking about rain in the west, Scott said, "Can't wait for my next vacation. Here again is Bryant Gumbel."

The show's executive producer, Marty Ryan, told the press after the program that he thought that Scott's remarks were "unfortunate" but that Gumbel "handled it well and got on with business." Ryan suggested that the saga was over and left it at that.

Gumbel never did make any move to apologize, and no one was

surprised. Ask Gumbel and he would have been the first to say that he hadn't done anything wrong. In subsequent days, although the on-air give-and-take began more typically, the strain on the set was still evident. Only after several weeks did it begin to fade, and then only because Gumbel consciously began to soften his image. He laughed more on the air, made fun of himself with varying success, and even pinch-hit for Willard Scott one morning, doing the weather and wishing a happy hundredth birthday to a great-grandmother from Kentucky. "Good-looking woman," Gumbel said between gritted teeth. He was not exactly sincere, but at least he was trying.

Off-camera, Gumbel was anything but happy. He felt that NBC had failed to support him during the memo scandal, making him look foolish when all he had done was follow Marty Ryan's instructions. He was particularly upset with Michael Gartner, who had done nothing to show agreement with the points Gumbel had made in the memo. The longer Gumbel allowed the situation to broil internally, the more disgusted he became with the way it was handled.

Unwilling to lose his temper with Gartner and unable to correct the situation, he broke off contact with the man who essentially ran the *Today* show from the top. Although Marty Ryan was in charge of the show, Gartner was in charge of Ryan, and as the months went on, it became obvious that Gartner was unable to do that job without the cooperation of the *Today* host. In the middle of July 1989, Bob Wright, the man General Electric had handpicked to replaced Grant Tinker and run NBC in 1986, took steps to defuse the situation. He brought in the president of NBC Sports, Dick Ebersol, to essentially take over responsibility for *Today and* Bryant Gumbel.

Ebersol was a wunderkind at NBC who had begun his climb to stardom in sports by assisting Roone Arledge when Arledge was a newcomer leading ABC Sports. Later, he had produced *Saturday Night Live*, a pro wrestling show, and Bob Costas's late-night NBC talkathon. Ebersol was smart, rich, and egotistical, and he was quick to jump at the opportunity when the unassuming Wright offered him the chance to run NBC Sports.

During his tenure at NBC, Wright had made few tactical errors, bringing in brilliant leaders to run his various broadcast divisions. But he made an error with Michael Gartner. A savvy newspaper editor, Gartner was hired to head the NBC News Division at a time when the network was paring down its resources while paying its anchors million-dollar-plus salaries. When the Gumbel memo scandal hit the *Today* show, Gartner handled it like any other business issue, without allowing for the enormous egos involved. It was a mistake from which he would never recover. Ebersol, who would have liked nothing better than to have headed both Sports and News at NBC (just as Roone Arledge did at ABC), saw his invitation to take over control of *Today* as the first step in that process.

At the time, even though *Today* was still leading in the overall ratings, it had once again taken a nosedive in its appeal to the all-important 18–49-year-old-female demographic group. While *Good Morning America* had risen 8 percent in that category since Charles Gibson's arrival, the *Today* show had fallen 12 percent among young women viewers. Ebersol's mandate was to raise that number and raise it quickly.

Ebersol and Gumbel were already old cigar-smoking buddies by the time Ebersol arrived at *Today* in August 1989 over Gartner's objections. The show's executive producer, Marty Ryan, who had essentially lost control of the show to Ebersol, could do little but stand by and watch as Ebersol made his first significant move—dumping John Palmer as the program's news anchor.

Ebersol thought the 53-year-old Palmer was bland and ineffective in the role, despite the fact that he was one of the most respected newsmen in the business and a twenty-six-year veteran of NBC. Ebersol wanted flash; he wanted pizzazz; he wanted a blonde, sexy, beautiful young woman named Deborah Norville. And Dick Ebersol *always* got what he wanted.

Norville had been delivering the headlines on *NBC News at Sunrise*, the ratings leader that preceded *Today*. Before joining that program, she had been a news anchor at WMAQ in Chicago, Jane Pauley's old alma mater. Norville had few viewers when she arrived at *Sunrise,* but among them was an important one—Bob Wright. "He saw in Deborah a blossoming talent," a *Today* research assistant remembers.

Ebersol knew Wright's feeling about Norville. He liked her style and ability to play the network game as well. Within days of his arrival, Norville was delivering the news on *Today.* Certain that the fresh news anchor would attract younger viewers, Ebersol encouraged Ryan to include her in the opening of each half hour, seated on the couch with Gumbel and Pauley. When Ryan balked at the maneuver, Ebersol was overheard to say that Ryan "couldn't produce a bowel movement" and insisted that Norville's presence on the program be increased.

No one noticed the attention being lavished on the newcomer more than Jane Pauley, who suddenly found new meaning in the old adage "Two's company, three's a crowd." Norville had no sooner taken up her position on the sofa than Pauley demanded an explanation from NBC. The quiet, prim Pauley was staking a claim to her territory, one that was very quickly being ripped out from underneath her.

Ebersol had heard countless stories about Pauley's on-air blunders from Bryant Gumbel and hardly expected to have much of a problem controlling her. With two and a half years remaining on her lucrative *Today* show contract, Ebersol anticipated that Pauley would do as she was told and toe the company line. He did not know Jane Pauley.

Perhaps it was the fact that Norville was criticizing Pauley behind her back, or that Gumbel was openly warm and outgoing with Norville on the air while being reserved and cold with Pauley. Whatever the motivation, Pauley got the message that her star had dimmed at NBC, and she asked to be released from her contract. More amused than threatened by her request, the old boys club of Ebersol-Gumbel refused to take her seriously, presuming instead that it was the first volley in an effort to get a raise.

When the network offered her more money, Pauley was only further incensed. She attempted to explain again: what she wanted was to leave, to sign off of the broadcast that had turned into a soap opera in front of millions of viewers. People magazine headlined NEWCOMER

DEBORAH NORVILLE STIRS THE LATEST IN THE *TODAY* SHOW'S COFFEE CUP, while calling her "NBC's great blonde hope."

Ebersol was quick to tell *Newsweek* magazine that he had brought in Norville "to appeal to women" at an annual salary of $1 million. But as *Newsweek* pointed out, "If he thinks hiring Norville at the expense of Pauley will appeal to the ladies, he may be in for a big surprise."

Carol Randolph, writing in the *Washington Times,* concurred: "NBC executives, in their infinite wisdom, tinkered with a show that didn't need fixing, and in doing so, turned off this loyal viewer. Apparently women anchors, even powerful, competent thirteen-year veterans like Jane Pauley, are vulnerable when the male powers that be decide a change is needed. Although the ratings didn't reflect a problem, Dick Ebersol, senior vice president in charge of the program, felt the show had become 'stale.' Apparently, one way of curing the problem is discarding the old, replacing it with something new, fresh. While that line of thinking works well with stale bread, I have a little problem applying the same course of action to people."

While Pauley insisted publicly that all was well between her and Norville—and indeed she was telling the truth, for she and Deborah did get along personally—that did not suggest that all was well on the show. What began as a request escalated to a demand as Pauley insisted on being able to leave the program. Yet, it wasn't until Tom Brokaw, Pauley's longtime friend and former on-air partner, sat down and heard her side of the story that NBC management finally considered her intentions. "Apparently coming from Tom Brokaw, Ebersol believed the same words that coming from Jane Pauley's mouth he could not," said a *Today* staffer.

Rather than lose Pauley altogether, the network offered to allow her to leave *Today* and become co-anchor of a new primetime news hour in development. *Broadcasting* magazine headlined JANE PAULEY: HERE AT *TODAY*, GONE TOMORROW in its October 16 issue, though the actual news wouldn't be mentioned on-air until the October 27 show.

"It has hurt to see two of my friends, Bryant and Deborah, assigned roles in this that they did not play," Pauley said that morning on *Today*. Looking at Gumbel, obviously proud of their long association, she spoke from the heart: "I'll have to say that what I am going to miss most is the pleasure I have taken in working with you."

Gumbel, looking about as comfortable as a blister on a foot, shifted in his seat before his rehearsed response—"Too many of our dawns have been clouded with idle, often erroneous speculation, much to the detriment of all of us here"—as though the ménage à trois had been going on for years rather than weeks. Calling Pauley his "buddy," he said that he would miss her as well, but quickly added, "I personally am looking forward to sharing my first cup of coffee with Deb, and I hope you are, too."

America would not be so easily fooled. Although Pauley passed Norville her alarm clock and the mantel of co-anchor that day, she didn't leave the program for two more months.

Pauley ended her run on December 29 with the same humility as she began it, thanking the network for "giving me this incredible front-row seat for the last thirteen years, and my colleagues for being more like family." There were tears, there were smiles, and there were commercial interruptions, as *Today* awkwardly attempted to pull itself into the nineties and leave behind its unsettling recent past. However, instead of the program's nightmare ending, the turmoil seemed to be just beginning, as the press and viewers alike refused to let the story die.

People magazine took a poll asking viewers to call in and vote: "Do you think Jane Pauley was treated fairly by NBC?" "Does Deborah Norville have enough experience to replace her?" When the votes were in, it was "no" on both counts. No matter how Norville behaved, nothing pleased *Today*'s fans. NBC executives were slow to realize that it wasn't Norville who was at fault, but rather the network itself, which had presumed that viewers would eat whatever was served on the *Today* show plate next to their morning cup of coffee and eggs-over-easy. But such was not the case. During Norville's first week with Gumbel, the ratings dropped like a sacred cow over a high cliff.

Anxious to get the show moving again, Ebersol had been meeting with *Entertainment Tonight*'s executive producer, David Nuell, who had helped to push *ET* over the top and keep it growing. Ebersol wanted Nuell to perform another miracle, this time for NBC. On the heels of the New Year, however, NBC's Michael Gartner slammed the door on the negotiations with Nuell, saying only that NBC was "unable to reach an agreement in a timely manner." Nuell's contract was being negotiated by his fiancée, Cynthia Riley, who also happened to represent *Good Morning America*'s Charles Gibson. Inside sources suggested that Nuell wanted NBC to guarantee him his full salary, even if he left the show before the three-year term specified by his contract. It was yet another ruckus for those attempting to deal with a battle plan that seemed to be short on ideas and long on leaders.

Quickly attempting to regroup, Ebersol reached out to KNBC's news director, Tom Capra, the son of directing legend Frank Capra and an old buddy of Ebersol's from his ABC days. Capra joined *Today* on January 28, 1990, shoving out executive producer Marty Ryan, the man who had begun it all by asking Bryant Gumbel to write a simple memo. Unlike the top-rated morning show that Ryan had inherited, Capra was handed a wounded and struggling program that was in desperate need of an executive producer who could motivate and energize. What it got was a man who was an expert at the mechanics of broadcasting, but who lacked creative inspiration. Rather than attempt to mold the program into something new and exciting, Capra decided to accentuate the old and familiar—in this case, Bryant Gumbel. "It ain't broke, but it needs a little tinker," said Capra, vastly understating the problem.

While Capra went to work "tinkering," the ratings told the true story. *Today* had fallen behind *Good Morning America* by nearly a full ratings point, while *CBS This Morning* remained a distant third. Reacting to *Today*'s slip, CBS moved to beef up its own arsenal, replacing Kathleen Sullivan with Paula Zahn. Zahn herself had replaced Steve Bell as the news anchor on *Good Morning America* and was now on the move again, this time jumping networks.

Just five days after joining CBS, Zahn found herself on-air next to Harry Smith, trying to avoid the effects of whiplash from the transition. "We'll have lunch with Harry Smith, and let them get to know each other," explained Erik Sorenson, who had taken over the reins as executive producer on the program. "Makeup, hair, wardrobe, and sit in the chair" is the way he described it, and just as quickly it occurred.

The timing of the move was seen as rather ironic, given that CBS's morning news program had posted a 20 percent gain in ratings during the past year, and Harry Smith had been selected to receive one of the Linda Ellerbee Awards for Distinguished Reporting given annually by the Media Research Center. Kathleen Sullivan, however, had begun to be a slight embarrassment to the network. She had to apologize when she uttered an expletive over an open mike, presuming she was off the air, and again when she referred to CBS as the "Cheap Broadcasting System" on an in-house closed-circuit television feed.

Often raging at staff members for their imagined shortcomings, Sullivan was as unpopular with the crew as she was becoming with the viewers. She had been under increasing personal pressure as well: her parents were nearly killed in a violent car crash, and her four-year marriage to Palm Springs architect Michael Kiner ended in a bitter divorce.

Sullivan had battled with a weight problem during her stint with CBS, while Paula Zahn was a fitness buff whose love of sports kept her 5-foot, 9-inch, 125-pound body toned and her energy level high. A graduate of Stephens College in Missouri, Zahn was on the varsity golf team (she was the first woman to play in the Houston Pro Am), competed in track and field in high school, and developed a love for alpine skiing. She was also a talented interviewer, which served her well from her first sunrise on *CBS This Morning*.

By March, NBC had placed into full motion its plan to restore Bryant Gumbel's popularity, highlighted by a primetime interview on ABC with former cohost of *Today* Barbara Walters. It was an unusual move, but these were unusual times that called for taking risks at all costs. Gumbel was uncomfortable addressing the memo scandal, not because he thought he was wrong, but because he thought he was right and knew others did not agree, Barbara Walters among them.

Knowing the press and the networks alike would be watching carefully for any sign of hedging on the critical questions, Walters made it clear that no subjects would be off-limits. She questioned Gumbel about his pompous attitude and his need to always be right. She cornered him on the Norville disaster and his role in it.

"I would say that Bryant Gumbel is an emotional guy and where possible we should capitalize on it, and where it hurts us, we should try to minimize it," he answered, as if talking about a person in some other room. "He's not the one who should be the heavyweight," he continued. "NBC should make the heavyweight decisions, and make sure that Bryant stays in the background."

Unwilling to let Gumbel talk around the issue, Walters asked directly, unemotionally, "If they could hire Jane Pauley back, if she would come back, would you like that . . . would you help?"

"To take *my* place or Deborah's?" Gumbel queried with a smile. "Oh, I don't know. I think it's always difficult to rewrite history, Barbara. I think the idea of bringing Jane back right now, while certainly a pleasant one for a lot of people to consider, would be fraught with so many difficulties involved and so many hurt feelings, and so much discomfort for all, including Jane, that I think it's kind of an unrealistic thing to consider."

If Walters's interview was supposed to help *Today*, it failed miserably. By May, *CBS This Morning* had risen in the ratings slightly, *Today* had fallen dramatically, and *Good Morning America* had easily beaten both shows. No longer content with Capra's "tinkering," Michael Gartner insisted that major changes take place on the air to reestablish a family feeling in the broadcast. Joe Garagiola, who was last seen on the program in 1973, was asked to return to smooth the rough edges, as the hard-to-know Gumbel and the brittle Norville attempted to find a common ground. Garagiola had done a guest shot on *Today* in January, and after the show, Gumbel had said, "You ought to come back soon." Little did he know how soon.

CBS's Faith Daniels was hired to take Norville's post reading the news, and NBC correspondent Katie Couric was added to the mix to report from Washington, D.C. At the same time, Dick Ebersol abruptly resigned from his *Today* show duties, taking full responsibility for the debacle that had occurred during his watch. "In order to stop this soap opera—and that's what it's become—somebody has to step up and take responsibility," he said. Since, as it happened, Ebersol *was* responsible for all the miscues on the show, no one argued with his decision, least of all Michael Gartner, who nevertheless still had to deal with Ebersol as senior vice president of NBC News and president of NBC Sports.

There was a certain urgency to the movement of talent on the *Today* set. NBC was hurting, robbed of the income it would have gotten had its early morning talk show stayed on top of the ratings. Every day it lost to *Good Morning America* in the ratings was another loss of between $300,000 and $400,000. The network needed a quick fix. One place it wasn't going to find it, however, was with Bryant Gumbel. The anchor remained adamant that his performance was unflawed, his criticism undeserved.

"Do I like what people have said about me in the last two years?" he asked. "Absolutely not. But in order to change that, if I've got to dislike who I look at in the mirror, it's not even close. I'll be damned if I'm going to do anything that forces me to look back and say 'Ugh.'"

As the *Today* set became more and more crowded, viewers found less to love, not more. "The show has just become too busy," *People* magazine reported. "While the busyness reinforces Gumbel's preeminent role (someone has to direct traffic), his patrician air has always been a liability. Look, there's no one on television more efficient or better prepared than Bryant Gumbel, but the fact is that viewers, especially women viewers, just don't go for his Autocrat-of-the-Breakfast-Table routine."

Yet, it wasn't Gumbel who was taking the most heat and the most pressure for the failure. That honor belonged solely to Norville, who went from heroine to villain in the course of a single month. The network that had pushed her onto a pedestal did nothing to help her when the pedestal began to topple, except place others around it. But these supports were there to catch the show, not the star.

When Norville first arrived on the *Today* set, she set the tone with her coworkers by sending out thank-you notes. To Norville, she was only doing what she was trained to do in the South. "A lady says 'thank

you' for kindness," Norville explained. However, her gesture of gratitude was perceived by the crew as a statement of superiority and pre-
tentiousness. They also were privately unimpressed when Norville
criticized Jane Pauley about her appearance, wardrobe, and hair.

"She was nasty," a cameraman remembered. "She was just naive
enough to be outspoken and critical of a lady we all loved," he said.

As viewers pushed Pauley toward "sainthood" and branded
Norville the "other woman" in an on-screen divorce, *Today*'s new
anchor was abandoned by the network, her cohost, and executive producer Tom Capra. "It was a daily hotbed of innuendo and hostility, all
coated in this forced politeness," said Gumbel's assistant at the time.
"Bryant went from thinking that Deborah was this wonderful, cute
addition to *Today* to cracking jokes behind her back. And he wasn't
alone. The guys all did it."

Yet, as personally unprepared as she may have been for the debacle that followed her entrance on *Today*, Norville was skilled as an on-
air talent. Having majored in broadcast journalism at the University of
Georgia while Jane Pauley was starting on *Today*, she had spent the subsequent thirteen years working her way up through the ranks of television news readers. She seemed peaked for success when she walked into
the maelstrom of hostility at Studio 3-B.

By the end of her first year on the program, Norville had been
nicknamed "the anchor that sunk." Observers called the move to put
her on the air "the worst executive decision since Classic Coke." She was
maligned by the press, hated by the viewers, ignored by her peers, and
ostracized by her network, which wanted to distance itself from her but
didn't know how. Soon afterward, it was motherhood that came to the
rescue. When Norville announced she was pregnant, Michael Gartner
privately exhaled a sigh of relief. What NBC executives had been unable
to do for over a year, Mother Nature accomplished in just eight
months. Her place on the couch was taken by Katie Couric.

During the entire time Norville was cohost of *Today*, the series
failed to beat *Good Morning America* even once. During her first week
of maternity leave, the show's ratings climbed from a 3.8 to a 4.3 (an
increase of half a million viewers). Whereas Norville was blonde and

seemed unnatural, Couric was brunette and exuded a girl-next-door image. When Norville grinned, her smile was frozen in place; when Couric grinned, the room smiled with her.

NBC executives stumbled over one another in their efforts to praise Couric, who just the previous month had been sent to Kuwait during Operation Desert Storm, where she interviewed General Norman Schwarzkopf and King Hussein of Jordan. She was a "unique talent," NBC said, and clearly one to be reckoned with. Norville would discover this the hard way, when, weeks after starting her maternity leave, NBC announced that she would be permanently replaced by Katie Couric.

When Bryant Gumbel had first introduced Norville to *Today*'s viewers in January 1990, he said he foresaw an "exciting new chapter in the rich history of this program." On April 4, 1991, he opened the *Today* show by welcoming Couric in a different manner. "Katie is now a permanent fixture up here, a member of our family, an especially welcome one. Deborah Norville is not."

If there was a more blunt way of dismissing a cohost, Gumbel had yet to discover it. There can be no denying that his phrasing was deliberate and meant to sting. A man used to winning, he was linking himself to the winning side, and the loser was left to pick up her own pieces and get out of town.

Just a week before NBC's announcement, Norville had made a rather startling statement of her own. Appearing in the cover story of *People* magazine breast-feeding her new baby son, Niki, Norville had described her months at *Today* as "more painful than childbirth—no comparison." She admitted that the hostility that had been directed toward her had caused shock, then devastation, then depression. "I can't tell you how depressed I was."

Rumors describing Norville's sudden fits of uncontrollable crying and hysteria were rampant. Edged out of the seat she had fought so hard to earn and keep, she wanted to run, but had no place to hide.

Perhaps Norville got the better of Michael Gartner, Bryant Gumbel, and all those at NBC who wanted to dispose of her when she no longer served their purposes. To the network's announcement that she would not be returning to *Today* as previously planned in order to become a full-time mother for a year, Norville replied that she wanted "to give [her] son the best possible start on life and practice good journalism. There is plenty of time for the latter, but . . . only one chance to do the former." Norville, the injured, forsaken, yet ultimately happy mother, disappeared—at least for a while.

She did, however, leave with a full purse. NBC continued to pay Norville her million-dollar-a-year salary for the next two years while she raised her young son in style. For the network, however, it was a small price to pay for a future that looked as though it was finally back on track. In reality, however, although one soap opera had ended, another was just beginning.

Only days after taking over the cohost reins, Couric announced that *she* was pregnant, making viewers and crew alike wonder what was stuffed in the couch on the *Today* set. Couric had been feeling queasy for weeks, but chalked up the nausea to all the traveling she had been doing for the show. Couric returned from her two-month leave— taken just before her daughter, Ellie, was born in July—with gusto and her ear-to-ear smile intact.

Viewers didn't have long to wait before experiencing Couric's renewed spontaneity. After Magic Johnson announced his HIV-positive status, the cohost described on-air the three commercial networks' policy against broadcasting condom advertisements. She then proceeded to show an ad for LifeStyles, a "sensually thin" prophylactic. Next, she interviewed Gwendolyn Florant, an AIDS counselor at Harlem Hospital, about safe sex. Florant brought along an anatomically accurate plastic penis and demonstrated the correct way to put on a condom. Said Florant, "The penis should be clean, the penis is going to be erect, and you are going to use a lubricated condom . . . with the spermicide nonoxynol-9."

No, Couric would never be confused with Deborah Norville. She was cute, some dared to call her "perky"—a powerhouse of personality, intelligence, spunk, and fun that brought *Today* back to life in a way that most observers would have labeled a "miracle."

Quite suddenly, *Today* found itself with a star—and an entirely new melodrama began to unfold. Now it was Couric who was getting all the attention, from both the network and the fans. The spotlight that found Couric in its center had just one limitation: it didn't include Bryant Gumbel. Only weeks passed before the host would discover that fact and make a move to bask once again in its glow—alone.

CHAPTER ELEVEN

THE WAR

When the *Today* show reached its fortieth anniversary in early 1992, NBC celebrated with a primetime special produced by Steve Friedman, whose attempt to launch the TV series *USA Today* had flopped and who had been rehired by the network to produce *NBC Nightly News*. At the celebration, John Chancellor revealed that he fell asleep on the air—but only once; Hugh Downs admitted that he never got used to the hours; and Jane Pauley said she now watched the show—in her pajamas. And Deborah Norville—well, Deborah Norville didn't say anything, because she hadn't even been invited.

Good Morning America, which had celebrated its fifteenth anniversary several months earlier, aired an equally good family-affair program, with the beaming Joan Lunden punching Charles Gibson jokingly in the arm when he referred to her real name, Joan Blunden (she had changed it when she first arrived at WABC in the seventies). For all the smiles, however, there was personal heartache wallowing just under the fancy Lilly Rubin suit that accented Lunden's legs. Lunden and her husband, Michael Krauss, had separated, although the official announcement would not come for a few more months.

Michael Castner, the senior producer of Lunden's *Everyday with Joan Lunden,* the renamed *Daytime* show from Paramount TV, blamed the failure of the syndicated series on the disintegration of Lunden's marriage. Lunden had attempted to continue on *GMA* while shooting *Everyday* and the resulting strain had aggravated what already was a tenuous relationship. *Everyday*'s failure after just one season dealt the final blow to a marriage that had deteriorated into co-existence.

"It's tough to juggle a marriage and a working relationship," Castner told *People* magazine. "It caused a lot of strain working together.
The tension was high, but Joan was very calm. Her idea of a temper
tantrum is to say 'Damn!' Michael, on the other hand, was very tough
to deal with." Lunden apparently agreed, for she moved out of their
home in Rye, New York, and into a rental house several miles away—
effectively ending their thirteen-year marriage. The couple split cus-
tody of their three daughters, who began to jockey between the homes.

Soon after, the supermarket tabloids latched on to Lunden and
Krauss, splashing their story across the checkout lines. One speculated
that Lunden was dating Alan Thicke, the star of ABC's *Growing Pains*
(in reality, they had only cohosted the "Disney Easter Parade" special
together). Krauss was said to be dating a redheaded "party girl"
(another unsubstantiated rumor).

The divorce turned ugly when Krauss succeeded in getting Judge
Nicholas Colabella of the White Plains, New York, State Supreme Court
to award him $18,000 a month in alimony support, after his attorney
Norman Sheresky successfully argued that Krauss was unemployed. "I
think this decision is a deplorable and shameful statement on how
working women are treated today when we've supported our families
and been totally responsible for our children. Why the courts don't tell
a husband who has been living off his wife to go out and get a job is
beyond my comprehension," Lunden remarked.

"It seems to be such an eminently fair disposition," Krauss's
attorney Norman Sheresky responded. "They rolled a big rock up the
mountain and now that they are at the top, she wanted to say, 'I'll take
it from here.' Here you have a man working side by side with his wife,
pushing her career, and suddenly she says, 'You should get a job.' That's
not so easy after fourteen years." Joan Lunden would not know.

Born Joan Elise Blunden near Sacramento, California, she was the
daughter of Dr. Erle Blunden, a surgeon whose parents were mission-
aries. He had spent his youth in China, and regaled his young daughter
and her older brother, Jeffrey, with stories of the Far East, instilling in
them his love of travel. An avid pilot, Dr. Blunden had just bought a
twin-engine Cessna 310 when his daughter turned 13. He had scheduled

a flight with his family to Los Angeles, where he was going to attend a medical convention, but his wife, Gladyce, objected to pulling the children out of school. She talked him into going alone and delaying the family outing.

On the day of the trip, Gladyce had a change of heart. Picking the children up early from school, she raced home to meet her husband in time for the departure. As they drove up the driveway, however, Dr. Blunden was taxiing the new Cessna down the dirt runway that he had built next to their country home. Gladyce and her children waved frantically to attract his attention, and watched as Dr. Blunden waved back, thinking they were saying goodbye. In reality, they were: his plane crashed into the canyons just north of Malibu. His death left an indelible impact on his young daughter.

When Joan Lunden married Michael Krauss, he was a producer of *Good Morning America*. Considerably older, in many ways he was a father figure to the struggling newswoman. As Lunden matured, however, Krauss became the dependent in the relationship, despite the fact that he exercised increasing control over her career and social life. Lunden, who projected the image of the "perfect woman" daily on *GMA*, had allowed her life to slide into emotional turmoil. Locked in a marriage that was suffocating her growth as an adult, she longed to extricate herself from the grip of a husband whose entire life revolved around her career. For the last three years of their relationship, Lunden pretended to be happy. The couple eventually went to a marriage therapist, with disappointing results.

Eager to begin a new life on her own, Lunden ended the relationship in January 1992. Although she had hoped to keep the details of her crumbling marriage out of the press, by February the newspapers— from *USA Today* to *The New York Times*—were carrying stories about her pending divorce, thwarting Lunden's attempts to avoid bringing her personal problems with her onto the *Good Morning America* set.

As it turned out, February was a disaster for *Good Morning America* for another reason. For the first time in 110 weeks, the *Today* show topped the ABC early morning entry in the ratings. *Today* was (once again) on location, in Cuba, when the crew received the news, having incurred $800,000 in expenses to broadcast live from Havana. The same week, the *Today* show named Jamie Gangel a national correspondent, moving her over from her former spot as a general assignment reporter at NBC News.

Tom Capra had been replaced as executive producer of *Today* the previous December with his senior producer, a 26 year old named Jeff Zucker, jokingly called "Doogie" by the cast after teenage doctor Doogie Howser, a character in an ABC series. *Time* magazine pointed out that Zucker's thinning hair and cool, confident manner "made him seem at least 30." Doogie's, er, Zucker's initial influence on the production was to allow segments to "find their own level." In TV parlance that meant that some segments would run substantially longer than originally intended when their subject warranted, and others would be abruptly halted when theirs didn't.

Rather than buy into the litany of those who preceded him as *Today*'s guiding hand—a credo built on the theory that viewers needed to be eased into their day—Zucker began to mold the show into a forum for breaking hard news that jolted viewers awake with a heavy dose of reality. Although the concept was not exactly on the cutting edge, it was a wake-up call for *Today*, if not for Americans.

Zucker allowed a fight-to-the-finish interview between Katie Couric and sometime–Ku Klux Klanner David Duke to run three extra minutes. If viewers had any doubts that Couric could hold her own in controversial situations, the Duke interview dispelled them. Couric bombarded Duke's rationale, prejudices, and attitudes about blacks and Jews. And while Couric redeemed herself with seeming ease, it would have been even more fascinating to see how Bryant Gumbel might have handled the face-off.

It was surprising that he didn't. Gumbel had begun to use the *Today* show as a platform to espouse his personal views, which, not surprisingly, were pro-black, left-wing, and very obvious. During the unrest in Los Angeles following the April 1992 announcement of the verdict in the case of Rodney King—a black man who had been beaten a year earlier by white police officers—Gumbel had an open mike. *Today* showed heartbreaking footage of the response to the verdict—marked by rioting that left the city in flames and destroyed neighborhoods and businesses. The program showed clips of children, some no older than two, accompanying their parents on nighttime lootings of appliance stores, shoe stores, clothing stores, and five-and-dimes, as well as exclusive portions of the privately shot video of the Rodney King beating itself. While speaking to a reporter from *The Washington Post*, Zucker boasted of *Today*'s newfound ability to move into action quickly as events warranted and keep pace with breaking news. He pinpointed the report of the Los Angeles riots as the kind of story that Gumbel and Couric were expert at covering. "Joan Lunden can't cover those stories," he added undiplomatically.

Good Morning America's executive producer, Jack Reilly, defensively shot back, "By my count, the man who questioned her credentials was 11 years old when Joan did her first story for *Good Morning America*. He probably was learning how to ride a bike." Regardless, Zucker made certain that videos of the pillage laced the morning newscast, providing ample fodder for Gumbel to defend the offenders.

Sam Donaldson, speaking on *Prime Time Live*, pressed California Congresswoman Maxine Waters to condemn the violent acts by constituents from her district. While others talked about the racist beating of a white truck driver that occurred in the wake of the verdict, Gumbel declared on *Today* that the act was "reminiscent of what happened to Rodney King." When critics pointed to the fact that the two black passengers in the car with King didn't get beaten and that King was drunk and driving at a high speed, Gumbel opted, "They probably perceived it that way because he was black."

The host gave examples of past racial discrimination, as if to justify the current situation. He had open session for two hours a day and used it freely. "Nice to be able to provide a forum, isn't it?" Couric said after one show.

"Yes. Nice to put it back on the front burner again," Gumbel responded.

Regarding the Rodney King verdict and its aftermath, Gumbel admitted on-air that he could not understand the logic of the jury that claimed to be impartial. He grouped himself with "any black American" who would find it impossible to understand how the jury could honestly believe that King "was directing the action in March of 1991. That takes a different kind of control, because people aren't tuning in to see you say, 'Hey, you're stupid, you're a racist. Shut up.'"

Yet, after 1992, the issue of race was never *off* of the front burner for Gumbel. While the abhorrence of discrimination in any form was to be championed, Gumbel saved his posturing for black issues at the expense of gays, Jews, Mexicans, Asians, and every other group that has felt the sting of prejudice. No longer a neutral journalist, Gumbel's personal politics were equated with those of the *Today* show, regardless of any attempts to appear nonbiased.

When conservative politician Pat Buchanan, running in the presidential election of 1992, appeared on *Today,* he was interviewed at length by Katie Couric. Couric disagreed with Buchanan's points of view and openly defended a left-wing position, albeit more for the sake of argument than personal belief. It was Gumbel, however, who polarized the segment when he closed with, "You just heard Pat Buchanan spouting the views of the far right. I don't want to give it any more time than it's worth."

By mid-1992, the presidential campaign had provided major grist for all three networks. George Bush, who was personally approached by Paula Zahn, fielded questions on *CBS This Morning* from "ordinary people" who were pulled from the tour line at the White House and seated next to the president in the Rose Garden. As guests in his house, none stepped over the line of decorum and asked any questions even remotely provocative.

Bush agreed to appear on the CBS entry only after the *Today* show had launched a live call-in broadcast with candidate Ross Perot. Although the segment was originally slated for one hour, Zucker impulsively expanded it to the entire two-hour broadcast. In doing so, he turned the program into a showcase for Couric, who was running interference between Perot and the callers.

Bob from Bowie, Maryland, asked Perot, "Have you ever had a desire to mind-meld with Howard Stern's penis?" While Couric danced around that question and Perot pirouetted around the answer, from the control room Zucker shouted an expletive into Katie's earpiece, adding "doesn't matter, doesn't matter" in rapid succession before directing her to move on to a call from Jane in West Alexandria, Ohio, a hopefully safer haven.

Zucker's prompts exploded into Couric's headset one second and came out of her mouth the next, phrased with poignant pauses, as if she had just thought of the concept. Seconds after Perot lambasted pollsters and their product, Zucker/Couric asked, "Didn't *you* spend $180,000 on a poll before you decided to entertain the notion to run?"

Perot originally was taken by Couric's magic, wondering, "Imagine if I had Katie as a running mate?" Only after the call-in program did he update his opinion, accusing her of "trying to prove her manhood."

Democratic candidate Bill Clinton also answered phoned-in questions on *Today*. Jockeying through callers like a well-rehearsed pro, he addressed each one by his or her first name, as if they were some long-lost relatives last seen at a reunion picnic. He and vice presidential candidate Al Gore would later appear on *CBS This Morning,* and Vice President Dan Quayle would be a guest on *Good Morning America*—pointing to the candidates' preference for "coffee cup journalism" rather than the standard Sunday morning news panels.

Joining them was President George Bush. Bush had refused to appear on *Today*—a show that diligently did not allow any interference in its content—but agreed to be interviewed on *Good Morning America* if, and only if, he could dictate the topics: taxes, crime, and health care. However, *Today* eventually got its moment with the president in a spontaneous interview led by Katie Couric, who was broadcasting from the Blue Room of the White House. Celebrating the two hundredth anniversary of the executive mansion, *Today* had arranged for Couric to tour the White House with the First Lady. When President Bush appeared at the Blue Room door, Couric cornered him, asking about the upcoming presidential debate, his rumor-mongering over Bill Clinton's character, and the Iran-Contra affair.*

On Zucker's prompting, Couric asked Bush if he had "any knowledge of the Iran-Contra arms-for-hostages deal while [he] was in office" as vice president. "I've testified 450 times under oath, some of them, and our staff 3,500, that, yes," Bush answered, later adding, "Yes, and I've said so all along; given speeches on it."

The next day, White House spokesman Walter Kansteiner attempted to rephrase Bush's answer, saying he misunderstood the question. Clinton seized on the *Today* interview as evidence that the president was altering his story on Iran-Contra, and Katie Couric found herself once again in the spotlight—albeit amid controversy—representing the NBC telecast.

Bryant Gumbel publicly embraced Couric's increased prominence on the program, but privately he ordered NBC's publicity department to turn down her exposure meter. "He was calling Couric 'the flavor of the month' behind her back, and then right to her face," a *Today* staffer recalled.

Meanwhile, Bryant Gumbel, who for four years had been pushing NBC to take the show to Africa, finally convinced the network that such a remote was not only affordable, but also necessary to fully expose the growth that had taken place on the continent. "I don't think anything about Africa makes American air," Gumbel had said. "I'm sure there are many Americans who think Africans all live in huts with lions walking around outside their door."

To dispel that illusion, Gumbel traveled with his teenage son Bradley and a crew from NBC to Zimbabwe during a *Today* hiatus. The

---

*To allow for the unexpected coup, Zucker bumped former NBC Entertainment president Brandon Tartikoff, who was on hand in Studio 3-B to plug his autobiography. "It's okay," Zucker suggested. "Brandon knows good television programming." He also knew the value of a *Today* show book plug, and insisted on being rescheduled.

show had gone off the air once again to allow for NBC's Olympics coverage—this time from Barcelona. For fifteen days, they journeyed through Zimbabwe, Botswana, Kenya, Egypt, and Senegal, taping segments in preparation of a future live broadcast from Zimbabwe for a week during the November ratings sweeps period.

Gumbel had succeeded in getting *Today* to Africa by writing another memo—this one thirty-five pages—to NBC News president Michael Gartner the previous Christmas. While claiming that the show was "more than a Nielsen safari" and referring to the hoped-for ratings bonanza, Gumbel alleged that he hadn't referred to ratings more than once in the memo. "My pitch has always been 'This is journalistically correct, warranted, breathtakingly beautiful, and exciting. And, by the way, it might do well in the ratings.'"

When at Masai Mara, a game reserve in Kenya, the Land Rover in which they were riding in pursuit of a hippopotamus rammed into a ditch, throwing Gumbel against the side of the vehicle. Gumbel tore ligaments in his wrist, but no one else was injured. The *Today* host, his arm in a cast, continued to play television tag with five assorted camera crews, which had been dispatched to capture him and Bradley in Matopos National Park; riding elephants through Botswana's Okavango Delta; hot-air ballooning across the arid Kenya plains; receiving first-aid advice from a *n'anga* (healer) near Victoria Falls (at 350 feet a dramatic sight); visiting a government school in Zimbabwe's capital, Harare; and using his handheld Canon 35mm camera to capture cave art in what was labeled the world's "first art museum."

Speaking of the experience of shooting in Africa, Gumbel pointed to the progress that blacks had made in Zimbabwe. "I think it's very difficult to go there and not come away a changed individual in terms of seeing not only what's already been accomplished, but what has yet to be accomplished. It stays with you for a while," he said—an understatement, particularly from the normally outspoken Gumbel.

By the time Gumbel had left for Africa again on November 11 for the live broadcast, he had met with African diplomats, written to the various embassies, held conferences with top-ranking members of the State Department, and entertained African officials. He had also gone out of his way to clarify to the press that the trip was unrelated to his African heritage.

"I was already taken to task by someone who seemed upset that I don't say, well, I wanted to go to Africa because I'm an African-American," he told *The New York Times*. While admitting that that played a small part in his pursuit of the location shoot, Gumbel added, "To suggest that it played a major part is to suggest that I've been derelict for ten years because we didn't go to Africa. This week isn't 'Bryant Goes to Africa.'" Perhaps not, but you could have fooled most of America.

With the panoramic skyline of Harare as the background of the *Today* set in Africa, Gumbel, as promised, challenged the American myth that the continent defined itself by "famine, animals, jungle, and discord." He could have added "Tarzan movies" but didn't.

A mini-bio of John Cecil Rhodes stated that Rhodes took African land by "force and deception," while fighting a ten-year war with African resistance fighters. It was Rhodes who first opened up Rhodesia (named after John Cecil, it was later renamed Zimbabwe) to European settlement. Gumbel blamed Rhodes for much of Africa's difficulties, then and now. Pointing out that Rhodes considered himself the builder of a nation, Gumbel editorialized, "In reality, he's dead—and he was wrong."

Gumbel neglected to give Rhodes the credit for building the network of tobacco farms that today account for the majority of Zimbabwe's agricultural exports and economic base. Overlooked as well was Rhodes's scholarship program at Oxford University, established from his 7-million-pound fortune that he bequeathed when he died at age 49.

On the show, Jimmy Carter pointed to America's lack of interest in the people of Africa, charging that the United States government "has much less interest in people who happen to be black or brown than we do in Europeans who are white. And we become obsessed when a few dozen people are killed in Bosnia, but we ignore tens of thousands that might be killed at the same time in, say, Mozambique or in Sudan, or, increasingly now, in Liberia." Many African-Americans might have found enlightening the fact that much of the region was settled in the early nineteenth century by freed American slaves, whose descendants dominated Libya's economics and policies until recently.

In his enthusiasm to set the record straight on the African continent, Gumbel erroneously located the west African nation of Côte d'Ivoire as being east of Zimbabwe, which would have placed it somewhere in the middle of the Indian Ocean or directly on top of Madagascar. There were other errors of basic economics and political oversimplifications that were arguably too complicated to be fully explained within the limited scope of the *Today* show's format.

Despite its shortcomings, the program did manage to present a serious overview of the region, one that brought human faces to the plight of its 700 million inhabitants but cushioned the horror of that message with images of the lush landscape and still-abundant wildlife.

During the week in which its African shows aired, *Today* did not beat *Good Morning America,* but it was a close second. More important for advertisers, the NBC series crept ahead in its appeal to women in the 18–49 age group, largely thanks to Katie Couric. *CBS This Morning* remained the also-ran, some 6 share points behind both its competitors.

Even more impressive was the fact that viewership was up for all three network shows. *Today*'s sales increased by $2 million over projections, and even *CBS This Morning* began to turn a profit— albeit a small one—for the first time in its history. It was amazing news for CBS, in particular, for the network had rallied despite being dropped by several of its affiliates, including WAGA-TV in Atlanta and WJBK-TV in Detroit.

By March, *CBS This Morning* had increased 23 percent from the previous year. New executive producer Ted Savaglio could not have been happier. "We've got momentum," he said. "We're a contender. *Today*'s run at *GMA* has stalled and we're in a position to continue growing."

Much of the credit for the improvement in *This Morning*'s numbers was given to the growing popularity of its hosts, Harry Smith and

Paula Zahn. By 1993, Smith had survived longer than any other host in the show's hot seat—five years. The man whom Americans knew as bald, bespectacled, and calmly self-deprecating had graduated from a small college in Iowa with a degree in communication. He had spent a summer as an English instructor in Taiwan, where he learned that he liked to teach and that he enjoyed helping others.

Even as *CBS This Morning* began its slow rise in popularity, Smith remained loyal to what he labeled as his "responsibility" and volunteered as a reading tutor in New York's public elementary schools. Every Tuesday, after *CBS This Morning* finished for the day, he went to Miss Anne Chase's first and second grade classes, and sat with youngsters eager to learn.

Smith met his wife, CBS sportscaster Andrea Joyce, when they were both co-anchors on the noon news at the network's Denver affiliate. It was his first job at CBS, which hired him, he claims, because he could write. "They didn't say, 'Gee, you've got a lot of hair.'"

Paula Zahn, on the other hand, did. She had the blonde locks of a pageant winner, which she was. Born in Naperville, Illinois, to an IBM sales manager and his wife, Zahn moved through news positions in Chicago, Dallas, San Diego, Houston, and Boston, where she met her husband, Richard Cohen, a real-estate executive. Both Smith and Zahn had three-year-old children, and in mid-1993, Zahn discovered she was pregnant, adding yet another female cohost to the collection of those who celebrated their pregnancies on the air. "If it worked for Jane Pauley and NBC, I'll use it," Savaglio said. In fact, he went one better than NBC. Harry Smith's wife was also expecting, and both women were due to deliver on the same date—October 23.

As it turned out, NBC had more to worry about in early 1993 than any competition from CBS. NBC News found itself on the defensive for rigging a test on a General Motors truck in a *Dateline* episode. Producers on the program had placed model rockets on the gas tank of the truck to ensure that it would explode on impact. In the ensuing debacle, Michael Gartner resigned as president of NBC News, ending his controversial tenure. Gartner's exit was announced with regret on *Today* on March 3.

One of the hardest hit by Gartner's departure was Jeff Zucker, who only weeks earlier had agreed, at Gartner's request, to replace Steve Friedman as executive producer of *NBC Nightly News*. Zucker continued to head the *Today* show as well, essentially working a sixteen-hour shift. Less than a month later, Gartner was gone and Zucker resigned the *Nightly News* position.

A month after his resignation, Zucker deflected some of the negative attention away from the NBC News scandal and back toward *Good Morning America*. The ABC series had no sooner announced its plans to produce shows from New Zealand and Australia during the May ratings sweeps period than *Today* revealed that it, too, had been offered a "barter-and-cash deal" to go Down Under but, under NBC News guidelines, had refused.

Without acknowledging the recent lapses in NBC News's ethics, *Today* suggested that there were improprieties at work at ABC. Phil Beuth, the ABC vice president in charge of *Good Morning America,* called the aspersions "sour grapes" and "dirty pool," while reminding NBC that the show was produced under the auspices of ABC Entertainment, a division that operated under different guidelines than the News Division.

"I have nothing to hide," Beuth suggested. "We've had these arrangements for six or seven years. It's very expensive to do shows like these. We make an arm's-length trade [with tourist boards]. They have absolutely no editorial control over what we do."

Good Morning America eventually traveled to Australia and New Zealand and won the ratings war for the month of May. *CBS This Morning* countered by presenting a déjà-vu video: President Clinton speaking from the Rose Garden of the White House with the folks plucked from the tour line at his front door. It was not unlike the show's program from the previous year, when a different president was in residence and a different party was in power.

Today made its own mark, of sorts, by bringing back former executive producer Steve Friedman, complete with his baseball bat and glove, to replace whiz-kid executive producer Jeff Zucker, who had been pulled off the firing line of *Today* by new NBC News president Andy

Lack to improve the ratings of the third-place *NBC Nightly News*. Lack thought that Friedman could pull another first-place run for *Today* out of his frantic energy. It took him only seven weeks on the job.

By the second week in July 1993, *Today* ended *GMA*'s thirty-four-week winning streak with a first-place finish. Bryant Gumbel could have claimed a piece of the victory trophy, but unfortunately he was on vacation when it happened, replaced next to Katie Couric by Stone Phillips. Blue ribbon in hand, Friedman put *Good Morning America* on notice. "This is their wake-up call," he said. "I intend to beat them on land or sea or wherever. They know how competitive I am and what happened the last time I was here," he added, failing to mention *CBS This Morning* in his war chant.

With millions of dollars in profit as the grand prize, the race to the finish line during the following November Nielsen sweeps weeks found both *GMA*'s Jack Reilly and *Today*'s Steve Friedman claiming ownership of the victory lap. By cold numbers alone, *Good Morning America* managed to top *Today* on the basis of some location stunts— a five-city California bus jaunt called "The Great Pacific Coast Highway Tour," followed a week later by two days in Puerto Rico. It wasn't Africa, of course, but it nevertheless did what NBC's stay in Zimbabwe did not—win the ratings.

Friedman, who stayed put during the all-important November ratings period, looked more toward trends than numbers. "If they want to say they're number one because they're one-tenth of a point ahead of us in the third quarter, so be it," Friedman said. "I say *we* are. The trend, my friend, is on our side. There's no question that this program is the one that's moving"—though not to any new locations. "As the man who invented the trips *GMA* used to scoff at, I'm glad they've learned their lesson. Imitation is the sincerest form of thievery," Friedman taunted.

In this war of words, Reilly countered, "I've heard better lines from Steve. He must be listening to Conan O'Brien," referring to NBC's new late-night host.

Many people on both sides of this ratings battle would miss the banter between the two executive producers when it ended, as it did in December. Reilly, 65 years old, retired from *GMA* and was replaced by his just-hired line producer, Bob Reichblum.

As both shows eased into the Christmas season and the New Year, *CBS This Morning* made some news of its own. The birth of Jared Brandon Cohen on October 16 gave Paula Zahn reason to be proud. Hillary Clinton seemed pleased as well when she sent a video greeting card that was aired on the program. "Hi Paula, and congratulations. I'm so excited for you and I can't wait to meet the newest addition."

On October 28, it was President Clinton who was sending best wishes to Harry Smith and his wife, sportscaster Andrea Joyce. Grady Thomas Smith weighed in at 8 pounds, 13 ounces, and the president announced the arrival on-air with, "This is an amazing contribution you are all making to the expansion of the American family, and I want you to know we are all very grateful for that."

While the president's greeting may not have made much sense, it certainly seemed more appropriate to most than the segment that Paula Zahn had taped right before she entered the hospital. Joining Marla Maples—the mistress of building magnate Donald Trump, who was pregnant with his child—the glowing mothers-in-waiting giggled over a line of high-end maternity clothes that carried Maples's signature. Maples made a point of saying, "People focus on the marriage when the important thing is bringing the child into the world."

No one at CBS—including Zahn, who knew better—corrected Maples's false impression. The network ignored the statistics from the previous year documenting the birth of over 1.2 million illegitimate babies, many of them born into poverty and ill health. By not offering that perspective, CBS seemed to be condoning the practice of unwed motherhood—or at the very least, attempting to paint it in the velvet cords of expensive maternity clothing. The White House refrained from commenting on that birth.

The White House was silent again at Christmastime, when all three series canceled their plans to tour the executive mansion with Mrs. Clinton, citing the White House's restrictions on questions regarding the president's personal life. Accepting restrictions about an interview "puts you on a very slippery slope," Bob Reichblum, *GMA*'s newly installed executive producer, said, even though the show had allowed such dictates from the executive mansion in the past.

Although early morning viewers did not get to see the White House Christmas tree, they nonetheless saw plenty of the mansion itself, as 1994 burst upon the sunrise set of all three programs with the Clinton inauguration. The changeover in the White House living quarters was mirrored by changes in the host chairs at CBS and NBC. Paula Zahn had returned from maternity leave and was preparing to travel to Lillehammer, Norway, with Harry Smith to anchor the CBS broadcasts of the Winter Olympics. The *Today* show got a new news anchor in the person of Matt Lauer.* At 36, Lauer had a model's good looks and was labeled "Hunka Hunka Mornin' Love" by *Entertainment Weekly.*

Simultaneously, Kathleen Sullivan—who once held Zahn's job and had burst upon the early morning broadcast scene during the 1984 Olympics in Sarajevo as an anchor for ABC—was making news of her own. After losing her job at CBS, Sullivan had turned to teaching golf for a living, gotten fat, and ended up as a spokesperson for Weight Watchers.

"One moment I'm a network anchor and the next, well, look at me," Sullivan exclaimed on her first commercial for the weight-loss regimen. She looked older, wiser, heavier, slower, and genuinely excited about losing a lot of excess pounds. "We're all in this together," she suggested, begging other overweights to join her on the scale.

For the next month, Sullivan weighed in weekly and the pounds flooded off—not unlike Dorothy Bryce, the Regimen Tablet girl from Garroway's *Today* show days, although Sullivan seemed to be more honest about the way she was losing weight. When Katie Couric grilled her on *Today* about crossing some mythical line between journalism and commercialism, Sullivan got what amounted to sweet revenge.

"Everyone says, 'Doesn't this hurt your colleagues?' Where were they the last three years?" Sullivan asked, smiling grimly. "Were they

---

*Lauer had taken over the position from Margaret Larson, who herself had assumed the chair temporarily taken when Faith Daniels left the news desk in May 1992.

helping me find a job? Were they saying wonderful things about me? Let's go back a couple years when I had to sit there and watch people trash me mercilessly in the press with no compassion and no regard for the truth." Sullivan added that Couric's and others' questions were sanctimonious, saying, "There can be no double jeopardy for pariahs."

Friend and fellow golfer Bryant Gumbel ignored Sullivan during her visit to *Today*. "He scorned me. We barely talked," she said. Likewise, her "good" friend and co-anchor on *CBS This Morning*, Harry Smith, became invisible after she was dropped from the program. "Not a call," Sullivan said. "He didn't phone to see if I was handling it well. He didn't phone to say he was sorry that it happened. He didn't phone, period." There were those, however, who *did* reach out—Joan Lunden, Barbara Walters, Nancy Reagan, and Joan Rivers among them.

Offering insight into life after the star of morning television dims, Sullivan said she was barely able to keep the bill collectors at bay after losing her $100,000-a-month salary nine months after her dismissal. Many pointed to poor fund management as the cause, but Sullivan told another story. At the time of her Lili Bart fall, she was building a home in East Hampton. She ended up taking a $400,000 loss on the place. She put her Manhattan apartment on the market; after four years, it finally closed, at another huge loss.

By the time Weight Watchers came calling, Sullivan had been reduced to living in a tiny one-bedroom apartment in Rancho Mirage, California. "You go down Frank Sinatra and turn right on Bob Hope and turn left on Gerald Ford," she said, "and if you hit Ginger Rogers or Dinah Shore, you went one block too far."

Sullivan's old stomping ground, *CBS This Morning*, had grown 44 percent over the past two years, hitting its highest ratings ever during the second week in January 1994, when Los Angeles was hit by a major earthquake. Paula Zahn's post-maternity return also contributed to a bounce in the numbers. However, it was too little, too late for Boston's WHDH-TV, which became the fourth CBS affiliate to drop the morning show in favor of local programming.

While *Good Morning America* still led the ratings in the season-to-date figures, by the last week in January, *Today* had surpassed it by two-tenths of a ratings point. The gain represented only about 150,000 more TVs turning to NBC, but as Steve Friedman quickly pointed out, "A win is a win."

Suggesting that NBC was now in the driver's seat, Friedman noted *Good Morning America*'s lack of competitiveness, which allowed *Today* to excel. "They didn't go for the jugular when they had the chance," Friedman explained. "They let *Today* stick around and we fixed a lot of our problems. We won't be as kind," he countered. Hardly rolling over and begging for mercy, *Good Morning America* traveled to Hong Kong during the second week of the Olympics, putting *GMA* back in the winning column.

With the ratings game continuing to generate more heat than an Indian summer, it fell to O. J. Simpson to provide the ultimate in viewer incentive for watching early morning television. The resulting intrigue and the scope of coverage would find viewership soaring—and Bryant Gumbel facing the most important decision of his entire career.

CHAPTER TWELVE

THE MURDERS

Brentwood, Calif.—Football great O. J. Simpson's former wife and a 25-year-old man were found apparently stabbed to death outside her Brentwood townhouse early Monday morning.

Los Angeles police said they were not ruling out anyone's possible involvement in the Sunday night slayings of Nicole Brown Simpson, 35, and Ronald Lyle Goldman, a waiter at a trendy Brentwood restaurant. Sources close to the case, who asked not to be named, said the football star is considered a suspect.

—*Los Angeles Times*, June 14, 1994

*B*ryant Gumbel first heard the news of the death of Nicole Brown Simpson on the morning of June 13, 1994, when he walked into Studio 3-B. Although he didn't know the details of the crime, he did know that his friend, sometime golfing partner, and *Today* show guest, O. J. Simpson, was not involved.

As the weeks went by and evidence supporting Simpson's alleged guilt was mounting, Gumbel remained steadfastly convinced of his friend's innocence. The rumors of a racially motivated police conspiracy made far more sense to Gumbel, who defended Simpson both on and off the air.

As Americans were turning on their television sets every morning to follow the unfolding Simpson murder saga, the *Today* show was

212 / MADNESS IN THE MORNING

making its own news. Three days after O. J. Simpson grabbed the nation's attention with his low-speed chase along the freeways and streets of Los Angeles; after he was subsequently arrested and charged with the Brown/Goldman murders; and after he moved into a jailhouse in downtown Los Angeles, the *Today* show found itself moving as well—into glistening new studio space with a huge window on New York.

The $15 million Studio 1-A, fronted by 100 linear feet of glass rising three stories high, was at street level on the corner of 49th Street and Rockefeller Plaza. The state-of-the-art facility was a gift from the network's parent company, General Electric. On opening day, President Bill Clinton was the first interview in an interactive question-and-answer session featuring passersby on the street. Using kiosks equipped with microphones and cameras, tourists and native New Yorkers became an instant part of the program, harkening back to the show's original days. As for the neck-and-neck early morning ratings, executive producer Steve Friedman said, "I expect this will put our neck ahead of theirs." *Today* failed, however, to beat *GMA,* despite a spike of about 22 percent in its ratings during opening week.

The set's window-on-the-world feature had one addition that the show's original studio had lacked: a mechanical wall that could be raised in place to block out the fans during any particular segment. Viewers at home got a firsthand view of the wall in action that first morning during a segment on the O. J. Simpson case. The wall was activated in the event that any sign-holders demanded that the sports star be freed—or executed.

"What are we going to call that hoojamajiggy that goes up and down?" Gumbel had questioned in a tour of the facility a few days earlier. "The drop," one person suggested. "The shade," another offered. "The wall," Katie Couric proclaimed, stating the obvious. And the wall it became.

By July, *People* magazine had referred to the set as "Gumbel under Glass," and Bob Reichblum at *Good Morning America* had countered all the press coverage of the new studio by saying that he wanted to "put a window across America, not on 49th Street." *USA Today* called it a "peep show for waving dorks." Unfortunately, the window failed to invigorate the ratings, and Steve Friedman found himself "moving to other assignments within NBC News" the following month. Replacing him, one more time, was Jeff Zucker.

Zucker had just taken over his new shift as the man in charge at *Today* when tragedy struck. As office workers watched helplessly, a *Today* stagehand was shot and killed outside the studio by a man with an AK-47 assault rifle who had attempted to gain entry to the set.

The stagehand, Campbell Montgomery, was 33 years old and had worked for NBC since 1990. The gunman, a Charlotte, North Carolina, native, was arrested as he sat calmly in his Ford Taurus on the street in front of the studio. He told police that NBC was spying on him by tapping his telephone and sending rays through his television set into his brain. Montgomery's wife later filed a $100 million lawsuit against Rockefeller Center, NBC's security service, and the manufacturer and importer of the assault rifle from which the bullet was fired.

Ten weeks after Zucker returned to *Today*, the series had beaten or tied *Good Morning America* eight times. Suddenly, Bob Reichblum took the challenge seriously and sent *GMA* out on another road trip, this one labeled "The Great Chesapeake Bay Bus Tour."

Reichblum, who had come to ABC from Miami—where he had been the news director on the network's local affiliate, WPLG—was nicknamed the Three Mile Island of executive producers for his intense work schedule. "Reichblum ought to give his adrenal glands to science," Charles Gibson said. "He's here from four in the morning till six at night. . . . It's an ironman, macho, guy thing."

As *Today* built a first-place strut into its gait, it introduced a new on-air slogan: "America's Favorite Morning Program." It was a line that caused Reichblum to react every time he heard it. "There's remarkable hubris over there," Reichblum said of his competition. "They call themselves 'America's favorite.' The question is, Are viewers calling them that as well?"

Zucker, who had not yet turned 30, countered, "He sounds nervous, Mr. Reichblum does. More Americans are watching *Today* than *GMA*. And if Bob can't figure that out, I'll send him over the ratings."

"I'll always be able to out-think the *Today* show," Reichblum shot back. "I'll always be able to do a better show than *Today.*"

"Out-think us?" questioned Zucker. "I have a lot of respect for Joan and Charlie, but in Bryant and Katie you've got the two sharpest people in morning TV." And so the children of the morning went back and forth for weeks.

Despite his outward confidence, Zucker was nervously watching the time clock as the seconds ticked away on what remained of Bryant Gumbel's contract. By December 1994, Gumbel's three-year, $7 million megadeal had expired, and he was now working without any contract at all. He was making no secret of the fact that he felt both underutilized by the network *and* underpaid (no small concept, considering Gumbel was then bringing in about $5,000 an hour in salary). According to rumors floating throughout the broadcasting industry, Fox TV's owner, Rupert Murdoch, was going to make an end run for the onetime sportscaster, showcasing him in a *Nightline*-patterned news hour. Other sources confirmed that CBS had offered the anchor $10 million for three years to jump free of the Peacock network.

Gumbel did eventually sign a new one-year deal with NBC—valued at nearly $3 million—and the network exhaled a collective sigh of relief. However, Gumbel was beginning to tire of the *Today* grind. He wanted new challenges, a larger audience, and more time to prepare in-depth pieces. On the *Today* show, all three were impossible to achieve.

As ABC assessed the reason for their loss of viewers, a survey conducted by a market research firm suggested that the "old family feeling" that had brought the show so many kudos a decade earlier now looked like a well-worn shoe. Early morning viewers were eager to find something new on television. Hoping for an instant fix, ABC's advertising agency, Grey Entertainment, created a reworked version of 26-year-old newcomer Des'ree's pop-rock hit "You Gotta Be." "Listen as your day unfolds," the song began, as snap clips of Lunden, Gibson, Christian, and news anchor Morton Dean flashed across the screen.

Despite the cheerful homogeneity of the song, life behind the scenes on *Good Morning America* was anything but happy. As Lunden continued to suffer the aftereffects of divorce, weatherman Spencer

Christian was shattered by an unexpected audit by the Internal Revenue Service. The IRS was questioning Christian's tax shelters, which, it claimed, were offering too much shelter and paying too little tax. As a result, the weatherman was forced to divest himself of nearly half of his exotic fine wine collection that he had been assembling since he first tasted a bottle of Chateau Lafite Rothschild in 1977. At one point his collection numbered 1,500 bottles.

By April, *Good Morning America* was running a consistent second to *Today* and could no longer deny that it seemed to have permanently slipped in the ratings. Citing its inability to compete effectively with a "serious news" program because it was governed by ABC's Entertainment Division, the network shifted control of its early morning program to the News Division. Alan Wurtzel, ABC's senior vice president for ABC News magazine and long-form programming, was placed in charge of the show from a management standpoint, while Bob Reichblum continued to receive the network's support as executive producer.

An ABC executive had remarked, "No one thinks the show is broken," but the statement was a lie. There wasn't a meeting at which one network executive or another didn't propose major changes, including one to totally rework the program from the bottom up. The first stop: Joan Lunden.

Lunden had enjoyed her role as both a crucial cog at *GMA* and—despite the network executives' emphasis on the future—the show's most enduring link to its past. However, as rumors about replacing her reached the cohost's ears, she threw herself into a regimen of self-improvement. Her unhappy home life had evidenced itself in a weight gain that she had only recently tackled successfully. In the year since her divorce, Lunden had dropped fifty pounds and had even released a workout video, *Joan Lunden's Workout America,* a self-proclaimed "cardio-dance and muscle conditioning" tape that seemed hopelessly caught in a disco time warp. As Joan did the Pony, waving her arms up and down, one reviewer suggested that the routine looked like a "cross between a talent show and a PTA fund-raiser." Yet, Lunden had dropped from a size 14 dress size to a size 8 and was looking better than she had in years.

Unfortunately, *Good Morning America* was not. Like most of the country, the show was caught up in "O. J. fever," hanging on every word of leaked evidence and presumed guilt or innocence in the controversial trial. For better or worse, the three breakfast shows were approaching their coverage of the trial from different angles that were reflective of their different perspectives.

While *Good Morning America* hyped each day's newscast with the latest shred of evidence or rumor, *CBS This Morning* presented testimony and scandal with equal neutrality. The *Today* show, meanwhile, assumed a more inside posture, dictated by Gumbel's relationship with O. J. Simpson.

Speaking with *TV Guide*, Gumbel clarified his position on Simpson's guilt or innocence. "O. J. was a friend," he told writer Janice Kaplan. "We've known each other for, I guess, twenty-one years, twenty-two years. Were we excessively close? No. Were we close enough to have dinner? Yes. Close enough to play golf together? Yes . . . I feel as most people would if a friend was accused of murder. Your initial reaction is 'No, my friend *couldn't* have done it.' Then, as you get into it, you hope that your friend *didn't* do it."

Gumbel's steadfast loyalty to his friend, despite what appeared to be overwhelming evidence to the contrary, was to many evidence itself of his arrogance and narrow-mindedness. It was a stamp that Gumbel had worn nearly all his professional life, yet it didn't stop him from bristling at its sound each time he heard it. "To suggest there's no racial aspects to judgments about me is naive," Gumbel told Kaplan. "I've said that if you lined up Ted Koppel, Barbara Walters, and Bryant Gumbel together and they all said the same thing in the same fashion, to most insecure critics, Ted would be confident, Barbara would be bitchy, and Bryant would be arrogant. Let's face it, there are a lot of people who are uncomfortable with the idea of a black man being their intellectual or economic or social equal or superior. It doesn't bother me, but I do think their judgments are warped."

Oliver North certainly would be one such person. During an on-air interview with the onetime Marine lieutenant colonel–turned–radio talk show host, Gumbel charged North with "denouncing" all the liberal guests he invited onto his show. "You know, Bryant, I don't think *anybody* ought to take themselves as seriously as you do every morning," North shot back.

"Oh, clearly not," Gumbel said defensively. "Perhaps the oath should have been taken a little more seriously before lying to the government, too," he added, referring to North's involvement in the Iran-Contra scandal. To Gumbel's credit, he later telephoned North and said he should have treated him better since, after all, he was a guest on the program, but he also added that he didn't regret the disagreement or its implications. Said Katie Couric of the jousting, "Boys will be boys."

Gumbel's cohost had little of his deep-seated need for respect, and even less of his pomp and circumstance. While Gumbel spent thousands of dollars on suits and custom-made shirts, Couric was happy to shop the sale racks (she even *rented* a formal maternity dress to wear to the White House). She drove a seven-year-old Honda, loved fishing, drank milk right from the carton, and preferred ordering takeout from Ollie's Noodle House on Broadway to eating in a fancy five-star restaurant.

"When I ride first class, it's always a little embarrassing to me," Couric said. "I'm just a coach kind of gal." Much of that everywoman charm emerged early in Couric's life. The daughter of a retired journalist–cum–public relations executive, Couric grew up in Arlington, Virginia, in a red-brick house surrounded by the proverbial white picket fence. The youngest of four children, she was surrounded by what her mother has since labeled a "creative disorder" ("I think she thought things straightened themselves out by magic"). She was suspended from Yorktown High School for smoking cigarettes, graduated with honors from the University of Virginia, and got a job as a desk assistant to ABC's Sam Donaldson, who once labeled her as "cream rising to the top."

Driven to get her shot as an on-air reporter, Couric moved to CNN, where at 23 she stood in front of a camera and reported live from the nation's capital. Moments after her broadcast, then–CNN president

Reese Schonfeld dictated a memo: "Katherine Couric is not to appear on television again—*ever.*" Over the next half-dozen years, Couric spent time reporting in local stations in Atlanta and Miami before landing a position at WRC, the NBC affiliate in Washington, D.C., where she was plucked from the line-up to become *Today*'s first national correspondent.

While at WRC, Couric met her husband, attorney Jay Monahan, at a party. She wore a tight black miniskirt; he passed himself off as a painter. A year later they were married, the organized Monahan cleaning up after his messy wife. He once found a bowl of half-eaten cereal his wife had stashed under his pillow and forgotten. "It was full of cat hairs," he said, not particularly surprised.

What did catch Monahan—and his wife—slightly off guard was Couric's second pregnancy, announced in July 1995, with a due date of January. The *Today* show redoubled its efforts to utilize Couric's talent before losing it once more for two months of maternity leave. As Al Roker, the weatherman on the show's weekend broadcasts who had taken over some of Willard Scott's map duty on the weekday series, wheeled on a flower-laden baby carriage, Couric exclaimed, "I know people think I need to lay off the jelly doughnuts because they haven't seen my waist in weeks."

Still mired in third place, *CBS This Morning* brought an audience back on its set as a means to lure viewers away from *Today*. "We've been in last place for thirty years," CBS News president Eric Ober reflected. "This is a way to differentiate our morning news program from the others. In effect to counterprogram." The network had tried the audience route once before, but Ober either neglected to mention that or forgot that it was a dismal failure.

Good Morning America had an even more acute problem. In a stock swap worth $19 billion, the Walt Disney Company was buying ABC, the second largest corporate merger in U.S. history. The deal was consummated on August 3, 1995. Charles Gibson was thirty minutes into the program that morning when Bob Reichblum alerted him through his earpiece that his current boss, Capital Cities chairman Tom Murphy, and his future boss, Disney chairman Michael Eisner, would be joining him live to announce the deal. It would not be Gibson's finest moment.

Murphy and Eisner strolled onto the set as if they owned it. Well, actually they did own it. After hearing about the financial details of the merger, Gibson tried to determine what effect it would have on the way the news was presented on ABC. Murphy answered by asking Gibson if he wasn't proud being a member of the Disney family. "I'm . . . I've never . . . ," Gibson sputtered.

"No, I'm serious . . . quite serious," asserted Murphy.

"I never thought I'd work for a guy named Mickey. Yes, sure, I'm . . . ," Gibson struggled to regroup.

"But it's *Snow White* and it's *The Lion King*," Murphy reminded him, as if perhaps Gibson was unaware of Disney products. "All those wonderful animated shows that they've done, all the creative energy in that company."

"No, there are . . . there are changes in the marketplace and in the regulatory rules which make this somewhat logical, and I guess everyone is surprised, in some ways not surprised." Huh? Come again, Charlie. "There was a sort of logic to this that . . . that has made sense," Gibson tried one more time. "I can't go to the tank and say, yes, this is great, you know, I mean, I have . . . I still have . . . here as an objective interviewer."

Not about to let him off the hook or even begin to understand Gibson's discomfort, Murphy laughed and said, "Kind of nice to get him, isn't it?"

"Well, he's fumbling around there," Eisner pointed out obnoxiously. "And on the air, too—it's perfect. So you don't like the deal, do you, Charlie?" Eisner asked pointedly.

"Don't you think this would be a good time for a commercial, everyone?" Gibson begged as the screen turned blank and an ad for Alpo dog food appeared—half-sponsor, half-savior.

• • •

Gibson wasn't the only cohost placed in a difficult position by his employer. Two months later, it was Bryant Gumbel's turn to be publicly humiliated by his boss.

On October 3, 1995, O. J. Simpson was found innocent of the murders of his ex-wife, Nicole, and her friend Ronald Goldman. No sooner had the verdict been announced than the victory party commenced at Simpson's home in Brentwood, California, where Simpson cornered his old friend, Don Ohlmeyer, president of NBC Entertainment West Coast. Simpson had decided he wanted to talk to the media and was offering the first interview to NBC.

Ohlmeyer went to NBC president Bob Wright, who in turn presented the offer to NBC News president Andrew Lack. Assured that there would be no restrictions on what NBC could ask of Simpson, and that Simpson could have his attorney present at the interview, Lack gave the "thumbs up" to the interview and called Simpson to advise him.

During their initial conversation, Lack told Simpson that he had selected Bryant Gumbel, Tom Brokaw, and Katie Couric to share the interviewing responsibility, since each would bring his or her unique perspective to the process. Simpson, reminding Lack that Gumbel was an old friend, said, "We go back a long way. We're friends . . . twenty years, golfing buddies. He knew Nicole. There might be a conflict of interest there."

Lack promised Simpson that he would give that point some thought, and he did. The following day, he alerted Gumbel that he was being pulled off the interview, citing the *appearance* of a conflict of interest. Gumbel was stunned. He argued that, as a professional broadcast journalist, he was able to separate his responsibility to NBC from his friendship with O. J. Simpson. "It was a very tough conversation," Lack later said. "Tough and brief."

The Simpson interview would be no ordinary interview. It would be extraordinary, one that would not only garner major ratings, but carry with it major prestige. Being removed from the process did more than devastate Gumbel—it made him question his entire career. The day following his conversation with Lack, Gumbel called in sick. News anchor Matt Lauer, substituting for Gumbel, made no mention of the reason for his absence. Gumbel was "sick" the next day as well, and the next. For an entire week, he remained at home. While perhaps not physically ill, he was emotionally and mentally upset, and unable to reconcile Lack's decision. As though moving in quarter-time, his mind played out the scenario over and over again, and each time it did, Gumbel returned to the same bottom line: it was time to leave *Today* and perhaps even NBC.

Simpson never did speak to Tom Brokaw, Katie Couric, or anyone else on NBC. The day after Brokaw and Couric flew to Los Angeles for the interview—a day before it was to take place live on NBC— Simpson's attorney Johnnie Cochran telephoned Andrew Lack. Given the fact that a civil case was still pending in the deaths of Nicole Simpson and Ronald Goldman, Simpson's lawyers thought it was a mistake for their client to be interviewed on television.

As NBC News attempted to wipe egg off its corporate face, Bryant Gumbel returned to the *Today* set a changed man. Having had the opportunity to review his career and his life over the past seven days, he had concluded that he was not getting the level of respect and adulation that he had anticipated and felt he deserved.

Initially, Gumbel made public his possible departure from *Today*. During the several months left on his contract, he had more meetings with Lack about the handling of the Simpson interview. Gumbel blamed Lack for his disregard for Gumbel's competence and thoroughness. Charges of racial bias once again surfaced, and while apparently unfounded, they were nonetheless only a gossamer breath beneath the surface.

When it came time to sign a new contract, Gumbel's representative, Ed Hookstratten, demanded and received a large raise for his client, pushing Gumbel past the $3 million mark for the next year's work. At the same time Gumbel signed the deal, he also announced that it would be his last for *Today*.

Although Gumbel had been hinting at leaving the show and his resignation was widely anticipated, NBC was nevertheless stunned by his announcement. Gumbel's feelings were both genuine and irrevocable. "Fifteen years is a long time in one place, and the world's too exciting to enjoy from one vantage point," Gumbel said without casting stones.

David Letterman was not so kind. Upon hearing about Gumbel's intention to resign from *Today*, the irrepressible Letterman listed the "Ten Reasons Bryant Gumbel Is Leaving the *Today* Show."

10. Found out that Gene Shalit borrowed his comb.

9. *Today* show Doctor Art Ulene's physicals last a little too long.

8. Has some grand plan about something called *The Yesterday Show*.

7. You try dealing with "Katie Perkie" every morning at 5:00 A.M.

6. Tired of sitting there helplessly while New Yorkers outside the window give him the finger.

5. He's pregnant.

4. Wants to get out of a town where guys sell bacon from a briefcase.

3. Got starring role in *The Greg Gumbel Story*.

2. Wants to have more sex on the Internet using the name "Giant Bryant."

1. He's getting out of the television business. He's going to work at CBS.

Gumbel and Letterman had had a history of strained relations after Letterman once interrupted a live primetime *Today* special in Rockefeller Center. Using a bullhorn, Letterman shouted down from his high-rise office: "My name is Larry Grossman [then-president of NBC News], and I'm not wearing any pants!" and caused Gumbel to stumble over his lines. Gumbel, unable or unwilling to see the humor in the moment, thought Letterman acted "unprofessionally," and so began a years-long feud.

In time, Gumbel did call a truce with Letterman and was invited multiple times on his show. Yet, a very real undercurrent of an unforgiven sin existed. On July 1, 1994, Letterman held a large sign against *Today*'s studio window proclaiming I LOVE YOU, BRYANT. Gumbel held up his own hastily written sign that read, BITE ME.

While NBC did its corporate best to regroup, *CBS This Morning* attempted to launch the studio audience version of its program. "They're rearranging the deck chairs on television's ever-listing *Titanic* again," *People* magazine said after the show's initial week. Reviewer David Hiltbrand said that "Paula [Zahn] and Harry [Smith] scuttle up and down the aisles with microphones to work the often-lifeless crowd like a couple of sleep-deprived Ricki Lake wannabes."

Apparently agreeing, and with mounting pressure to raise *CBS This Morning* and *The CBS Evening News* from their third-place ratings, CBS fired Eric Ober, president of CBS News, and replaced him with Andrew Heyward, a twenty-year veteran of the network. Officially, the change in command came at the request of executives from the Westinghouse Electric Company, which had bought the network in a $5.4 billion acquisition the previous November.

Hoping to seize upon what it saw as discord at NBC and stupidity at CBS, ABC, only weeks earlier, had replaced Bob Reichblum, the executive producer of *Good Morning America*, with the series's senior producer, Marc Burstein. By coincidence, Burstein's wife, Lori Beecher, had spent two years as an associate producer at *GMA* and was at that moment the primary talent booker on *Today*.

At the start of the new year of 1996, Hillary Rodham Clinton became a prime candidate for a guest spot on all three networks, as the First Lady eagerly made the media rounds to promote her book, *It Takes a Village and Other Lessons Children Teach Us*. With her image fraying due to ever-enlarging investigations into her involvement in Whitewater and White House travel office affairs, Mrs. Clinton was an open target for probing queries. Instead, the early morning not-exactly-news shows decided to treat her appearance as a "love-in."

With Katie Couric having just given birth to a 7-pound, 10-ounce baby girl, *Today* called on Maria Shriver to interview Hillary Clinton.

Calling the book "terrific," Shriver veered the segment away from politics and into a question-and-answer exploration of family relationships and life's lessons learned.

On *CBS This Morning*, Paula Zahn and Harry Smith fared slightly better, directly asking the First Lady if she knew how documents sought in the Whitewater investigation had "mysteriously" been discovered in a room next to her office in the White House. "Did you put them there?" Zahn wondered.

"Of course not," Mrs. Clinton stated emphatically, adding that her husband knew nothing about them either. Zahn and Smith pursued the First Lady's denials no further. Instead, they passed the microphone to their new, even less confrontive audience.

The first woman selected to ask a question simply told Mrs. Clinton how wonderful she was, saying "You're a model for women everywhere." When an 80-year-old woman wanted to know if Mrs. Clinton would ever run for president, the First Lady responded, "Not in this lifetime," and then asked for the woman's address so that she could send her a birthday card from the White House.

Good Morning America passed on interviewing the First Lady so that Barbara Walters could question her on *20/20* in primetime. Although Walters touched on the problems Hillary Clinton faced as subcommittees second-guessed her every move, there was more shmoozing than follow-up questions from the interviewer Mrs. Clinton called "a dear friend." Dear friends are like that.

Good Morning America had not given up its fight for first place, or the top guests, however. If anything, it took on new glamour status with the sudden transformation of Joan Lunden, who had regained the self-esteem that she had buried under the pressure to balance family and career. Helping the transformation was a new relationship—with actor Kevin Costner.

Costner himself had just been granted a divorce from his wife of nineteen years. Though the split was amicable—despite the $80 million divorce settlement—Costner was eager to launch into a new romance, specifically one with Lunden, whom, he claimed, he had wanted to meet for years. Costner rented a private yacht and the pair sailed around Manhattan on their first dinner date. Although others would follow, an extended romance between the two was unable to withstand the bright lights of media attention.

Nevertheless, Lunden's self-confidence had already blossomed. As if freed from some thorny prison of contempt, Lunden laughed and bubbled through the hours on the set of *Good Morning America,* infusing the entire production with her happiness and helping to create the family that *Today* had hoped to become. As Gibson, Lunden, and Christian brought their warmth beyond the set and into viewers' homes, a gaggle of new correspondents—among them designer Tommy Hilfiger and computer expert Gina Smith—came along to join the party.

Yet, no sooner had the ensemble acclimated to its new freedom and new upbeat tempo than fate moved in. News anchor Morton Dean left the program and was replaced with former NBC *Today* news anchor Elizabeth Vargas. Although Dean had previously read the news from Washington, D.C., Vargas was added to the "family" in New York, right along with a new set designed to accommodate the new arrival.

Gone was the living room of old and in its place was a loft apartment. On the second level were Vargas's news desk and Spencer Christian's weather map. Christian and Vargas hit it off immediately, sharing a love of wine and rock music, but it wasn't the weatherman and the newscaster who generated the gossip. In a scenario reminiscent of the Pauley/Norville debacle, Vargas's intentions on *Good Morning America* were interpreted as plays to replace Joan Lunden on the sofa.

ABC News chief Roone Arledge did little to squash the rumors by calling Vargas the "heir-apparent" to Lunden in a *Newsweek* article. There was also a leak within the trade press that a clause in Vargas's contract with ABC stipulated that she would be paid $1 million if she was not named cohost of *Good Morning America* within her first two years on the show.

Both Lunden and Vargas went out of their way to be overtly friendly on the air. Vargas was even called in to replace Gibson when he went on vacation soon after her arrival on the set. "I wouldn't have done that if everybody wasn't getting along," executive producer Marc

Burstein told *TV Guide.* Yet, the more everyone denied that anything was going on, the more certain everyone seemed to be that something was, indeed, amiss.

In the same odd way that a roadside accident causes drivers to rubberneck in curiosity, so too did viewers begin to tune in to see if they could pick up on any discord between the two women, taking the show's stagnant ratings up one notch and the blush off CBS's plans to revitalize its own breakfast fare.

CBS News president Andrew Heyward had installed Jim Murphy as *CBS This Morning*'s newest executive producer in April 1996 and created still another game plan to move the network's ratings forward. Gone was the studio audience that only months before was extolled by the network's executives as the key to success. In its place was "affiliate participation," in which the stations that carried the telecast could program about two-thirds of the first hour of the show, taking what they wanted from the network feed and inserting their own local news or anchors as they saw fit. The second hour would remain in the hands of the network alone, with the exception of the traditional breakaway for local news on the half hour.

Gone, too, were anchors Harry Smith, who was sent packing to points unknown within CBS News, and Paula Zahn, who was assigned a Saturday spot on *The CBS Evening News* and a role as occasional substitute for Dan Rather in that show's anchor seat during the week. Replacing them were Mark McEwen—the onetime stand-up comic, weatherman, and most recently the program's entertainment editor, a post he had occupied since 1992—and Jane Robelot, who had only recently been signed to the show as the news anchor. Before moving to *CBS This Morning,* Robelot had been a news anchor at the network's Philadelphia affiliate, WCAU-TV.

Not content with the typical twosome in the spotlight, CBS added a third cohost, Jose Diaz-Balart, who was hired away from NBC's Miami affiliate, WTVJ-TV. Prior to joining that station, Diaz-Balart had been a correspondent in Europe and Washington, D.C., for the Spanish-language Telemundo network. Replacing Robelot at the news desk was Cynthia Bowers, onetime anchor with CNN in Atlanta.

Despite the new faces, new set, new name (*This Morning* preceded by the local stations' own call letters), and new theme music, the show retained the same old ratings. When the new series premiered on August 12, 1996, the *Today* show remained in first place, *GMA* was second, and CBS was still a distant third. The same day, Fox Broadcasting, the fourth network in some circles, debuted its own morning gabfest titled *After Breakfast** between 9:00 and 10:00 A.M.—a timeslot typically dominated by the syndicated *Live with Regis & Kathie Lee.*

The shows debuted in the middle of a presidential campaign that pitted incumbent Bill Clinton against former Republican Senator Robert Dole. As the underdog, Dole attempted to mount the podium of the early morning shows as often as possible, given the restraints of the federal policy controlling equal access.

Appearing on *Today,* Dole utilized the show as a pulpit upon which to lash out at the media and its propensity to distort what Dole labeled "fact." In the interview, conducted by Katie Couric, Dole was given an open mike to expand on his charges that the "liberal media" were following the Democrats' lead in questioning his earlier statement that tobacco may not be addictive.

"You can't respond," an agitated Dole told interviewer Couric. "The media has already made up their mind. I've said I don't know whether it's addictive. I'm not a doctor. I'm not a scientist. People shouldn't smoke, young or old. Now what else do you do?" he asked.

The question of Dole's alliance to the tobacco industry was continuously placed at the center of the presidential campaign, and Dole's pundits had hoped that a pleasant interview with Couric might soften and broaden his image. Instead, Dole leaped off the screen with hostility—and without any regard for the political consequences.

The Republicans had been at odds with NBC for several months

---

* *After Breakfast* had previously run on Fox's cable outlet FX for two years. It was hosted by Laurie Hibberd, Tom Bergeron, and a puppet named Bob. Making the mix all the more interesting, Hibberd was the girlfriend of Michael Gelman, the executive producer of *After Breakfast's* competition, *Live with Regis & Kathie Lee.*

228 /   MADNESS IN THE MORNING

at this point, after Bryant Gumbel's remarks during the network's coverage of the funeral of Secretary of Commerce Ron Brown, who was killed in a plane crash in Croatia. Gumbel, who was in Washington, D.C., interviewing House Democrat Charles Rangel for the *Today* show, said, "Although many have praised Ron lavishly, I understand no Republicans have yet expressed condolences to the Brown family. Is that politics as usual, or is that just plain bad manners?"

Republican National Committee Chairman Haley Barbour immediately expressed his outrage, emphasizing that he had personally conveyed his sympathies to Brown's family. The day following Gumbel's remarks, news anchor Ann Curry ended her news reading with, "Wednesday, we said that the family of Ron Brown had not received condolences from any Republican. That is not the case. In fact, messages of condolence were expressed by some Republicans and we regret the error."

While that satisfied the Republicans and should have ended the issue, Gumbel wasn't at all pleased. He felt that viewers might attribute the apology to him. In a personal statement issued later, Gumbel said that "out of respect for the memory of Ron Brown and his grieving family, I am not anxious to prolong this story. Like most people, I had hoped that decency would prevail over politics. Those involved will have to live with the truth." Presumably, Gumbel was including himself in that group.

Gumbel spent the remainder of his contract on a diet, convinced he was going to leave NBC as trim as when he arrived. Weatherman Al Roker had placed what Gumbel called "a major squeeze play" on his own waistline, dropping from 315 pounds to 255 in eight months. Roker was more or less humiliated into dieting by his young daughter Courtney, who announced to her father one day, much to his embarrassment, that he had "enormous breasts." Apparently, he agreed with her and decided to trim down to a less exclamatory size. While still not slim by any measure, at least he was less likely to have a stroke while pointing to high-pressure areas over the Midwest. "I'm never going to be svelte," he admitted. "My family has a low center of gravity."

Regardless, Roker's image apparently fit his career plans, for he admitted to *People* magazine that a weatherman "should generally be the goofiest-looking person on the newscast." On the *Today* show, of course, the "goofiest" title could have gone to any number of hopefuls, including Willard Scott, who would have happily taken the honor. Scott remained in "semi-retirement," content to appear on only a couple of shows a week.

Roker had picked up the slack without difficulty and was actually becoming quite effective as a sidewalk correspondent, working the crowd outside of the *Today* studio. He had graduated from the State University of New York at Oswego on Lake Ontario, having majored in television and radio. Although he was told he had "the perfect face for radio," Roker got a job at the local CBS affiliate in Syracuse as a weekend weatherman. He then moved to Washington, D.C., and independent station WTTG. Next came a five-year weather stint for the NBC affiliate in Cleveland, followed by a move to Manhattan and WNBC and the on-air forecasts for *Weekend Today.*

By the time Roker relieved Willard Scott of some of his *Today* show duties, the brouhaha over Bryant Gumbel's memo had died down. Scott's wound, however, had not healed. "The odd thing is they're much alike," Roker confided to James Brady in *Parade* magazine. "Both are perfectionists."

Today's executive producer, Jeff Zucker, could have easily worn that label as well. The task of putting the series back on top of the Nielsen pack was not an easy one, despite the way it might have looked on-air. Responsible for literally thousands of details, Zucker was unstoppable. The long hours and stress seemed to wash off his shoulders, as week after week he fed on the show's success. In October 1996, however, Zucker learned he was not as invincible as he thought. At the age of 31, he was diagnosed with colon cancer.

The news stunned the show's stars and staff. With their leader wounded and possibly dying, the team united as never before, redoubling its efforts to continue the momentum Zucker had brought to the show. Hit particularly hard by the news, Katie Couric picked up the mantle of Zucker's personal health. Channeling her resources, she located the top colon cancer specialist in New York and insisted Zucker utilize him as his primary physician. She walked him through the horrors of surgery and subsequent chemotherapy and rejoiced with him when his doctors reported that they had succeeded in removing all traces of malignancy. Word of Zucker's condition was kept out of the press and by December, he was back at grappling speed, just in time to give Bryant Gumbel his exit cue.

The seemingly unflappable Gumbel was finally realizing that his days on the program where he had spent the past fifteen years were fast drawing to a close. Now eager to respond to what he perceived as the media's malicious criticisms, Gumbel appeared as a special guest on Oprah Winfrey's syndicated talk show on December 2. Winfrey turned the program into a veritable "This Is Your Life, Bryant Gumbel." Katie Couric, Al Roker, and Matt Lauer showed up for the salute. Willard Scott did not.

There were clips of former altar boy Gumbel as he was greeted by the Pope, as well as his final interview with the dying Arthur Ashe. Gumbel commented on the fact that during the interview he had failed to address the issue that his old friend Ashe was dying of AIDS. "I wrestled with it and was satisfied I wasn't derelict in my duty," Gumbel told Winfrey. "This was not a case of national security."

When Winfrey touched on his controversial 1989 memo, Gumbel retained his sense of propriety and lack of guilt. "In retrospect, the only thing I regret is a poor choice of words. [The memo] was to respond to a producer's request."

On being labeled "arrogant," Gumbel tapped a familiar litany: "I think some of it is color-related. In today's society an African-American man who exhibits a degree of confidence is viewed as arrogant."

And on his aborted O. J. Simpson interview: "It wasn't that I wanted it so badly. What I was offended about was that I could interview people associated with the trial [but then couldn't interview Simpson]. I was not going to promote an interview on that day with a big smile."

Two weeks before Gumbel's departure, NBC News named news

anchor Matt Lauer as cohost of *Today*. NBC News chief Andrew Lack had offered Couric the title of solo anchor, which she turned down, preferring to share the anchor duties with Lauer. Both hosts enjoyed many of the same personality traits—they were attractive, intelligent, and quick to laugh. They also shared a certain down-to-earth quality, a characteristic previously in short supply during the Gumbel-run administration.

For Gumbel, the always impeccable, always technically precise anchor, it was time to use up some leftover vacation days with a trip to Bali, where he hoped to find a vision of the future. None, however, would be forthcoming. On January 3, 1997, with more than three thousand *Today* shows packed away in his photographic memory, Gumbel admitted that it was, as he often said on the program, "time to move on."

THE FUTURE

*N*ew York City, January 3, 1997: Bryant Gumbel was uncomfortable. The man who had spent one-third of his life as host of NBC's top-rated early morning talk/news show was about to anchor his final two-hour broadcast. And he was clearly anxious—not so much because he was leaving the show, but rather because he didn't know what executive producer Jeff Zucker had planned for his last program.

"I'm okay," he said, attempting to camouflage his anxiety by taking a quick sip from a china mug. "A bit apprehensive. This is the first time I spent the night before broadcast with nothing to do."

In reality, he had much to occupy his mind. Bryant Gumbel *always* had much on his mind. Despite his repeated claims that he "had the best job in the world," it was still simple for him to find fault around him. Criticism came easily, and this day was no exception.

"I'm a bit of a control freak," he admitted on that last show.

"Oh, really," cohost Katie Couric laughed. "This just in." The sound of laughter around the studio echoed in bittersweet reinforcement of the truth of the statement.

Ironically, of course, the person Gumbel controlled the most was himself. Never wanting to be caught unprepared, over the past decade and a half he had worked harder and longer than anyone on the program. He had researched, read, studied, and made lists. Lots of lists. Legal pads of lists, written in different colored inks that corresponded to different guests.

The pads were lined up neatly before each show. The pens were arranged just so, next to them. His suit, tie, shirt, socks, cufflinks, and underwear were color-coordinated in an effort to conform to a rigid set of self-imposed standards. A man whose talent was as large as his ego, he was often misunderstood in his quest for perfection, even up until his final broadcast.

Those who dared to get close to the exacting keeper of regimens were likely to be rebuffed in any serious attempt at friendship. It was not so much that Gumbel disliked people. It was more that he didn't care to make time to tolerate their inadequacies. Those friends that he did manage to cultivate were more likely to be found on the golf course than in a television studio—golf being his sport of choice. All of which meant that NBC was left to throw a goodbye party for a man who instinctively disliked parties, surrounded by people who were there by mere accident of time, place, and NBC's hiring practices.

The finale was one day short of Gumbel's fifteenth anniversary in the anchor chair. He had begun his reign with an Afro and attitude, and was ending it in tears and with emotion during a salute that included taped tributes from Hillary Rodham Clinton, former President George Bush, John Travolta, Tom Cruise, Jeff Daniels, and Sandra Bullock.

The artist formerly known as Prince dropped by, costumed in copycat Gumbel attire of perfectly coordinated suit and silk tie, impeccably ironed pocket square, and slicked hair. The effect was more pimp than fashion plate, but nobody seemed to mind. Muhammad Ali and wife Bonnie gave Gumbel a scrapbook of photos with the champ; comedian Tracey Ullman brought Bryant a golf bag complete with liquor flask; artist Leroy Neiman painted the cohost a portrait that made him look younger and thinner; and Katie Couric wrote him a poem in which she described him "perspicacious, pugnacious, persistent, and proud." She could have added panoptic, Pantagruelian, paronomastic, patriarchal, and philopolemic—but she didn't.

Willard Scott kissed Gumbel, twice—"the European way"—and said that among the staff and crew, "everybody loved Bryant Gumbel." He seemed to mean it. Joe Garagiola and Gene Shalit joined the family in time for a champagne toast, and offered kind words of reflection that they also fashioned sincerely. Jane Pauley called Gumbel the yin to her yang, or vice versa, remembering their travels around the globe.

Then it was Gumbel's turn. With only moments left to the end of his final *Today* show, Gumbel pulled on his left ear, stroked his chin, and filled with tears as he remarked that he was "humbled," "grateful," and "proud" to have such friends and colleagues. "I don't want to make more of this than it is . . . ah . . . Television is not medical research," he reminded us all. And then he proceeded to hyperventilate.

"Fifteen years is not a lifetime. Fifteen years has been about a third of my life," he added, blowing nervously into his cheeks. "It's been . . . ahh . . . It has been . . . ahh . . . ahh . . . It's been a real pleasure and a genuine privilege to represent this program and the wonderful, wonderful people who put it on.

"I've had a great time. I really have. I've had a great time," Gumbel added, as if anyone needed convincing. "I hope that you've enjoyed it nearly as much—even a fraction as much as I have," he concluded, attempting to keep his composure. "And thank you all very much. I mean that."

As Al Roker led a standing ovation, and all hoisted champagne glasses, Gumbel's run on *Today* faded into the history books. Matt Lauer, standing on Gumbel's left, was poised to take the throne. Yet, at the moment, he was left to be content with the future, for Gumbel nearly failed to acknowledge his successor at all. At the end of one segment midway through the program, Gumbel threw an aside to Lauer: "You're gonna do terrific." There would be no passing of alarm clock; no handshake of reassurance.

The air on *Today* hung thick with the heady tribute, buoyed by Gumbel's own acknowledgment of his success and talent. Though few could equal Gumbel's own opinion of himself, several tried, including Betty Winston Baye. Writing for the Gannett News Service in the *Louisville Courier-Journal*, a paper once edited by former NBC News president Michael Gartner, Baye said that "Bryant Gumbel's work ethic, his competence, his positive self-awareness, his unwillingness to take less than he deserved, and his courage in daring to be his own man at all times are characteristics, not just to be admired, but to be duplicated."

Sometime Gumbel critic Marvin Kitman of *Newsday* joined

those who rushed to exalt the departing cohost. The columnist who had once labeled Bryant Gumbel "Bryant Gumball" and "Bryant Fumble" recanted, "Above all he is very smart. That was part of his problem. He was never able to disguise the fact too well, no matter how hard the make-over people at NBC worked on him."

That Gumbel was intelligent was never a question. Nor was his ability to conduct an interview and time it perfectly to the second. Yet, feelings of warmth and compassion—even after a decade and a half on the show—were missing from both the man and those who had come to honor him that day. They said he was loved, but everyone kept his or her distance. They said he would be missed, yet the following week, with Lauer in place, the show not only kept pace, but actually increased its ratings.

The on-air joviality between Lauer and Couric was a marked departure from the starched rapport shared between Couric and Gumbel. There was no straining to meld sweet and sour. The recipe turned into a meringue of froth and fun, tempered by the serious foundation delivered by NBC News. There was no talk of Gumbel after his exit. At least not at first.

Gumbel occupied his time playing golf and eating . . . both to excess. In the first month following his *Today* finale, he packed on fifteen pounds and grew a full beard. By the time he joined Clint Eastwood, Kevin Costner, and Bill Murray for the Pebble Beach National Pro-Am Golf Tournament in Carmel, California, in February, he looked less like a television star than a retiree. Only days later, he would astound NBC and most others with the announcement that he had signed a contract with CBS News that guaranteed him $7 million a year (more than double his NBC salary) to do a primetime newsmagazine series.

In fact, Gumbel had been participating in serious talks with all three networks. He had been flown by the General Electric corporate jet to Seattle to meet with Microsoft chief Bill Gates to discuss opportunities with the NBC/Microsoft joint venture, MSNBC cable network.

NBC had also offered Gumbel the opportunity to host its *National Geographic* series five times a year, a spot as a once-a-week anchor on *Dateline,* and a syndicated series for local NBC stations.

In the end, however, it was CBS's offer to joint venture a syndicated series through its Eyemark Entertainment division that attracted Gumbel. "I was impressed with the executives at CBS, and I'm excited about the chance to create a newsmagazine from scratch and to be a partner in a syndication company where I can come up with ideas for programming," Gumbel said. The fact that he would *own* a percentage of the programs wasn't mentioned, but, according to insiders, it played a major role in his decision.

In the meantime, *Today* without Bryant Gumbel was loosening its necktie and becoming nearly giddy with its own success. While the show began to inch even further ahead in the ratings, and the time was ripe for celebration, the pall of tragedy hit the series once more—this time aimed at its newest family member.

Less than a month after Matt Lauer climbed into the chair that Gumbel built, he received word that his father was dying of lung cancer. At 74, Ralph Lauer lived in retirement in Palm Beach Gardens, Florida, and had successfully kept the extent of his illness from his son. Finally, however, in February, when it became apparent that his cancer had spread, the elder Lauer confided that his illness was terminal. With little time to enjoy the excitement of his *Today* show triumph, Lauer began a secret weekly commute, leaving New York at the close of the show on Friday morning at 9:00 and returning to Manhattan in time for his 5:30 A.M. call on Monday.

According to Lauer's sister, April Stone, their father continued to watch the *Today* show every morning until he lapsed into a coma and died in the spring. "I can't tell you how important that was to me," Lauer later said with a mixture of sadness and pride.

Ralph Lauer had lived long enough to see his son succeed in a way that several years earlier would have seemed all but impossible. In 1992, Lauer was living with Walden, his golden retriever, in a small cottage in North Salem, New York. He had been out of work for a year and a half and was in so much debt that he had answered an ad for a job with a tree-trimming company in Greenwich, Connecticut, where his mother lived.

His résumé was a checkerboard of TV magazine shows that had been canceled or from which he was fired, the last of which, from 1989 to 1991, was a low-budget, three-hour, live interview show called 9 Broadcast Plaza. Although the program made little impression on most viewers, it nevertheless stuck in the mind of Bill Bolster, the general manager of WNBC-TV, who offered Lauer the anchor position on Today in New York, one of the station's news broadcasts. Bolster's call to Lauer beat the tree-trimming service by some four hours.

It was Steve Friedman who discovered Lauer on the local station and moved him into the national spotlight as Today's news reader. On those occasions when Lauer substituted for Bryant Gumbel, his unintimidating charm stood as welcome relief to Gumbel's often-terse interview style. Whereas Gumbel needed to show his intelligence and preparation, Lauer allowed the subject's story to unfold in its own fashion.

Lauer's success as Gumbel's replacement did more than impress the producers of Today and the executives at NBC News; it also attracted the attention of ABC executives, who began to work quietly in the background, in the hopes of recruiting Lauer to join Good Morning America. Despite offers of an increased salary and stock options, Lauer rebuffed the network, content to wait for his moment in the spotlight at NBC.

When he moved into the anchor seat permanently, Lauer's coupling with Couric brought a comfort to the Today show that lit up the switchboard, the fan mail, and the ratings. With Al Roker taking on most of the weather assignments, and Ann Curry moving over from NBC News at Sunrise and MSNBC to replace Lauer at the news desk, the Today show suddenly seemed fun once more, and viewers took notice.

Out from under Gumbel's overbearing glare, Katie Couric blossomed. She was always feisty and quick to show no fear before Gumbel, but with Lauer as her cohost she dropped the armor of self-protection she had worn around his predecessor and replaced it with an authentic curiosity that worked well in everything from political interviews to cooking demonstrations.

By May 1997, Couric was hiding her own personal tragedy. In an ironic twist of fate, her husband, Jay Monahan, had himself been diagnosed with colon cancer. Pulling out the information she had assembled for Jeff Zucker the previous year, Couric threw herself into his treatment as well. On June 6, Monahan was operated on. The prognosis seemed excellent for a complete recovery.

At this point, both *Today* show hosts could have taken a page from Joan Lunden's new book that was published that spring. Titled *Joan Lunden's Healthy Living: A Practical, Inspirational Guide to Creating Balance in Your Life,* her message suggested a new maturity and serenity to go along with her snazzy new look. The woman who had in the past doubted her talent and questioned her mind was now informing others that "we are all in charge of our own happiness." It was as simple as it was comprehensive, a lament that Lunden would soon be called upon to apply to herself, when she was advised that she was being replaced on *Good Morning America* after seventeen years on the show. Despite the fact that she was doing her job as well as ever, viewership on the series was continuing to fall. Lunden became ABC's scapegoat of the moment, and the network did little to camouflage the fact. ABC did allow her to make the official announcement, which said, in part, that she was "moving on to primetime in September." Given the fact that Lunden had no specific deal for a newsmagazine or specials other than four *Behind Closed Doors* hours in the next year and a half, the announcement posed more questions than it answered.

Unofficially, ABC wanted Lunden off *Good Morning America* to allow the network to revitalize the show with new talent. A fresh face was the network's answer to its hemorrhaging ratings. Lunden, it was believed, had lost touch with her audience. Her new image was more playgirl than mother, more guru than friend, and did little to endear her to ABC News president Roone Arledge, who never had been a fan of Lunden's and thought of her more as an entertainment talent than a news journalist.

Lunden placed a positive spin on her termination by suggesting that it was a creative challenge for her to develop projects that would showcase her abilities. Fortuitously for her bank account, she had nearly two years remaining on her ABC contract and the network was obligated to pay her regardless of on-air performance.

Elizabeth Vargas's name was immediately tossed into play as a candidate for Lunden's replacement by those who were operating from an old score card. *TV Guide* had recently run an unflattering item about Vargas, suggesting that her ego had gotten too large for her talent on a recent location shoot during which she had demanded, and received, star treatment. The *TV Guide* article leaked portions of a putative internal ABC memo, which claimed that Vargas demanded such treatment as "two-camera shoots whenever it involves her interviewing somebody," "hair and makeup at location," "she doesn't want to be there if you're shooting B-roll" (background shots), and "always assume that she will be running a bit late (15–30 minutes)."

Despite Vargas's flat denial that she demanded special treatment, her future on *Good Morning America* was over. Wanting to avoid another Deborah Norville debacle, ABC moved quickly, following up the announcement of Lunden's departure with one about Elizabeth Vargas. Vargas, too, would be leaving *GMA*, ABC said, to become a special correspondent on *20/20* and *Prime Time Live*. At least on the surface, Vargas received the better deal with a guaranteed position within ABC News. Columnist Liz Smith characterized the switch as "another good example of a controversial TV personality failing upwards."

ABC News wasted little time in replacing Vargas in the news reader chair with Kevin Newman, onetime co-anchor of *Good Morning America/Sunday*. Newman, like ABC's Peter Jennings, had honed his skills with the Canadian Broadcasting Corporation.

Vargas was stunned by the move, having bought wholesale into her own publicity and fully expecting to find herself sitting in the cohost position on *GMA*. That honor, however, was awarded to Lisa McRee, the 35-year-old news anchor from ABC's Los Angeles affiliate, KABC. In selecting McRee, ABC gave the nod to a news journalist with poise and refinement, as well as statuesque legs and a face that apparently had been restructured by plastic surgery to broadcast perfection.

The network did not make any attempt to duplicate the whole-some charm of Katie Couric. ABC News president Roone Arledge labeled McRee a "tremendous talent" and said that she combines the "skills of a serious journalist with an unmistakable warmth and sense of humor," but he could also see a side of her that had yet to reveal itself to viewers.

McRee had graduated from the University of California at San Diego majoring in communications and went to work at the local NBC affiliate soon after. Jobs in Bakersfield, California, and Dallas, Texas, fol-lowed before ABC plucked her in 1992 to anchor its *World News Now* program. Later, McRee also did spots for the former ABC News maga-zine *Day One* before heading to Los Angeles to anchor the evening news telecasts there.

If anything, the announcement of Lunden's replacement, made months in advance of her September departure, suggested that TV's hard-headed executives had learned a lesson about viewers' loyalties and early morning habits. "We stayed too long with a lot of things we should have been changing over time," Alan Wurtzel, ABC's senior vice president of newsmagazines, said. "Everything in this program is under review . . . everything."

Unfortunately for ABC, the man who most clearly picked up on that message was Charles Gibson. The last of the Old Guard, Gibson began to make noises that he, too, wanted out of the program. Sud-denly, *Good Morning America* seemed more like a house under renova-tion than the familiar shoe that audiences had grown to love and wear, albeit in shrinking popularity.

The mood greeting Lunden's departure was considerably dif-ferent from that at Bryant Gumbel's final program some nine months before. Just days earlier, Princess Diana had been killed in a tragic car crash that had sent the early morning shows sprinting for coverage. In ABC's case, newcomer Lisa McRee was launched on her *GMA* career by being pressed into action and flown to London. On Friday, September 4, 1997, while the competition was concentrating on the princess's funeral preparations, McRee flew back to New York and joined the outgoing Lunden in the studio for the formal transfer of power.

It was a day that Joan Lunden had secretly dreaded. Despite her public pronouncements that she was looking forward to the creative challenges that lay ahead, the fear of her unknown future hung heavily on her. Yet, by the time the fateful day finally arrived, the woman who had anchored daytime television longer than any other was amazingly calm—or at least she was until she discovered that ABC had failed to dispatch her usual limousine, or *any* car and driver for that matter, to transport her from her home in Greenwich, Connecticut, to the station. Apparently, an overeager transportation dispatcher had actually canceled her limo pickup one day too soon. Long past being frantic at this point, Lunden managed to find the irony in her situation and ended up driving herself into Manhattan, where she was greeted by a standing ovation for what had been nicknamed "Lunden's Last One" by the staff.

In a clip montage of her seventeen years on the program, she was shown bungee jumping off a bridge above a New Jersey river, riding horseback on a narrow trail along deep gorges in Montana, rappeling down Mendenhall Glacier in Alaska, and traveling through some of the most beautiful country in the world—the Grand Canyon, an Australian sheep ranch, a vineyard in Aix-en-Provence, France.

John Travolta offered his taped goodbye, calling her "darling"; his wife, Kelly Preston, lamented how amazing Lunden had been for the past seventeen years; Michael Douglas suggested that he would miss seeing her in Santa Barbara, as if she would no longer be invited; Michael Bolton couldn't say goodbye because he saw her often; and Vice President Al Gore congratulated her on moving to "better hours and bigger projects," although none was booked at the time.

Spencer Christian, who was assigned the street detail, met "people gathered here from all over the country who want to say goodbye to Joan." There was Christian and Mickey from West Palm Beach, Florida; Crystal from Washington state; Connie from Salem, Oregon; and Rita and Chuck from Toledo, Ohio. Amazingly, despite their geographic distances, each had made up a matching placard eulogizing Lunden, written in a similar style of handwriting, and had brought it to the same corner an entire city block from the studio.

The ladies of news—Diane Sawyer, Paula Zahn, and Barbara Walters—all saluted Joan as the on-air trailblazer she was, with Walters assuring her that there was, indeed, "life after breakfast." Lunden's smile suggested that she wasn't totally convinced as she handed off her alarm clock to Lisa McRee.

President Clinton thanked Joan for "always presenting news in a positive light," whatever that meant. He was not the only one to pay taped respects. George Bush said his goodbyes along with wife Barbara; so, too, did Gerald and Betty Ford. Actors Candice Bergen and Billy Crystal did as well, while Tom Selleck, known for his long legs, revealed that his knees had rubbed Lunden's during their interviews and that he had been "thrilled." David Letterman offered a Top 10 list of Lunden's future plans, including "split a case of Old Milwaukee with Hugh Downs," and Celine Dion made a personal appearance to sing "Because You Loved Me" while holding Lunden's hand. One who was noticeably absent from the tribute was *Good Morning America*'s original host, David Hartman, with whom Lunden had worked for seven years. He was mentioned only briefly in passing, during Lunden's long list of closing thank-yous that ended with, "And, of course, David Hartman, who showed me the ropes here."

Finally, with the clock ticking down to the last seconds of the longest reign in the annals of early morning television, Lunden's eyes filled with tears. Surrounded by her real family and her television family, who seemed equally as touched by the moment, Lunden said goodbye: "This has been a very rare and privileged seat from which to view this world and be where history is being made. And it's more than anyone could ever hope for in a lifetime."

As Lunden moved to take her place in television history, Charles Gibson welcomed his new cohost just as he, himself, had been welcomed a decade earlier. Any question in his mind that the network was serious about replacing him as well disappeared with the arrival of Fox TV's *After Breakfast* host Tom Bergeron,* who was given multiple on-air tryouts during Gibson's vacation later that year.

To Bergeron's disappointment, none of his test runs particularly impressed ABC or improved the show's ratings, perhaps because his coupling with Lisa McRee was awkward at best. "Their chemistry couldn't fill a test tube," one producer observed. Ironically, while the Bergeron-McRee mix fell flat, the Gibson-McRee repartee flowed easy and fresh, allowing the veteran host to jockey for position within ABC News.

As 1998 began, all of Washington and much of the rest of the country became transfixed by the news that Linda Tripp, a chain-smoking single mother and employee at the Pentagon, had recorded a conversation with her best friend, Monica Lewinsky, at the deserted bar of the Arlington, Virginia, Ritz-Carlton Hotel. Lewinsky claimed to have had a sexual relationship with President Bill Clinton in the Oval Office and for the past several months had been revealing intimate details of their love trysts to Tripp over the phone. Tripp took her news to Independent Counsel Kenneth Starr, who already had the president under a microscope for his involvement in the shady land deal known as Whitewater.

It was the type of scandal that had the three early morning network shows reaching for any angle that would shed even the tiniest shred of new controversy on the emerging story. Since Monica Lewinsky and Linda Tripp weren't personally available, their lawyers and spokespersons made appearances on all three programs, attempting to keep the direct glare of the spotlight off of their clients and on the White House. For his part, President Clinton denied having had an

*His former cohost on *After Breakfast,* Laurie Hibberd, had been hired for occasional "Morning Buzz" gossip segments on *Good Morning America.*

affair with Lewinsky. Although Clinton wasn't making any early morning talk show appearances either, the First Lady was.

Weeks before Lewinsky's allegations wafted through the White House like nerve gas, Hillary Clinton had been scheduled to speak on both *Today* and *Good Morning America*—first with Katie Couric on January 27 (the subject was to be child care) and the next day with Lisa McRee (about the previous evening's State of the Union message delivered by the president). But the Lewinsky scandal prompted the First Lady to give her first public response to the allegations on national TV.

Katie Couric had been preparing for the interview during the week prior to the telecast, reviewing with Jeff Zucker the tone that the interview would take as well as specific questions to ask concerning the suggestion of infidelity in the Oval Office. No one shared her excitement at the opportunity more than Couric's husband, Jay Monahan. He also knew what the world did not—that they were sharing their own private drama. Jay Monahan's cancer had returned and he was fighting the increasing agony of his disease.

After the Friday, January 23 *Today* show, Couric went to Monahan's bedside at Manhattan's Lenox Hill Hospital, near the apartment they shared with their daughters, Elinor, 6, and Caroline, 2. Jay Monahan died the following day.

Matt Lauer, barely warmed to the co-anchor seat, was still in a state of shock as he explained Couric's absence from the set to viewers on Monday, January 26. The following day he was called in to interview the First Lady and attempted to strike a position that was "dignified and compassionate," according to Zucker. He apparently achieved this goal, for after the broadcast, Mrs. Clinton thanked Lauer for his "treatment of the subject."

Dressed in a brown suit, accented by a gold necklace and eagle pin, the First Lady credited a "right-wing conspiracy" for the intense probe into her husband's sex life, adding, "a lot of this is deliberately designed to sensationalize charges . . . because everything else they've tried has failed." As she alternated between hushed confidentiality, philosophical tolerance, and stern rebuke, Mrs. Clinton laid the blame for the scandal at the feet of Ken Starr and a cabal of others. "The best thing to do in these cases," she suggested, "is just to be patient, take a deep breath, and the truth will come out."

The following day on *GMA*, the First Lady was still unapologetic and equally emphatic. "I have talked to my husband about everything," she said. "I can state unequivocally that, as my husband has said, these are false allegations." Asked if she thought that the president had told her the whole story, she answered firmly, "I know he has."

When Couric returned to *Today* four weeks later, she tugged at Lauer's hand as she thanked him and said, "It's great to be back." The signature grin that had often widened in laughter across the screen made an attempted appearance, but failed to convince. This was Katie Couric, widow, now. "Words, of course, will never describe how devastating this loss has been for me and my daughters and all of Jay's family as well. But the heartfelt and compassionate letters and cards that so many of you have sent to me were enormously comforting, and I'm so grateful," she managed. She then launched into the program, in which she interviewed former Secretary of State James Baker regarding the Iraqi showdown over United Nations inspections. On a chain around her neck: her husband's wedding band.

During the weeks ahead, Couric and Lauer continued to strike that special balance between familiarity and respect, with viewers responding in ever increasing numbers. *Today's* audience peaked at 7.2 million people, the most viewers at any time in the show's history, and more than *Good Morning America's* and *This Morning's* combined.

For all her attempts to appear as if she were moving on with her life, Couric instinctively shared the sadness in her heart through eyes that sparkled less, yet said more, reflecting a new maturity and inner strength that only the survival of a tragedy can bring. Her grace and resolve inspired with a quiet dignity; her smile edged with memory.

Realizing that *Good Morning America* was falling deeper in a black hole with no escape route in sight, ABC announced in March that effective May 4, news reader Kevin Newman would replace Charles Gibson in the co-anchor chair next to Lisa McRee. Shelley Lewis was

246 / MADNESS IN THE MORNING

named as the show's new executive producer, replacing Mark Lukasiewicz, who himself had been in the job only less than a year.

One of Lewis's first challenges was orchestrating *Good Morning America*'s coverage of the opening of Disney's Animal Kingdom in Orlando, Florida. Since Walt Disney Studios was the parent company of ABC, Lewis had hoped to extract an exclusive behind-the-scenes tour of the property. As it turned out, however, each of the morning talk shows was invited to cover the grand opening.

For its part, *GMA* sent Lisa McRee to handle the assignment. Stationed in the African Village in front of the Tree of Life, McRee held forth from the centerpiece of the newest Disney theme park, informing viewers that there were 1,200 animals living at the park, representing 400 species, "er, 200 species," she quickly corrected.

McRee cornered Disney chairman Michael Eisner, but not before *Today*'s Katie Couric had had her way with him. Pointing to the fact that a pair of nearly extinct cranes had been run over accidentally and killed, Couric asked, "What can you say to animal activists?"

"I do have the bad news to tell that all of the animals here will die at some point," Eisner drolly countered.

By the time Eisner made it to the Tree of Life, he was eager for a friendly smile. He found it in McRee, who gushed with enthusiasm, using words like "amazing" and "fabulous" before adding, "I hate to do a shameless plug." She then proceeded to do an amazing and fabulous one by suggesting that not since the Book of Genesis had such creative juices flowed. She even cooed up to Eisner and asked, "Shall I call you my liege?" From his pursed lips, the answer apparently was no.

This Morning had the sense to keep Jane Robelot in her anchor seat back in her air-conditioned studio in Manhattan. On the scene, Mark McEwen and Jose Diaz-Balart sweated in the humidity and spouted enthusiasms through perspiring lips.

But it was to fall to Lisa McRee to really make the morning complete by stating, "If they could only figure out how to make hair spray to keep your hair up in the Florida humidity, these Disney people would be geniuses"—clearly not her finest moment, though Charles Gibson never gave a hint of distress back at home base in New York.

For Gibson, the clock was ticking, and nothing—especially not a

Disney theme park—was spoiling his ride into the sunset. On the day before Gibson was to retire from *Good Morning America,* an ad in *USA Today* read: "He's a journalist who opened our eyes to the world every morning. Thank you, Charlie." Across the bottom of the page it added, "Thanks for bringing such wit, charm, and above all, intelligence to our mornings. From all of us at ABC and from all of America . . . sleep late, Charlie, you deserve it."

Gibson had made it through eleven years on the program, the same tenure as David Hartman. Without pointing fingers, he said of the show's declining ratings, "I think we made some decisions a couple of years ago, where the audience lost its assurance of exactly what the show is all about. We were doing too much experimenting." He might have been referring to the show's movement from ABC's Entertainment Division into the News Division. More likely, he was placing the blame on the Disney ownership.

Of his favorite shows, Gibson pointed to two special weeks—one broadcast from Saudi Arabia in 1990 during the Thanksgiving holiday, when U.S. soldiers were preparing to launch the Gulf War; the other after the bombing of the Federal Building in Oklahoma City in 1995, when he broadcast live from the roof of an abandoned bookstore and saw "the best side of humanity in response to the worst."

As the studio was being torn apart for still another new set, *Good Morning America* broadcast its goodbye party to Charles Gibson from the Tavern on the Green restaurant adjacent to Central Park. It was a celebration that brought out all the series's regulars, present and past, this time including David Hartman. Joan Lunden was back, as was medical editor Dr. Tim Johnson, science editor Dr. Michael Guillen, legal editor Professor Arthur Miller, entertainment correspondent Chantal Westerman, medical correspondent Dr. Nancy Snyderman, and special correspondents Bill Ritter and Steve Fox.

President Clinton dropped in via tape to say that "Hillary and I are sad to see you go." From Gibson's favorite baseball team, Baltimore Orioles superstar Cal Ripken Jr. retired the number oo, giving it to the outgoing host. And Barbara Walters stopped by to welcome Gibson to ABC News, where he was headed to join her on the restructured ABC News nighttime magazine shows.

Ted Koppel could not help but razz Gibson about the upcoming move in his taped tribute: "I read somewhere the other day, Charlie, that you were a little worried about tearing up on your last show. Well, let's take inventory. You don't have to go to bed at seven anymore. You don't have to get up at three. And as I understand it, they are going to pay you a fortune for working one day a week. I can see why you are choked up about that. . . . Newman's the guy who ought to be crying."

Kevin Newman wasn't crying that day. In fact, he accepted with anticipation and pride an eleven-year blank journal as a gift from Gibson. There were tears, however, from Gibson's longtime assistant, Grace Wong, who was saluted by her boss for selfless devotion. Gibson's recognition of Wong and all the other behind-the-scenes staffers who put on his 2,640 shows was typical of Gibson's style—honest, humble, and very, very thankful. He had "so many memories, such wonderful times, and [it was] such a privilege to have been part of this broadcast."

Gibson saved his last thoughts for his audience, however, expressing "sincere gratitude. You have always shown us such kindness. Television is a crazy business and it sometimes catches us by surprise . . . that we have millions of friends that we don't know."

The following week, as the ratings sweeps began, *Good Morning America* unveiled its new set—larger and more expansive than ever— just when *Today* was becoming more intimate. In the hope of keeping any loose viewers from tuning in to its competition, the *Today* show sent Matt Lauer out on the road to five different countries, turning the trip into the contest "Where in the World Is Matt Lauer?" The contest awarded the first ten viewers who guessed the answer over the Internet Matt Lauer T-shirts "valued at less than $20.00." According to the rules, "Taxes, if any, are the responsibility of the winners."

While Americans were busy guessing where Lauer was traveling, they missed an even bigger secret: the identity of his traveling companion. Lauer was accompanied on this trip by his girlfriend, Dutch model Annette Roque, whose professional name, Jade, alluded to her Indonesian heritage. Roque had been placed on the *Today* payroll under "Makeup." Over a romantic dinner in Venice, Lauer asked Roque to be his wife and slipped a diamond engagement ring on her finger.

At the same time, Kevin Newman had a secret all his own. While vacationing in Venice, Italy, prior to taking over *GMA,* and eating with his wife at Harry's Bar, Newman overheard two *Today* show producers laying out the various stops along Lauer's entire trip. Upon learning of Newman's silence, *Today* executive producer Jeff Zucker suggested it showed a lot of class.

Katie Couric's class was also evident the following month, when she signed a new contract to remain at *Today* for four more years. When asked how much NBC had raised her salary, Couric responded that her mother told her never to talk about money. Particularly not when you have more than enough. Couric's new salary rose to $7 million a year, while Lauer earned just over $1 million.

Bryant Gumbel was said to be unimpressed when he learned of Couric's salary increase. But then, Gumbel was busy licking his wounds from the cancellation of his *Public Eye* series from CBS. A casualty of low ratings, CBS had pulled the show from the air in February to keep the network's Nielsen numbers from being hurt by the newsmagazine. Further embarrassing the onetime *Today* host was the fact that his former series had only increased in viewership since the day he vacated the anchor seat.

At the time, CBS had more problems than Gumbel's series. Its own *This Morning* was showing no signs of picking up any viewers who had tuned out of *Good Morning America,* sending CBS executives into the dance known as "The Ritual," in which the network took another serious look at its morning show format to identify the changes that would breathe life into the corpse.

Barely breathing itself, *Good Morning America* tried reverting once more to a gossip format to energize its ratings, adding the queen of Manhattan table talk, Cindy Adams, to its roster of regulars. Newly appointed ABC News president David Westin continued to give Newman and McRee a vote of confidence, while calling "fixing *GMA*" his number-one priority.

One star who would not be on Westin's list for the future was weatherman Spencer Christian. Unable to get assurances of a long-term contract, the veteran regular of the series announced his intention to leave the program by January 1999 for a position in San Francisco at ABC-owned KGO-TV. With Christian's departure, the landscape of *GMA* would be populated totally by newcomers, a serious loss to a series that once labeled itself as "comfortable as an old shoe."

In July 1998, *Cosmopolitan* magazine published its "lust survey," which was topped by NBC's Matt Lauer, who received 44 percent of the vote. Lauer, anything but impressed by his sex-symbol status, had previously described himself to *People* magazine as a guy who "had a large nose and an overbite, whose hair in the back is disappearing, and who's losing his butt." Others on *Cosmo*'s lust list included Peter Jennings (scoring 13 percent of the vote), Tom Brokaw (9 percent), Bryant Gumbel (8 percent), and Dan Rather (6 percent). Kevin Newman didn't make the cut.

Neither, of course, did Charles Gibson, who by this point had settled into ABC News and was redeeming himself on his new national canvas with spectacular results. In August, Gibson temporarily replaced Peter Jennings in the anchor chair on *ABC World News Tonight* and not only proved his ability as a newsman, but actually won his final week in the ratings race against *NBC Nightly News* and *The CBS Evening News*.

Back in the upper echelon of ABC News, while Gibson was being elevated to Jennings's primary substitute, talks were being held with Connie Chung and her agents about taking on a permanent anchor position on *Good Morning America*. Having already had her taste of the dawn patrol, Chung turned down the offer, as did ABC news reporter Meredith Vieira.

As David Westin was becoming increasingly frustrated by the lack of positive movement on *Good Morning America*, he was facing a network impatient for results. Patricia Fili-Krushel, head of ABC's Daytime Division, had been promoted to the presidency of ABC Television in July 1998; included among her responsibilities were all of ABC News and ABC Entertainment. If Westin could not correct *GMA*'s problems, he knew that Fili-Krushel would find someone within ABC Entertainment who would be willing to try.

While *Today*'s executives looked at the disintegration of their once-mighty competitor with little more than smug amusement, the producers of CBS's *This Morning* saw ABC's tumble as a chance to finally get out of the basement. In an effort to recharge their own morning program, CBS News executives called upon a familiar name as a consultant: onetime *Today* executive producer Steve Friedman, who was working as general manager of New York's WCBS-TV.

Friedman's idea for a new CBS morning show centered on an old name: Bryant Gumbel. Out of work but being paid $5 million a year, Gumbel had interested various CBS executives, including CBS Television president Leslie Moonves and CBS News chief Andrew Heyward. The biggest obstacle to getting Gumbel to return to the early morning grind, however, was Gumbel himself. Hardly a team player, Gumbel is an individualist who places his own priorities at the top of any list.

It would take more than sweet talk to convince Gumbel that stepping back into the dawn patrol was a positive move for his stalled career. Inside sources suggested that Gumbel wanted a guarantee of the profits from the program and editorial control over it—not unlike Dave Garroway's deal at NBC nearly fifty years earlier.

In an overall effort to improve its news presence, CBS made plans to construct a new studio complex on Fifth Avenue near Central Park. Artists' renderings of the projected complex showed a $30 million glass-and-steel showplace that would eventually house the news broadcasts for the network's local affiliate station and network series under the news banner.

Given the failing production that *Good Morning America* had become, critics were amazed that CBS hadn't moved quickly to take advantage of the competitive opportunity. Television critics began calling *Good Morning America* the Hindenburg of morning shows, pointing to the lack of chemistry between the struggling hosts. Lisa McRee and Kevin Newman shared little in common, either on or off the set. Part of the problem could be traced to Newman's Canadian background. "Lisa reached for her napkin; Kevin called his a *serviette*. It was a cultural thing," said a *GMA* researcher. During a summer in which most of America was caught up in the major-league race between Mark

McGwire and Sammy Sosa to break Roger Maris's sixty-one home-run record, Newman remained aloof to the excitement and made no effort to understand it. Uncomfortable on-air with McRee and off the air with his loss of privacy, he compensated by eating, packing on ten pounds of fat in three months.

As the ratings continued to inch down week after week, staff members began to search for back-up employment opportunities. By December, even Newman realized that a tough situation was about to become intolerable as the cast and crew rallied to bid bon voyage to weathercaster Spencer Christian. Charles Gibson's appearance on the program was a harbinger of things to come.

As Lisa McRee prepared to take a week's vacation, the lion's share of the show shifted to Newman, who demanded to speak with network executives, asking them pointedly about their intentions for the broadcast. What Newman needed to hear was unilateral support from a news division that had been vacillating for months. What he received instead was confirmation that David Westin and his news team were uncertain not only about the direction of the program, but also about Newman's own future on the broadcast.

Unable to accept the network's noncommitment, and ignorant of its plans to bring back Charles Gibson into the anchor seat along with the star power of Diane Sawyer, Newman requested his release from the broadcast. When he finally received official word of the network's decision, his reaction was one of relief coupled with disbelief. His sentiments were echoed by most at ABC and many critics across the country.

In making the official announcement, Westin conceded that ABC News, rather than individual anchors or producers, was to blame for the ratings demise of the series. "ABC News management tried to change the show without having a clear enough vision about where it should go," he said. He then confirmed that ABC News still had no solid long-range plan for the series. Even the Gibson-Sawyer assignments were labeled as "temporary." When Westin first asked Sawyer to join the dawn patrol, she was agreeable, if not eager. He stated, "She said, 'If you really need me to do this, if the News Division needs me to do it, I will do it,'" albeit on a short-term basis.

Lisa McRee never returned to her *GMA* anchor chair. Rather, she cleaned out her dressing room the day following the announcement, while Elizabeth Vargas filled in for her on-air. Kevin Newman exited earlier than expected as well, disappearing from sight during the second week of January. By the time Charles Gibson and Diane Sawyer were saying "Good morning, America" on their first broadcast together—January 18, 1999—Newman had driven his leased BMW z3 across the border to Canada for a visit with his mother and sister.

As expected, the Sawyer-Gibson anchor team appeared relaxed, confident, and personable on their first week of shows. Inspired largely by the curiosity of viewers piqued by the marketing campaign that preceded the broadcasts, the program's ratings moved up, attracting 4.3 million viewers (compared to *Today*'s 5.7 million). With newsman Antonio Mora added to the *GMA* family as the news anchor, and WABC weatherman Sam Champion handling the forecasts,* *Good Morning America* began to feel like a comfortable place to visit once more. The hosts sat in a comfortable living room decorated with antiques, its walls lined with well-worn books. Even the gas-burning fireplace, which had disappeared from the set during the Gibson-Lunden days, was back, center stage.

The mood in the executive meetings that followed those initial broadcasts was upbeat, if not cohesive. Westin wanted to return some of the folksy charm to the broadcast, while McGrady pushed for harder news to utilize Sawyer's strengths and contacts. Yet, still no decisive direction was determined. Perhaps, one executive suggested, they should just "wait and see."

"Do nothing?" came the response. And then the room fell silent.

---

*Tony Perkins, a weathercaster with WTTG-TV, Fox's Washington, D.C., affiliate, and cohost of *Fox Morning News*, took over as *GMA*'s permanent weatherman on March 8.

THE REALITY

On May 4, 1999, CBS made it official: Bryant Gumbel was returning to early morning television as the host of a totally restructured *This
Morning* program. At the network's press conference detailing its plans
to revitalize the early morning series, Gumbel tried to put a positive
spin on his career back-track. "I'm not necessarily sure I'd ever look at
hosting two hours of live television as a comedown," he said. "The
primetime venture didn't work out. It's not the end of my life." Apparently not.

The moment smacked of déjà vu, as Gumbel sat side-by-side with
Steve Friedman, his former executive producer at *Today*, whom CBS
was bringing aboard as senior executive producer of the new *This
Morning*. It seemed fitting that Friedman, who had guided *Today* back
to its ratings pinnacle from a new street-level studio in Rockefeller Center, was present as CBS News president Andrew Heyward officially gave
the green light to create a new window-fronted studio in the General
Motors building on Fifth Avenue. By the time Gumbel would take over
the revamped CBS entry on November 1, 1999, ABC's *Good Morning
America* would be in its own new ground-level studio in Times Square.
By setting up new studios overlooking prime Manhattan locations,
both networks have joined NBC in what appears to be a winning formula for attracting tourists and viewers alike. Yet CBS's effort to turn
This Morning into a new and improved version has been tried before
and no doubt will be attempted again, in the endless cycle of madness
in the morning.

Now, forty-five years after Dave Garroway first alerted viewers to a "revolution" in television, the networks are finally beginning to get the point. Mornings are a time of ritual, of familiar steps and welcome aromas. Sudden jolts and aggressive moves are irritations that serve to aggravate rather than improve.

"We want to catch these people in their underpants," Pat Weaver said in 1952. The networks have only now begun to realize that to be welcomed in that process requires sensitivity to viewers' early morning vulnerabilities. As network news loses viewers to cable TV and the Internet, early morning programming remains the sole area of growth. As such, it keeps the attention of those interested in delivering the news as well as those excited by increasing profitability. It also has been targeted by independent local stations, which can develop inexpensive, customized counterprogramming to steal individual viewers away from the networks.

"The key is to reinvent yourself before it's too late," *Today*'s Jeff Zucker maintains, now looking wiser than his years, the effects of a decade spent on the network fast track. Apparently that reinvention means dropping those who have stayed too long and become too familiar, those whose loyalty and talent are rewarded by being discarded like a sagging mattress.

Early morning television has become the habit of millions of viewers who find it the elixir for opening their eyes, literally and figuratively, to a world in which communication has become less a luxury than a necessity. It has turned into an industry that provides hundreds of millions of dollars in profits to networks that find such profits increasingly rare. Pat Weaver's original concept of an electronic newspaper has found its time, if not its way, and regardless of the individual personalties involved, is destined to remain a part of the small screen wake-up call to America.

> And we are going to bring you the great stories in the news just as often as we possibly can on this program—over your breakfast table, just as regularly as coffee is served.
>
> —Jack Lescoulie, 1952

SOURCE NOTES

The majority of this book was compiled from interviews with those who spent their lives rising before dawn to work behind the scenes in early morning television. The crews and staffs of *Today, A.M. America, Good Morning America, The CBS Morning News,* and *CBS This Morning* provided the backbone not only of this chronicle but also of the shows themselves. For that, they have my gratitude and admiration. Those who refused to be interviewed gained my respect as well, for in their effort to protect their privacy, they sought to protect the illusion of early morning television itself. In all cases, those who spoke off the record remain uncredited, but appreciated for their candor.

In addition, the following articles, books, and references were used to create a timeline of events that when linked one day to the next, formed the guideposts to the incredible legacy that early morning television has become. Articles appearing without bylines carry no author reference. Page numbers refer to East Coast late editions. Page numbers in other editions may differ. Sources of direct quotations are often not credited, for to do so would have become tedious within the structure of the work.

"ABC, CBS Hope to Gang Up on Sleeping *Today.*" *Television/Radio Age,* September 19, 1988, p. 20.

"ABC Morning Show Switches Departments." *New York Times,* April 6, 1995, sec. C, p. 24.

"ABC to Replace *A.M. America* with *Good Morning* Magazine." *New York Times,* October 15, 1975, p. 57.

ADALIAN, JOSEF. "A Primetime Return for Kathleen Sullivan." *Washington Times,* June 14, 1994, sec. C, p. 14.

———. "Channel Surfer." *Washington Times,* February 21, 1994, sec. C, p. 17.

ADAMS, VAL. "NBC-TV Is Off Air Two Hours in Dispute." *New York Times,* April 28, 1959, p. 37.

———. "From Night Owl to Rise-and-Shiner." *New York Times,* February 3, 1952, p. 37.

ADLER, JERRY, WITH SUE HUTCHISON. "A Case of Morning Sickness." *Newsweek,* March 13, 1989, p. 81.

ADLER, JERRY, WITH RENEE MICHAEL, MICHAEL REESE, AND NIKKI FINKE GREENBERG. "The Wheels of Fortune." *Newsweek,* November 4, 1983, p. 81.

ALLIS, TIM, WITH TOBY KAHN. "Rookie of the Year." *People,* August 17, 1992, p. 89.

ALTER, JONATHAN. "Behind the NBC News Blues." *Newsweek,* October 16, 1989, p. 88.

"A.M. America." Variety, January 15, 1975, p. 42.

AMORY, CLEVELAND. "Review: *Today." TV Guide,* September 28, 1974, p. 40.

——. "You Are Cordially Invited." *TV Guide,* March 31, 1962, p. 15.

——. "Review: *Good Morning, America." TV Guide,* January 17, 1976, p. 34.

ANDERSON, LORRIN. "Guilt and Gasoline." *National Review,* June 8, 1992, p. 35.

ANDERSON, SUSAN HELLER. "Chronicle." *New York Times,* February 21, 1990, sec. B, p. 4.

——. "Chronicle." *New York Times,* March 7, 1990, sec. B, p. 4.

——. "Chronicle." *New York Times,* August 21, 1990, sec. B, p. 6.

——. "Chronicle." *New York Times,* November 17, 1990, p. 48.

——. "Chronicle." *New York Times,* May 15, 1991, sec. B, p. 4.

ANDREWS, PETER. "With a Folksy Flavor . . ." *TV Guide,* February 26, 1977, p. 26.

APPLE, R. W. "The Clinton Budget: A Victory Most Precious." *New York Times,* May 28, 1993, p. 1.

"As NBC's Cross-Board 7 to 9 A.M. Today. " *Variety,* January 21, 1953, p. 15.

ASCHER-WALSH, REBECCA. "Taking It to the Streets." *Entertainment Weekly,* June 17, 1994, p. 7.

ASKIN, STEVE. "*Today* Beams Diverse Grandeur of Africa into U.S. Homes." *National Catholic Reporter,* December 11, 1992, p. 23.

ASSOCIATED PRESS REPORTER. "*Today* Televises a Vatican Mass." *Los Angeles Times,* April 2, 1985, sec. VI, p. 9.

——. "News Division Won't Run Early Show, CBS Says." *Atlanta Constitution,* July 26, 1986, sec. A, p. 2.

——. "ABC, NBC Compete to Interview Cathy Webb, Dotson Together." *Atlanta Constitution,* May 15, 1985, sec. B, p. 9.

——. "Shriver, Sawyer: A Bad *News* Day." *Los Angeles Times,* August 8, 1986, sec. VI, p. 25.

——. "With Lesson from Gumbel, Lauer Did Homework for *Today." Maui News,* December 24, 1996, sec. B, p. 4.

——. "Will Rogers Jr., Humorist's Son, Soldier, Politician and Actor, 81." *New York Times,* July 11, 1993, p. 36.

——. "S. Kritsick, 42, Vet on Talk Show." *Philadelphia Inquirer,* January 17, 1994, sec. A, p. 12.

As We See It. *TV Guide,* May 11, 1957, p. 4.

——. *TV Guide,* February 9, 1963, p. A3.

——. *TV Guide,* February 25, 1967, p. A4.

——. *TV Guide,* October 15, 1977, p. A4.

AUCOIN, DON. "Gumbel's Transition a Rough One." *Boston Globe,* December 29, 1997, sec. D, p. 2.

AULETTA, KEN. "The Network Takeovers: Why ABC Survived Best." *New York Times,* July 28, 1991, sec. G, p. 20.

"Auto Aide Relieved in Belafonte Case." *New York Times,* March 11, 1968, p. 82.

AVERBUCH, GLORIA. "Morning Star." *Runner's World,* February, 1991, p. 31.

BAKER, DENISE. "Gumbel to Moderate Affirmative Action Panel." *Nation's Cities Weekly,* September 4, 1995, p. 1.

BALDWIN, HANSON W. "Reforms Pressed at West Point; Sports Shake-Up Due in Scandal." *New York Times,* January 14, 1952, p. 1.

"Barbara Walters: New *Today* Co-Host." *New York Times,* April 23, 1974, p. 87.

"Barbara Walters Signed to 3-Year NBC Contract." *New York Times,* July 31, 1973, p. 74.

"The Bare Facts." *New York Times,* September 6, 1980, p. 46.

BARK, ED. "ABC Fires Three Salvos in Ratings War." *Dallas Morning News,* July 17, 1985, sec. F, p. 1.

——. "CBS Decides to Let Kurtis Get Some Sleep." *Dallas Morning News,* June 10, 1985, sec. E, p. 1.

——. "Weatherman Finds Humor Amid the Heat." *Dallas Morning News,* August 24, 1984, sec. A, p. 23.

BARNARD, CHARLES N. "Some Questions for Miss Walters." *TV Guide,* December 30, 1972, p. 26.

BAROL, BILL, with MARY BRUNO AND MARTIN KASINDOAR. "Taking *Today* to the Top." *Newsweek,* February 24, 1986, p. 66.

BARRON, JAMES. "Bright Lights, Big City, Live Cameras." *New York Times,* June 15, 1994, sec. B, p. 1.

——. "Rifleman Kills an NBC Stagehand in Rockefeller Center." *New York Times,* September 1, 1994, sec. B, p. 1.

——. "The Last U.S. Hostage." *New York Times,* December 5, 1991, p. 21.

BARTHEL, JOAN. "He Gets Richard Burton, She Gets an Expert on Head Lice." *TV Guide,* June 11, 1983, p. 35.

——. "Joan Lunden: TV's Morning Glory." *Cosmopolitan,* October 1990, p. 202.

BARTLEY, DIANE. "She Won't Be a '5th Wheel.'" *USA Today,* August 13, 1986, sec. W, p. 3.

BAUDER, DAVID. "There's Always Tomorrow, But for Gumbel, No More *Today.*" *Maui News,* January 3, 1997, sec. B, p. 4.

——. "*Today* Relishes Its Morning Rout." *Rocky Mountain News,* July 7, 1997, sec. D, p. 2.

BEATTY, JEROME. "Garroway's Gold Mine . . . He Makes People Like Him." *American Magazine,* April, 1954, p. 40.

BECKWITH, RUFFIN. "Fairway Interview with Bryant Gumbel." *Golf Magazine,* February, 1982, p. 135.

BENNER, RALPH. "Is This -30- for 'Scoop' Rona?" *Los Angeles,* December 1982, p. 254.

BENNET, JAMES. "Despite Dole's Best Effort, Softer Side Loses Ground." *New York Times,* July 3, 1996, sec. B, p. 6.

BENSON, JIM. "KNBC News Director Capra Taking Over *Today* Show." *Variety,* January 17, 1990, p. 3.

BERGER, WARREN. "A Bold Old Hand Reshapes CBS News." *New York Times,* April 28, 1996, sec. B, p. 36.

BERKE, RICHARD L. "President Backs a Gay Compromise." *New York Times,* May 28, 1993, p. 1.

"Betty Furness Dead of Cancer." *Washington Times,* April 4, 1994, sec. A, p. 5.

BEUTEL, BILL. "Beutel Defends Moscow Report." *New York Times,* December 14, 1975, sec. B, p. 33.

BIANCULLI, DAVID. "Feelin' His Oats: Willard Jabs Back at Bryant." *New York Post,* March 14, 1989, p. 77.

——. "TV Tonight." *Philadelphia Inquirer,* April 27, 1994, sec. G, p. 6.

"Black Collectors." *Ebony,* January 1995, p. 52.

BLUM, DAVID. "Life of Bryant." *New York,* March 20, 1989, p. 28.

——. "*Today*'s Man: Bryant Gumbel's Different Strokes," *New York,* August 4, 1986, p. 30.

BODDIE, ELLEN. "Great Scott!" *Fifty Plus,* December 1987, p. 30.

BODLEY, HAL. "Crack of the Bat Draws Hartman Back to Camp." *USA Today,* March 13, 1985, sec. C, p. 2.

BOEDEKER, HAL. "A Vigorous Challenge in Morning TV." *Philadelphia Inquirer,* February 14, 1994, sec. E, p. 1.

BOROUGHS, DON L., DAN McGRAW, AND KEVIN WHITELAW. "Disney's All Smiles." *U.S. News & World Report,* August 14, 1995, p. 32.

BOZELL, L. BRENT, III. "Paucity of Quotes . . . Plethora of Sound Bites." *Washington Times,* January 1, 1994, sec. D, p. 3.

BRAATEN, DAVID. "Regan Exchanges Hisses with Nancy via *Today* Show." *Washington Times,* October 24, 1989, sec. A, p. 3.

BRADY, JAMES. "In Step with Al Roker." *Parade Magazine,* January 5, 1997, p. 18.

BRINLEY, MARYANN BUCKNUM. "Jane Pauley: The Frustrations of a Working Mother." *McCall's,* November 1984, p. 68.

"Brokaw Replacing Chancellor? NBC Mulls News Changes." *TV Guide,* November 26, 1977, p. A1.

BROOKE, JILL. "More Tube Time for Lunden." *New York Post,* March 7, 1989, p. 77.

——. "Someone's Out to Get Bryant." *New York Post,* March 1, 1989, p. 69.

BROWN, BEN. "But So Far, the Reception Is Lukewarm in the USA." *USA Today,* May 7, 1985, sec. D, p. 3.

BROWN, LES. "Ailing *A.M. America* on ABC-TV Is Forging a New Format." *New York Times,* September 12, 1975, p. 66.

BROWN, PATRICIA LEIGH. "Now, on Talk Radio, Remodeling Tips." *New York Times,* May 31, 1990, sec. C, p. 1.

BROWN, RICH. "More Musical Anchors at *Today.*" *Broadcasting,* April 8, 1991, p. 25.

BROZAN, NADINE. "Can Shriver Co-Anchor in Marriage and on TV?" *Atlanta Constitution,* October 31, 1985, sec. C, p. 5.

——. "Chronicle." *New York Times,* October 5, 1991, p. 22.

——. "Chronicle." *New York Times,* August 14, 1992, p. 26.

——. "Chronicle." *New York Times,* June 10, 1992, sec. B, p. 7.

——. "Chronicle." *New York Times,* August 5, 1992, p. 21.

——. "Chronicle." *New York Times,* October 19, 1993, sec. B, p. 2.

——. "Chronicle." *New York Times,* October 29, 1993, sec. B, p. 7.

——. "Chronicle." *New York Times,* August 19, 1995, p. 20.

——. "Chronicle." *New York Times,* November 28, 1995, sec. B, p. 5.

——. "Chronicle." *New York Times,* December 22, 1995, sec. B, p. 7.

——. "Chronicle." *New York Times,* December 18, 1996, p. 29.

BRYANT, CARLETON R. "Hostage Talks to Wife by Phone." *Washington Times,* October 23, 1991, sec. A, p. 12.

"Bryant Gumbel Announces He Will Leave *Today* Show After One More Season." *Jet,* January 22, 1996, p. 37.

"Bryant Gumbel Exits *Today.*" *Mr. Showbiz,* January 3, 1997. >www.mrshowbiz.com<

BUCHALTER, GAIL. "To Wake Up Its Sluggish *Early Today* Show, NBC Anchors Its Hopes on Connie Chung." *People,* June 13, 1983, p. 34.

BUCHANAN, PATRICK. "Some Unanswered Questions About John Dean Interview." *TV Guide,* December 11, 1976, p. A7.

BUMILLER, ELISABETH. "What You Don't Know About Katie Couric." *Good Housekeeping,* August 1996, p. 72.

BURDICK, TOM, AND CHARLENE MITCHELL. "Look Over Your Shoulder for Norville." *Washington Times*, December 14, 1989, sec. C, p. 2.

BURSTEIN, MARC. "ABC's Disney Report Was a Legitimate Story." *New York Times*, May 22, 1996, sec. A, p. 16.

"Bush to Appear on Morning Show." *New York Times*, June 30, 1992, p. 21.

CALHOUN, JOHN. "*Today* on the Street." *Theatre Crafts International*, August–September 1994, p. 12.

CALTA, LOUIS. "Hugh Downs Leaving *Today*, McGee Successor." *New York Times*, April 27, 1971, p. 87.

"Can a Few Good Former ABC Types Wake CBS Up in the Morning?" *Television/Radio Age*, December 7, 1987, p. 28.

"Capra Says *Today* Needs Tinkering." *Broadcasting*, February 5, 1990, p. 30.

CARMAN, JOHN. "CBS Exec May Quit if Turner Succeeds." *Atlanta Constitution*, June 10, 1985, sec. B, p. 1.

——. "Forrest Tries Too Hard to Outshine Phyllis." *Atlanta Constitution*, August 20, 1985, sec. B, p. 7.

——. "Sawyer Is Substitute Co-Host for *The CBS Morning News*." *Atlanta Constitution*, August 9, 1985, sec. P, p. 19.

CARMODY, JOHN. "*Good Morning America* Made Part of ABC News." *Philadelphia Inquirer*, April 7, 1995, sec. E, p. 16.

CARTER, BILL. "After *Today*, an Uncertain Tomorrow." *New York Times*, December 18, 1996, sec. C, p. 15.

——. "CBS Likely to Replace Producer." *New York Times*, February 13, 1991, sec. C, p. 18.

——. "CBS's Ruptured Ties to Affiliates." *New York Times*, September 14, 1992, sec. D, p. 1.

——. "For *Today*: Cloudy." *New York Times Magazine*, June 10, 1990, p. 26.

——. "Gumbel Signs New *Today* Contract." *New York Times*, December 4, 1991, sec. C, p. 26.

——. "Gumbel to Leave *Today* after One More Year." *New York Times*, January 5, 1996, sec. D, p. 26.

——. "Lauer Named to Replace Gumbel on *Today*." *New York Times*, December 24, 1996, sec. C, p. 18.

——. "Morning News Programs Draw the Young and Mobile." *New York Times*, April 5, 1993, sec. D, p. 1.

——. "NBC Losing Morning Race as Ratings of *Today* Drop." *New York Times*, February 26, 1990, sec. D, p. 1.

——. "NBC Names Executive Producer of *Today*." *New York Times*, December 3, 1991, sec. C, p. 17.

——. "NBC to Reimburse Disney for *Today* Show Junket." *New York Times*, October 8, 1991, sec. C, p. 20.

——. "New Producer for *NBC Nightly News*." *New York Times*, May 12, 1990, p. 46.

——. "On the Set with Bryant Gumbel." *New York Times*, November 11, 1992, sec. C, p. 1.

——. "Sawyer Makes a New Deal with ABC." *New York Times*, February 17, 1994, sec. C, p. 22.

——. "Surprise Interview with Bush for *Today*." *New York Times*, October 14, 1992, p. 22.

——. "Ted Koppel Says *Nightline* in Jeopardy." *New York Times*, June 4, 1992, sec. C, p. 20.

——. "*Today* Gives Perot Two Hours to Answer Queries." *New York Times*, June 12, 1992, p. 14.

——. "*Today* Producer, 26, Hopes Youth Equals Success," *New York Times*, December 9, 1991, sec. C, p. 11.

——. "*Today* Show Moving to Storefront Studio." *New York Times*, November 9, 1993, sec. C, p. 21.

——. "TV's Late-Night Landscape Blurs." *New York Times,* May 17, 1994, sec. C, p. 17.

——. "Women Anchors Are on the Rise as Evening Stars." *New York Times,* August 12, 1990, sec. B, p. 27.

CARVAJAL, DOREEN. "First Lady Is Treated with Care by Audience." *New York Times,* January 20, 1996, p. 10.

"*CBS This Morning* Co-Anchor Kathleen Sullivan Is Being Removed." *Broadcasting,* February 12, 1990, p. 64.

"CBS to Revamp *Morning News.*" *New York Times,* May 17, 1973, p. 71.

"CBS-TV Sets *Jayne Mansfield Story.*" *New York Times,* October 13, 1980, sec. C, p. 22.

"Celebrity Mother: Talks about What She's Learned." *Glamour,* May 1983, p. 108.

CHASE, CHRIS. "Bryant Gumbel: *Today*'s Dynamic Anchor." *Cosmopolitan,* February 1986, p. 162.

——. "Katie Couric: TV's Morning Star." *Cosmopolitan,* May 1992, p. 238.

"Chasing the Clouds Away." *People,* October 7, 1996, p. 42.

CHASTAIN, SUE. "Jean Harris Says She Got Educated Quickly in Jail." *Philadelphia Inquirer,* February 15, 1994, sec. F, p. 2.

"The Chimpanzee & The Queen." *Variety,* June 3, 1953, p. 13.

CHRISTY, MARIAN. "The Prime of Phyllis George." *Boston Globe,* February 6, 1985, p. 65.

CLARITY, JAMES F. "Notes on People." *New York Times,* October 6, 1972, sec. B, p. 3.

CLARK, KENNETH R. "February Holds a Goodbye for Host of *Good Morning.*" *Chicago Tribune,* October 3, 1986, sec. E, p. 5.

——. "Changes Ahead for *Morning News.*" *Chicago Tribune,* July 4, 1986, sec. E, p. 10.

——. "*Morning News* Doctor Loses Patience with CBS." *Chicago Tribune,* July 30, 1986, p. 4.

——. "Phyllis George Gets Down to Business in CBS Debut." *Chicago Tribune,* January 16, 1985, sec. E, p. 5.

——. "Phyllis George Resigns Post on *Morning News.*" *Chicago Tribune,* August 31, 1985, p. 3.

——. "TV News Gentle to Dotson, Webb." *Chicago Tribune,* May 16, 1985, p. 4.

CLARKE, GERALD, WITH LESLIE WHITAKER. "Amiable Joe." *Time,* May 28, 1990, p. 72.

COFFEY, RAYMOND. "A Showbiz Mass: Is Nothing Sacred?" *Chicago Tribune,* March 31, 1985, sec. E, p. 3.

COHEN, SHERRY SUIB. "Katie Couric: Early Morning's Brightest Star." *McCall's,* June 1995, p. 86.

COINER, JILL BROOKE. "Hey Hey Paula." *Family Circle,* June 8, 1993, p. 24.

COLLINS, MONICA. "A Roman Holiday for *Today.*" *USA Today,* April 3, 1985, sec. D, p. 3.

——. "Bryant Gumbel's Big Thaw." *USA Today,* June 5, 1989, sec. D, p. 3.

——. "CBS Starts Over Again—Minus Phyllis George." *USA Today,* September 3, 1985, sec. D, p. 3.

——. "CBS' Bland Breakfast Show." *USA Today,* December 1, 1987, sec. D, p. 1.

——. "Day 1: Ed Murrow's Spirit and Phil Collins' Big Fan." *USA Today,* May 7, 1985, sec. D, p. 3.

——. "Everyman David Hartman." *USA Today,* June 18, 1985, sec. D, p. 3.

——. "From the Vatican to Vietnam." *USA Today,* April 1, 1986, sec. D, p. 3.

——. "Getting the Royal Runaround." *USA Today,* May 8, 1985, sec. D, p. 3.

———. "Gibson, ABC's New *Good* Guy." *USA Today,* March 2, 1987, sec. D, p. 1.

———. "Gumbel Soars with the Ratings." *USA Today,* April 11, 1985, sec. D, p. 3.

———. "Lunden, Co-Host at Last." *USA Today,* August 6, 1986, sec. D, p. 3.

———. "Maria and Forrest, Out of the Woods." *USA Today,* July 31, 1986, sec. D, p. 3.

———. "Memo to NBC: We Love Scott." *USA Today,* March 1, 1989, sec. D, p. 1.

———. "Phyllis George at Ease on CBS." *USA Today,* May 9, 1985, sec. D, p. 3.

———. "Shriver and Sawyer: CBS' *Morning* Stars Are Rising." *USA Today,* January 14, 1986, sec. D, p. 3.

———. "Ten Years of Tradition, with a Smile." *USA Today,* November 4, 1985, sec. D, p. 1.

———. "*Today* Romances the Rail." *USA Today,* May 20, 1985, sec. D, p. 3.

———. "*Today* Wakes Up to No. 1." *USA Today,* March 29, 1985, sec. D, p. 1.

———. "*Today* Will Come to Sunday." *USA Today,* June 18, 1986, sec. D, p. 1.

"Combat 'Veteran' Bell Relives Battlefield Memories." *USA Today,* April 22, 1985, sec. D, p. 3.

"Company Town: TV Ratings Report." *Los Angeles Times,* January 17, 1997, sec. D, p. 4.

"The Complete, Uncensored Bryant Gumbel Memo." *Seven Days,* March 22, 1989, p. 7.

CONAWAY, JAMES. "How to Talk with Barbara Walters about Practically Anything." *New York Times Magazine,* September 10, 1972, p. 40.

"Coronation and Commercials." *New York Times,* June 9, 1953, p. 26.

"Coronation TV Shows in U.S. Anger British." *New York Times,* June 8, 1953, p. 1.

"Correction." *Mediaweek,* August 5, 1996, p. 3.

COSTIKYAN, BARBARA. "*Today*'s Jane Pauley Today." *Cosmopolitan,* November 1984, p. 42.

COX, ALLAN. "Seize Opportunities for Greatness and Make the Times." *Atlanta Constitution,* November 24, 1986, sec. C, p. 11.

CRONKITE, WALTER. *A Reporter's Life.* New York: Random House, 1996.

CUMMINGS, JUDITH. "Notes on People." *New York Times,* August 18, 1980, p. 82.

CUNNINGHAM, KIM. "Family Viewing." *People,* March 6, 1995, p. 102.

———. "The Gravity Gene." *People,* November 4, 1996, p. 150.

CYCLOPS. "After a Few More Tomorrows, *Today* May Be In for Trouble." *New York Times,* August 19, 1973, sec. D, p. 15.

DALE, ARDEN. "Shooting Stars Gets Seconds in the Sun, as *Good Morning America* Visits Shoot." *Back Stage,* February 16, 1990, p. 6.

DALEY, STEVE. "Kurtis Says Goodbye to News Show." *Chicago Tribune,* June 8, 1985, p. 5.

DALLOS, ROBERT E. "Incident at TV Taping Irks Belafonte." *New York Times,* March 7, 1968, p. 87.

DANIELS, LEE A. "Hughes Rudd, TV Correspondent for Two Networks." *New York Times,* October 14, 1992, sec. B, p. 10.

DARRACH, BRAD. "Goodbye *Today,* Hello Tomorrow." *Life,* December 1989, p. 46.

"Dave and the Chickens." *Newsweek,* January 25, 1954, p. 56.

"Dave Garroway." In *Current Biography.* New York: H. W. Wilson, 1952.

"Dave Garroway's Death Recalls How He Boosted Blacks during His Career." *Jet,* August 9, 1982, p. 15.

"David Hartman." In *Current Biography.* New York: H. W. Wilson, 1981.

Davidson, Casey. "Births/Adoptions." *Entertainment Weekly,* January 26, 1996, p. 15.

Davidson, Casey, with Ben Hellwarth and Andrew LePage. "Exits." *Entertainment Weekly,* January 19, 1996, p. 11.

Davis, Gerry. *The* Today *Show.* New York: Quill William Morrow, 1987.

DeBlois, F. "Review: *Today.*" *TV Guide,* June 11, 1960, p. 23.

Dendy, Larry B. "Deborah Norville: *Today's* Rising Star." *Saturday Evening Post,* March, 1990, p. 44.

Diamond, Edwin. "All About Deborah." *New York,* October 23, 1989, p. 28.

———. "The Couric Effect." *New York,* December 9, 1991, p. 20.

Diamond, Edwin, and Jack Link. "Surprise! TV's Morning Shows Aren't What You Think They Are." *TV Guide,* May 21, 1983, p. 4.

"Died: Dave Garroway." *Newsweek,* August 2, 1982, p. 63.

Doan, Richard K. "The Doan Report." *TV Guide,* May 8, 1971, p. A1.

———. "The Doan Report." *TV Guide,* June 9, 1973, p. A1.

———. "The Doan Report." *TV Guide,* July 28, 1973, p. A1.

———. "The Doan Report." *TV Guide,* September 8, 1973, p. A1.

———. "The Doan Report." *TV Guide,* November 3, 1973, p. A1.

———. "The Doan Report." *TV Guide,* July 20, 1974, p. A3.

———. "The Doan Report." *TV Guide,* August 3, 1974, p. A5.

———. "The Doan Report." *TV Guide,* February 15, 1975, p. A3.

Dobyns, Lloyd. "Producer to Reporter: 'Think Weird, Think Live, Good Luck.'" *TV Guide,* February 14, 1987, p. 36.

Donahue, Deirdre. "Steinem, Ms. Anchor on A.M. TV." *USA Today,* September 10, 1986, sec. D, p. 1.

Donlon, Brian. "A Bad Start for CBS' Day." *USA Today,* August 13, 1987, sec. D, p. 3.

———. "ABC Tries for Sunnier *Morning.*" *USA Today,* March 17, 1986, sec. D, p. 3.

———. "ABC's Affable Morning Man Is Signing Off." *USA Today,* February 19, 1987, sec. D, p. 1.

———. "A Good Start for *Morning.*" *USA Today,* December 2, 1987, sec. D, p. 3.

———. "A Quick Look at the Ratings War." *USA Today,* May 16, 1986, sec. WE, p. 5.

———. "Bill Kurtis' Farewell: Today Is His A.M. Sign-Off." *USA Today,* June 14, 1986, sec. D, p. 3.

———. "CBS A.M. Ratings Wake Up." *USA Today,* January 23, 1987, sec. D, p. 1.

———. "CBS Names Its New A.M. Contender." *USA Today,* November 16, 1987, sec. D, p. 1.

———. "CBS: 32 Years of Early-Morning Malaise." *USA Today,* May 15, 1986, sec. D, p. 3.

———. "CBS Toasts a Year of Morning Stability." *USA Today,* November 28, 1986, sec. D, p. 3.

———. "CBS' A.M. Ratings Rise and Shine." *USA Today,* December 29, 1987, sec. D, p. 1.

———. "CBS' Winston: Dashed Hopes." *USA Today,* July 29, 1986, sec. D, p. 1.

———. "Charles Gibson Will Be *Good Morning* Co-Host." *USA Today,* January 29, 1987, sec. D, p. 1.

———. "Forrest Sawyer Exits CBS." *USA Today,* September 25, 1987, sec. D, p. 1.

———. "*GMA* May Get a Face Lift." *USA Today,* October 8, 1986, sec. D, p. 3.

——. "*GMA* Wins Week, Not the War." *USA Today*, March 28, 1986, sec. D, p. 3.

——. "*Good Morning* Begins Life with Hartman." *USA Today*, February 23, 1987, sec. D, p. 3.

——. "Gumbel, the $7 Million *Today* Man." *USA Today*, August 8, 1988, sec. D, p. 1.

——. "Hartley Gets a Partner for A.M. Show." *USA Today*, November 14, 1986, sec. D, p. 1.

——. "Hartley May Wake CBS' A.M." *USA Today*, October 21, 1986, sec. D, p. 1.

——. "Hartman Says No to Gumbel." *USA Today*, February 17, 1987, sec. D, p. 3.

——. "Hostages Dominate CBS' A.M." *USA Today*, June 19, 1985, sec. D, p. 3.

——. "Is *Today* the Morning Show of Tomorrow?" *USA Today*, January 14, 1986, sec. D, p. 1.

——. "Lunden OKs New Contract." *USA Today*, July 22, 1987, sec. D, p. 3.

——. "Lunden Plans to Leave ABC." *USA Today*, September 10, 1987, sec. D, p. 1.

——. "Marty Ryan, Taking It One *Today* at a Time." *USA Today*, August 11, 1987, sec. D, p. 1.

——. "*Morning* Hits 14-Year Low for CBS." *USA Today*, March 27, 1987, sec. D, p. 1.

——. "*Morning* Is Good and Getting Better for Gibson." *USA Today*, August 18, 1987, sec. D, p. 3.

——. "New Plan for CBS' *Morning*." *USA Today*, April 9, 1986, sec. D, p. 3.

——. "On *Today*, It's Kiss and Make Up." *USA Today*, March 14, 1989, sec. D, p. 1.

——. "Past Comes Back to Haunt Gumbel." *USA Today*, March 2, 1989, sec. D, p. 3.

——. "Quarterback: From Boos to Applause." *USA Today*, January 14, 1987, sec. A, p. 1.

——. "Rivals Try to Cash In on *Today* Break." *USA Today*, September 12, 1988, sec. D, p. 1.

——. "Scott's Jabs Irk NBC." *USA Today*, April 5, 1989, sec. D, p. 3.

——. "Sun Sets for CBS in A.M." *USA Today*, July 28, 1986, sec. D, p. 1.

——. "The Mood Backstage at *Today*." *USA Today*, March 2, 1989, sec. D, p. 3.

——. "*This Morning* Premieres—Minus Hoopla." *USA Today*, November 30, 1987, sec. D, p. 1.

——. "*Today* Show Forecast: Stormy Weather." *USA Today*, March 1, 1989, sec. A, p. 1.

——. "*Today*: So Hot Willard's Wig Almost Melted." *USA Today*, March 25, 1986, sec. D, p. 1.

——. "*Today* Stays Up Tonight." *USA Today*, August 19, 1985, sec. D, p. 3.

——. "Twelve Years of Rise-and-Shine on *Today*." *USA Today*, October 11, 1988, sec. D, p. 1.

——. "Wake Up to Deja Vu on CBS." *USA Today*, June 25, 1986, sec. D, p. 3.

——. "Will Winston Work A.M. Magic?" *USA Today*, May 15, 1986, sec. D, p. 3.

——. "Winston to Leave CBS." *USA Today*, July 30, 1986, sec. D, p. 1.

Donlon, Brian, and Peter Johnson. "Great Scott, You're Loved." *USA Today*, March 2, 1989, sec. A, p. 1.

Dowd, Maureen. "Dieting with Kathleen Sullivan: With a Will and a Weigh." *New York Times*, January 12, 1994, sec. C, p. 1.

Downey, Maureen. "Lunden's Morning Light Will Brighten." *Atlanta Constitution*, December 10, 1986, sec. B, p. 1.

"Downs to Be *Today* Host." *New York Times*, May 24, 1962, p. 71.

DOWNS, HUGH. *On Camera: My 10,000 Hours on Television*. New York: G. P. Putnam's Sons, 1986.

DRAKE, ROSS. "The Day Harry Truman Chewed Him Out." *TV Guide*, March 10, 1973, p. 18.

DREHER, ROD. "Celebrity-Watches: Double Cheese, Please." *Washington Times*, August 29, 1993, sec. D, p. 3.

DREYFUSS, JOEL. "A Man for Today." *Black Enterprise*, April 1982, p. 32.

DUFFY, MIKE. "*Today* Show Clicks to Climb Rating Ladder." *Atlanta Constitution*, April 5, 1985, p. 11.

DUNKEL, TOM. "Gumbel & Son Take the Show on the Road." *Travel & Leisure*, November 1992, p. 87.

DUPREE, SCOTTY. "Morning Becomes Eclectic." *Mediaweek*, June 24, 1996, p. 13.

"Early to Rise . . ." *TV Guide*, January 28, 1956, p. 8.

EFRON, EDITH. "New Girl on *Today*." *TV Guide*, May 16, 1964, p. 24.

ELLIOT, SUSAN. "Katie Couric: *Today's* Good News with a Mile-Wide Smile." *Woman's Day*, September 3, 1991, p. 58.

ELLIOTT, STUART. "A Vaseline Commercial that Looks Like News." *New York Times*, November 29, 1991, sec. D, p. 5.

——. "CBS for Breakfast, but Does 'Marcy' Like It?" *New York Times*, August 26, 1991, sec. D, p. 6.

——. "Pop Music Takes Center Stage in a *Good Morning America* Campaign to Attract Younger Viewers." *New York Times*, March 6, 1995, sec. D, p. 8.

ELM, JOANNA. "Jane Pauley: My Life After *Today*." *TV Guide*, March 10, 1990, p. 28.

ELVIN, JOHN. "Inside the Beltway." *Washington Times*, August 4, 1989, sec. A, p. 6.

——. "Inside the Beltway." *Washington Times*, December 17, 1990, sec. A, p. 6.

——. "Inside the Beltway." *Washington Times*, June 24, 1991, sec. A, p. 6.

"Emily Boxer Joins *Home* Show." *Publishers Weekly*, September 20, 1991, p. 17.

"Emily Boxer Leaves *Today* Show After 12 Years and 3,500 Authors." *Publishers Weekly*, August 30, 1991, p. 16.

"Emily Jordan Boxer, Television Producer, 65." *New York Times*, January 12, 1994, sec. B, p. 7.

"End of an Era." *New York Times*, March 8, 1992, sec. D, p. 7.

"Erma Bombeck Drops Out of ABC's *Good Morning America* Regulars." *Los Angeles Times*, September 20, 1986, sec. V, p. 14.

"Excerpts from Clinton's Question-and-Answer Session in the Rose Garden." *New York Times*, May 28, 1993, p. 14.

"Fair and Wet." *TV Guide*, February 4, 1956, p. 12.

FARINET, GENE. "Frank McGee: 1921–1974." *TV Guide*, April 24, 1974, p. A3.

FINK, MITCHELL. "The Insider." *People*, August 19, 1996, p. 41.

——. "The Insider." *People*, October 7, 1996, p. 45.

FIRESTONE, DAVID. "The Crash of Flight 800." *New York Times*, July 20, 1996, p. 26.

"First Lady Gives TV Viewers Tour of the White House." *New York Times*, February 16, 1968, p. 19.

"Five Years in a Goldfish Bowl." *TV Guide*, January 19, 1957, p. 14.

FLANDER, JUDY. "Catching Up with Katie Couric." *Saturday Evening Post*, September–October 1992, p. 38.

FOWLE, FARNSWORTH. "Frank McGee of NBC Dead; Newsman and *Today* Host, 52." *New York Times*, April 18, 1974, p. 44.

"Frank Blair Resigns." *New York Times*, December 14, 1974, p. 42.

"Frank Blair, 79, Ex-*Today* Anchor." *New York Times*, March 16, 1995, sec. B, p. 14.

FRANK, STANLEY. "The Sweatshirt Guy Who's Become a Breakfast Egghead." *TV Guide*, March 15, 1969, p. 32.

"Friedman Steps Down from *Today.*" *Broadcasting*, June 8, 1987, p. 34.

FRIEDMAN, STEVE. "When Jane Pauley Kissed My Ring, I Knew We Were on Our Way." *TV Guide*, January 16, 1988, p. 26.

FRIEND, TAD. "Would You Buy a Used TV-News Show from This Man?" *Esquire*, December 1990, p. 155.

FULLER, JOHN G. "Trade Winds." *Saturday Review*, February 8, 1958, p. 6.

FUNT, PETER. "How Jim Hartz Won the Great TV Host Hunt." *New York Times*, September 22, 1974, sec. B, p. 1.

"Future of CBS' Morning Programs Is Still Up in the Air." *Atlanta Constitution*, September 28, 1982, sec. B, p. 7.

"Gabor Voted Year's Top Whiner." *Washington Times*, December 27, 1989, sec. A, p. 2.

GALLOWAY, PAUL. "Instead of Helping to Take Off Pounds, Fat Squad Put the Media On." *Chicago Tribune*, May 16, 1986, sec. E, p. 2.

GARROWAY, DAVE. "Actors by Dawnlight." *Theatre Arts*, November 1953, p. 20.

"Garroway No Longer Will Work by the Dawn's Early Light." *TV Guide*, August 11, 1959, p. 20.

"Garroway Today." *TV Guide*, July 10, 1953, p. 15.

"Garroway Upset." *New York Times*, November 5, 1959, p. 3.

GATES, ANITA. "Books in Brief." *New York Times*, October 15, 1995, sec. G, p. 21.

GAY, VERNE. "Gumbel OKs a Big Deal for One More Year of *Today*s." *Newsday*, January 5, 1996, sec. A, p. 2.

———. "How Bryant Gumbel Approaches the Next Chapter of His Career May Well Mean the Difference Between Greatness and Mere Competence." *Newsday*, January 19, 1997, sec. C, p. 8.

———. "Off Camera: It's a Lousy Job at CBS, But Someone Has to Do It." *Newsday*, January 3, 1996, sec. B, p. 49.

GEHMAN, RICHARD. "Portrait of a Tormented Man." *TV Guide*, July 15, 1961, p. 12.

———. "Portrait of a Tormented Man." *TV Guide*, July 22, 1961, p. 24.

GENDEL, MORGAN. "*Morning News* Continues to Soften." *Los Angeles Times*, June 10, 1985, sec. F, p. 8.

"Gene Shalit Will Replace Joe Garagiola on *Today.*" *New York Times*, January 5, 1973, p. 63.

GENT, GEORGE. "Jessel Is Cut Off on TV Show over References to Newspapers," *New York Times*, July 31, 1971, p. 49.

GERARD, JEREMY. "CBS New Division President Is to Announce His Departure." *New York Times*, August 23, 1990, sec. C, p. 15.

———. "*CBS This Morning.*" *Variety*, September 2, 1996, p. 33.

———. "Few Tears over Changes at CBS." *New York Times*, August 24, 1990, sec. C, p. 3.

———. "*Today* Staff Is Shuffled to Restore 'Family.'" *New York Times*, May 16, 1990, sec. C, p. 21.

GERSTON, JILL. "How a Bright Ex-Model Made It Big." *New York Times*, May 12, 1996, sec. L, p. 59.

——. "Mr. Warhol Meet Mr. Barnum." *New York Times*, April 29, 1990, sec. G, p. 35.

"Getting Older." *New York Times*, December 4, 1994, sec. F, p. 29.

"Gibson, Mudd: New Jobs." *Los Angeles Times*, January 30, 1987, sec. F, p. 1.

"Gibson's Last Show on *Good Morning*." *Maui News*, May 1, 1998, sec. B, p. 16.

GLIATTO, TOM, WITH SUE CARSWELL. "Facing the Sunset." *People*, January 10, 1994, p. 86.

GLIATTO, TOM, WITH ALAN CARTER. "*Today*'s Latest Coo." *People*, March 25, 1991, p. 66.

GLIATTO, TOM, WITH ALAN CARTER, LISA RUSSELL, AND JOANNE KAUFMAN. "With Deborah Norville Switched to the Mommy Track, *Today* Has Arrived for New Coanchor Katie Couric." *People*, April 22, 1991, p. 72.

GLIATTO, TOM, AND SUE MILLER. "Top of the Morning." *People*, December 22, 1997, p. 109.

"*GMA*'s Lunden to Leave Show." *Broadcasting*, September 14, 1987, p. 117.

"Good Morning." *Variety*, February 22, 1956, p. 16.

"*Good Morning, America*." *Variety*, November 5, 1975, p. 62.

GOODWIN, BETTY. "Screen Style." *Washington Times*, September 14, 1993, sec. C, p. 15.

GOLD, HERBERT. "'I Need My 15-Minute Fame Fix.'" *TV Guide*, July 2, 1977, p. 12.

GOLDBERG, KAREN. "Page Two Extra." *Washington Times*, January 11, 1990, sec. D, p. 2.

GOLDBERG, ROBERT. *Anchors: Brokaw, Jennings, Rather and the Evening News*. Secaucus, N.J.: Carol Publishing, 1990.

GOLDFARB, MICHAEL. "*Today* Counts on Royal Chap." *USA Today*, February 11, 1987, sec. D, p. 2.

GOLDMAN, KEVIN. "And, Back on *Today* . . ." *Newsday*, March 7, 1989, sec. B, p. 7.

——. "Bryant and Willard Make Up." *Newsday*, March 8, 1989, sec. B, p. 7.

——. "Gumbel's Memo to Boss Gives NBC *Today* Staff Poor Ratings." *Newsday*, "February 28, 1989, p. 5.

GOODMAN, MARK, WITH TOBY KAHN. "Yesterday and *Today*." *People*, January 20, 1992, p. 83.

GOODMAN, WALTER. "Arthur Kent Has a Tryout on *Today*." *New York Times*, August 22, 1991, sec. C, p. 20.

——. "Beauty and the Broadcast." *New York Times*, January 26, 1992, sec. B, p. 29.

——. "Candidates Run to the Puppy Dogs." *New York Times*, October 26, 1992, sec. C, p.16.

——. "Explosion Aboard TWA Flight 800." *New York Times*, July 19, 1996, sec. B, p. 10.

——. "Fine-Tuning a Sweet Formula." *New York Times*, January 21, 1990, sec. B, p. 1.

——. "First Lady as Star of the TV Talk-Show Circuit." *New York Times*, January 10, 1996, sec. C, p. 19.

——. "For News-Magazine Fans, a Double-Feature Opportunity." *New York Times*, June 1, 1994, sec. C, p. 18.

——. "In a 'Lone Ranger' Role, Perot Builds an Audience." *New York Times*, April 23, 1992, p. 23.

——. "New Co-Host on *Today* Eases Her Way Into the Job." *New York Times*, January 9, 1990, sec. C, p. 18.

——. "New Co-Host on *Today* Gets Off to Affable Start." *New York Times*, April 22, 1991, sec. C, p. 16.

——. "Pearl Harbor, as Both Sides Saw It." *New York Times*, December 5, 1991, sec. C, p. 22.

——. "Rating the Interviewers in Hillary Clinton's Blitz." *New York Times*, September 27, 1993, sec. C, p. 16.

——. "Some *Today* Segments Bigger than Bite-Size." *New York Times*, March 2, 1992, sec. C, p. 14.

——. "*Today* Celebrates Itself, at Night Yet." *New York Times*, January 14, 1992, sec. C, p. 11.

——. "What's on Court TV and CNN after O. J." *New York Times*, October 18, 1995, sec. C, p. 22.

"*Good Morning America*—Live from QE2, July 1–4," *Travel Weekly*, June 19, 1986, p. 5.

"*Good Morning* Drops Hartman as Its Anchor." *Chicago Tribune*, September 26, 1986, p. 4.

"Good Times, Just Like Old Times, for *Today*." *Broadcasting*, February 2, 1986, p. 49.

GOULD, JACK. "Comment on *Today*." *New York Times*, January 20, 1952, sec. B, p. 11.

——. "TV: Garroway Departs." *New York Times*, July 18, 1961, p. 59.

——. "TV: Politics for Early-Bird Viewers." *New York Times*, November 8, 1963, p. 62.

GRAHAM, JEFFERSON. "*Today* Apologizes; Gumbel Has His Say.'" *USA Today*, April 12, 1996, sec. D, p. 3.

GRANGER, ROD. "New Dawn for *Today*?" *Broadcasting*, May 21, 1990, p. 50.

GREANEY, DAN. "Elliot's Rock Talk Plays Well in the Morning." *USA Today*, July 14, 1988, sec. D, p. 3.

"Great Scott! TV's Favorite Weatherman." *Ladies' Home Journal*, November 1987, p. 62.

GREEN, ABEL. "Jessel Was to Announce Show Biz Retirement on NBC-TV *Today* but Edwin Newman Hastened It." *Variety*, August 4, 1971, p. 35.

GREENE, DONNA. "Pressing Country Clubs to Accept Blacks." *New York Times*, February 3, 1991, sec. XII, p. 3, West Coast edition.

GREGORY, DEBORAH. "All Talked Out?" *Essence*, April 1996, p. 64.

GREPPI, MICHELE. "*GMA* Weatherman Spencer Christian Is Sunny and Smart." *Atlanta Constitution*, August 7, 1988, p. 4.

——. "Herd Mentality at Animal Kingdom." *New York Post*, August 11, 1998, p. 42.

——. "Memo to Marty." *New York Post*, March 2, 1989, p. 101.

——. "Who Is Harry Smith and Why Is He Up for Early Mornings?" *Atlanta Constitution*, August 14, 1988, TV supplement, p. 4.

——. "Willard Hurtin' Over Memo." *New York Post*, March 2, 1989, p. 101.

——. "Willard Seals Scrap with a Kiss." *New York Post*, March 14, 1989, p. 77.

GRIFFITH, THOMAS. "Television News without Blinkers." *Time*, April 29, 1985, p. 72.

GRIMES, WILLIAM. "Bob Looks Back on His Partnership with Ray." *New York Times*, May 7, 1992, p. 15.

GUILDER, ELIZABETH. "Clauses K.O. Nuell as *Today* Topper." *Variety*, January 3, 1990, 29.

"Gumbel Inks 3-Year Pact, *Today* Worth $7 Million." *Jet*, August 22, 1988, p. 18.

GUNTHER, MARC. "Lightweights Steps Into Key Spots at CBS." *Dallas Morning News*, September 23, 1985, sec. E, p. 1.

——. "The Bush Media Plan: Avoid Hard Questions." *Philadelphia Inquirer*, October 3, 1992, sec. A, p. 4.

HALL, GLADYS. "Mr. & Mrs. Dave Garroway." *Ladies' Home Journal*, July 1960, p. 54.

HALL, JANE. "A Roller Coaster Ride from Morning to Night." *Los Angeles Times*, July 6, 1994, p. 2.

——. "David Hartman Leaves *GMA* after a Decade Run that Rarely Showed the Muscle behind His Mild Manner." *People*, October 20, 1986, p. 59.

——. "David Hartman's Silent Partner No More, Joan Lunden Wins New Status on *Good Morning America*." *People*, August 18, 1986, p. 52.

——. "Fighting Off a Few Guilty Tears, Jane Pauley Leaves Her Kids at Home and Heads Back to Work on *Today*." *People*, October 27, 1986, p. 108.

——. "It's War as Jane Pauley and Bryant Gumbel Take *Today* on the Road to Trounce David Hartman." *People*, May 6, 1985, p. 107.

——. "Smith Likely Out When CBS Revamps *Morning*." *Los Angeles Times*, March 7, 1996, sec. F, p. 2.

——. "Starring in a Twin Bill." *People*, December 5, 1983, p. 124.

HAMBURGER, PHILIP. "Morning Call." *New Yorker*, January 2, 1954, p. 55.

——. "Rise and Shine." *New Yorker*, February 2, 1952, p. 60.

HARDING, HENRY. "For the Record." *TV Guide*, July 15, 1961, p. A1.

——. "For the Record." *TV Guide*, December 2, 1961, p. A1.

——. "For the Record." *TV Guide*, June 2, 1962, p. A1.

——. "For the Record." *TV Guide*, June 30, 1962, p. A1.

——. "For the Record." *TV Guide*, September 5, 1964, p. A1.

HARRIS, JOANNE. "Questions, No Doubt." *American Visions*, October–November 1992, p. 22.

"HBO Show for Gumbel." *New York Times*, February 7, 1995, sec. B, p. 19.

"Helen O'Connell Obituary." *Washington Times*, September 10, 1993, sec. B, p. 2.

HELLMICH, NANCI. "Watching Kathleen Sullivan Watch Her Weight." *USA Today*, January 5, 1994, p. 5.

HENNINGER, DANIEL. "The Anchorman Chronicles: Geneva." *Wall Street Journal*, January 11, 1985, p. 18.

HEVESI, DENNIS. "Anita Colby, 77, a 'Supermodel' Who Also Wrote on Beauty, Dies." *New York Times*, March 28, 1992, p. 30.

HICKEY, NEIL. "He Starts His Day with Homework." *TV Guide*, August 1, 1964, p. 4.

——. "Peace, It's Wonderful!" *TV Guide*, January 25, 1975, p. 8.

——. "The Man with the $175,000 Smile." *TV Guide*, January 30, 1965, p. 20.

——. "The Not-So-Hard Times of a Newscaster." *TV Guide*, February 28, 1972, p. 44.

——. "*Today*'s Yesterdays." *TV Guide*, January 11, 1992, p. 14.

——. "Too Big Too Soon?" *TV Guide*, August 27, 1977, p. 23.

HIGGINS, GEORGE V. "What's News Got to Do With It?" *Wall Street Journal*, August 4, 1986, p. 13.

HILL, DOUG. "Watch Out for Her Surprise Offensive." *TV Guide*, September 2, 1989, p. 12.

HILTBRAND, DAVID. "The *Today* Show." *People*, July 2, 1990, p. 7.

——. "Tube." *People*, November 6, 1995, p. 15.

HILTON, RONALD. "ABC and the Kremlin." *New York Times*, December 21, 1975, sec. B, p. 35.

HINE, AL. "Garroway at Home." *Holiday*, March, 1955, p. 14.

HOBAN, PHOEBE. "The Loved One." *New York*, July 23, 1990, p. 24.

HOFFMAN, JAN. "Doctor, Doctor, Give Us the News." *New York Times*, October 27, 1991, sec. B, p. 29.

———. "There's Been a Change in the Weather." *New York Times*, July 29, 1990, sec. B, p. 25.

"A Holocaust Survivor Remembers on *GMA*." *USA Today*, May 7, 1985, sec. D, p. 3.

HUGHES, MIKE. "Cracks in CBS Coverage." *Gannett News Service*, February 15, 1994, sec. D, p. 1.

"'I'm a Lord-Knows-What.'" *TV Guide*, January 2, 1965, p. 12.

IRVINE, REED, AND JOE GOULDEN. "Commentary." *Washington Times*, May 14, 1992, sec. G, p. 4.

"It Pays to Monkey Around." *Variety*, March 7, 1956, p. 31.

"It's Extravaganza Cross-the-Board in CBS-TV's Bid for Breakfast Mob." *Variety*, April 28, 1954, p. 15.

"It was Different on *GMA*." *Newsday*, March 13, 1989, sec. B, p. 7.

"Jack Lescoulie, *Today* Show Pioneer, Dies." *Los Angeles Times*, July 23, 1987, sec. A, p. 3.

JACOBS, A. J. "Gumbel's Gamble." *Entertainment Weekly*, December 9, 1994, p. 10.

JAHR, CLIFF. "A Voice for Today." *Parade Magazine*, June 9, 1985, p. 4.

JAMES, CARYN. "How Keaton Commanded His Life's Last Stage." *New York Times*, October 6, 1996, sec. B, p. 48.

JENSEN, ELIZABETH. "Great Scott! Gumbel Becomes a 'Diplomat' on Return." *New York Daily News*, March 7, 1989, p. 7.

"Jim Hartz Is Named a Co-Host of *Today*." *New York Times*, July 23, 1974, p. 67.

"Joan Calls It Splits." *People*, February 10, 1992, p. 42.

"Joan Lunden." In *Current Biography*. New York: H. W. Wilson, 1989.

JOHNSON, PETER. "A President and a Protest Greet *Today* Studio." *USA Today*, June 21, 1994, sec. D, p. 3.

———. "ABC Chief Sticks with Embattled *GMA* Team." *USA Today*, July 14, 1998, sec. D, p. 3.

———. "Amid *GMA* Storm, Christian Taking Off." *USA Today*, July 16, 1998, sec. D, p. 3.

———. "Brinkley's ADM Ads Air Again during His Old Show." *USA Today*, May 11, 1998, sec. D, p. 3.

———. "CBS Gets Gumbel at $5M at Year." *USA Today*, March 13, 1997, sec. D, p. 1.

———. "CBS Still Gumbel's Address." *USA Today*, May 21, 1998, sec. D, p. 3.

———. "CBS Studies New Dawn for Old *This Morning*." *USA Today*, July 20, 1998, sec. D, p. 3.

———. "*Dateline* Star's Deal Second to Brokaw's." *USA Today*, June 18, 1998, sec. D, p. 3.

———. "Dawning of a New Format for *CBS Morning News*." *USA Today*, May 5, 1996, sec. D, p. 3.

———. "Different Hours, More or Less, for Newsmags." *USA Today*, May 18, 1998, sec. D, p. 4.

———. "ESPN Anchor May Be in Running for *GMA* Job." *USA Today*, December 17, 1996, sec. D, p. 4.

———. "Katie Couric Expecting 2nd Child." *USA Today*, June 27, 1995, sec. D, p. 3.

———. "Kondracke and Barnes Bid McLaughlin Bye-Bye." *USA Today*, May 5, 1998, sec. D, p. 3.

———. "Lauer Avoids Rumor in Interview with Hillary." *USA Today*, September 6, 1998, sec. D, p. 3.

———. "Matt Lauer Steps Up as *Today* Co-Anchor Jan. 6." *USA Today*, December 24, 1996, sec. D, p. 3.

———. "MSNBC to Add Delay after Showing Suicide." *USA Today*, May 4, 1998, sec. D, p. 3.

———. "Network News Shuffle." *USA Today,* March 14, 1997, sec. D, p. 1.

———. "New *GMA.*" *USA Today,* April 30, 1998, sec. D, p. 3.

———. "Rooney Still Steamed About 1990 Suspension." *USA Today,* December 23, 1996, sec. D, p. 3.

———. "*20/20, PrimeTime* Officially One Newsmag." *USA Today,* May 20, 1998, sec. D, p. 3.

———. "Zahn, Smith Bid Adieu to the *Morning* Beat." *USA Today,* June 17, 1996, sec. D, p. 3.

JOHNSON, PETER, AND ALAN BASH. "Child-Death Case Grabs Talk Shows, Newsmags." *USA Today,* November 7, 1994, sec. D, p. 3.

———. "McEwen Senses Upturn On CBS' New *Morning.*" *USA Today,* August 12, 1996, sec. D, p. 3.

JOHNSON, PETER, AND BRIAN DONLON. "Scott's Cloudy Mood." *USA Today,* March 3, 1989, sec. D, p. 1.

JOHNSON, PETER, MATT ROUSH, AND ALAN BASH. "E! Entertainment Axes an Unsuspecting Sullivan." *USA Today,* July 11, 1996, sec. D, p. 3.

JOHNSON, PETER, AND ANN OLDENBERG. "CBS' New *Morning* May Leave Smith Out in Cold." *USA Today,* March 6, 1996, sec. D, p. 3.

JOHNSTON, LAURIE. "Notes on *People.*" *New York Times,* March 24, 1976, p. 28.

JOHNSTON, LAURIE, AND ALBIN KREBS. "Rona Barrett Bids *Good Morning* Goodbye, NBC Hello." *New York Times,* July 25, 1980, sec. D, p. 12.

JULIAN, JESSICA. "How Are Hughes and Sally Doing?" *New York Times,* September 2, 1973, sec. B, p. 10.

"Julia Roberts—From Pretty Woman to Party Woman?" *Mr. Showbiz,* September 10, 1996. >www.mrshowbiz.com<

KAITER, JOANMARIE. "Good-Hearted or Ruthless—or Both?" *TV Guide,* September 5, 1987, p. 26.

———. "List-Maker Bryant Gumbel Strives to Control Every Aspect of His Life, and Boils Over If He Can't." *TV Guide,* June 15, 1985, p. 26.

KANE, MARY. "NCL Hopes *Today* Broadcasts Will Create a Wave of Bookings." *Travel Weekly,* May 29, 1986, p. 1.

KAPLAN, JANICE. "Bryant Gumbel: A Talk with the *Today* Anchor at the Top of His Game." *TV Guide,* June 17, 1995, p. 26.

———. "Joan Lunden Takes On Her New Life." *TV Guide,* March 30, 1996, p. 20.

———. "Morning Television: The Mayhem Behind the Scenes." *Cosmopolitan,* July 1989, p. 158.

KAPLAN, PETER W. "Hartman Reassuring in 'Future Is Now.'" *Dallas Morning News,* June 3, 1985, sec. E, p. 1.

KASINDORF, JEANIE. "The *Today* Show—Yup and Coming." *New York,* August 26, 1983, p. 17.

"Katie Couric." In *Current Biography.* New York: H. W. Wilson, 1993.

"Katie Couric: *Today*'s Savvy Co-Anchor Put Her Show Back on Top by Excelling." *People,* December 28, 1992, 74.

KAUFMAN, JOANNE. "Katie Couric Today." *TV Guide,* February 6, 1993, p. 10.

KAUFMAN, JOANNE, AND ALAN CARTER. "Newcomer Deborah Norville Stirs the Latest Tempest in the *Today* Show's Coffee Cup." *People,* October 9, 1989, p. 48.

KAYE, ELIZABETH. "The Cat Is Back!" *Mademoiselle,* February 1990, p. 120.

KAYLIN, LUCY. "Zucker Unbound." *Gentlemen's Quarterly,* October 1992, p. 193.

KELLOGG, CYNTHIA. "Television Jill-of-All-Trades." *New York Times,* October 18, 1953, sec. B, p. 12.

KELLY, JAMES, WITH LAWRENCE MONDT. "Snap, Crackle, Pop at Daybreak." *Time,* June 24, 1985, p. 88.

KELLY, KATY. "CBS Gets Angel of the Morning." *USA Today,* February 17, 1994, p. 8.

KENNEDY, DANA, WITH JENNIFER PENDLETON. "*Today* Tomorrow." *Entertainment Weekly,* March 29, 1996, p. 6.

KESSLER, JUDY. *Inside Today: The Battle for the Morning.* New York: Villard Books, 1992.

KING, BILL. "Sandi Freeman Turns Up on ABC." *Atlanta Constitution,* May 17, 1985, p. 19.

———. "Sawyer Has the First-Day Jitters in Debut on CBS' *Morning News.*" *Atlanta Constitution,* July 9, 1985, sec. B, p. 9.

———. "Sawyer May Replace CBS Co-Anchor." *Atlanta Constitution,* May 29, 1985, sec. D, p. 1.

———. "WAGA Cancels Low-Rated *CBS Morning News.*" *Atlanta Constitution,* August 6, 1986, sec. B, p. 1.

———. "Worst Morning News Shows." *Atlanta Constitution,* September 11, 1986, sec. B, p. 10.

KIRK, DON. "For News Correspondents, Visit to Vietnam Is a Rerun." *USA Today,* April 29, 1985, sec. A, p. 9.

KIRKPATRICK, DAVID. "Advertisers Crash Crowd Outside *Today.*" *Wall Street Journal,* April 24, 1996, sec. B, p. 1.

KISSELOFF, JEFF. *The Box: An Oral History of Television, 1920–1961.* New York: Viking Penguin, 1995.

"Kissinger Is Guest Weatherman." *Washington Times,* May 22, 1991, sec. A, p. 2.

KITMAN, MARVIN. "A Slice of Gumbel Pie." *Newsday,* March 7, 1989, sec. B, p. 7.

———. "Audience Can't Revive *CBS Morning Show.*" *Newsday,* October 26, 1995, sec. B, p. 65.

———. "Coming Clean: Bryant Gumbel Was Misjudged." *Newsday,* January 3, 1997, sec. B, p. 2.

———. "Katie vs. Deborah: A Case of Charisma." *TV Guide,* May 11, 1991, p. 30.

———. "Nobody Can Steal Their Thunder." *TV Guide,* July 6, 1991, p. 24.

KLEINFIELD, N. R. "The Networks' New Advertising Dance." *New York Times,* July 29, 1990, sec. C, p. 1.

KLEMESBUD, JUDY. "Oh, How She Loves to Get Up in the Morning . . ." *New York Times,* July 2, 1967, sec. B, p. 15.

KLOER, PHIL. "New Contract Won't Humble NBC's Gumbel." *Atlanta Constitution,* August 8, 1988, sec. D, p. 1.

KOLBERT, ELIZABETH. "From the Rose Garden, the Bush TV Show." *New York Times,* July 2, 1992, p. 14.

———. "Perot Takes Issue, While Clinton Takes On Issue." *New York Times,* June 12, 1992, p. 14.

———. "Sticking to the Rose Garden to Avoid Thorns in the Side." *New York Times,* May 28, 1993, p. 15.

———. "Talk Shows Wrangling to Book the Candidates." *New York Times,* July 6, 1992, p. 10.

———. "*Today* Producer Called Ready to Drop News Job." *New York Times,* March 16, 1993, sec. C, p. 18.

KOVACH, BILL. "Big Deals, with Journalism Thrown In." *New York Times,* August 3, 1995, p. 25.

KOWET, DON. "Media Found Flat-Footed in Gorbachev Ouster." *Washington Times,* August 20, 1991, sec. B, p. 7.

———. "Scanning the Airwaves." *Washington Times*, February 7, 1991, sec. E, p. 1.

———. "Scanning the Airwaves." *Washington Times*, February 18, 1991, sec. E, p. 1.

———. "Scanning the Airwaves." *Washington Times*, March 1, 1991, sec. E, p. 1.

———. "The Return of Uncle Feelgood." *Washington Times*, July 27, 1990, sec. E, p. 1.

KOWET, DON, GARY ARNOLD, AND DAVID COIA. "Scanning the Airwaves." *Washington Times*, February 20, 1991, sec. E, p. 1.

KREBS, ALBIN. "CBS Picks Woman as Half of Its Team for *Morning News*." *New York Times*, June 22, 1973, p. 71.

———. "Notes on *People*." *New York Times*, July 6, 1971, p. 10.

———. "Notes on *People*." *New York Times*, October 12, 1971, p. 40.

———. "Notes on *People*." *New York Times*, January 15, 1972, sec B, p. 3.

———. "TV: Rudd and Miss Quinn in Debut on CBS News." *New York Times*, August 7, 1973, p. 74.

KRIPKE, PAMELA GWYN. "TV Anchor with a Hint of Mischief." *New York Times*, August 21, 1994, sec. XIII, p. 9, West Coast edition.

KRUPP, CHARLA. "Deborah Norville: Southern Belle or Steel Magnolia?" *Glamour*, December 1990, p. 168.

———. "The *Today* Show's Katie Couric: Score One for Real Women." *Glamour*, July 1991, p. 110.

KUBASIK, BEN. "Tension Nags *Today* Staff." *Newsday*, March 14, 1989, p. 6.

KURTZ, HOWARD, AND DAVID S. BRODER. "In Tobacco Flare-Up, Echoes of the Old Dole." *Washington Post*, July 4, 1996, sec. A, p. 1.

LAMPERT, LESLIE. "Katie's Place." *Ladies' Home Journal*, May 1994, p. 168.

LASKIN, DAVID. "A Change in the Weather." *New York Times*, February 18, 1996, sec. B, p. 36.

"Last Week NBC's *Today* Was Celebrating the Program's Longest Winning Streak." *Broadcasting & Cable*, September 16, 1996, p. 93.

LAWSON, CAROL. "Can a Kosher Snack Climb to Stardom?" *New York Times*, July 31, 1996, sec. C, p. 1.

LEV, MICHAEL. "Forgoing Copywriter Fame to Feed for TV's 'Dragon.'" *New York Times*, December 26, 1991, sec. D, p. 5.

LEVIN, ERIC. "TV Teletype: New York." *TV Guide*, January 5, 1974, p. 34.

LEVIN, GARY. "Webs Serve Morning Fare with Fresh Mugs." *Variety*, July 1, 1996, p. 23.

LEVIN, GARY, AND PETER JOHNSON. "Four More Years, $7M for Couric." *USA Today*, June 29, 1998, sec. D, p. 1.

LEVINE, IRVING R. "Instant Celebrity." *TV Guide*, October 30, 1971, p. 29.

"Lew Wood Replacing Frank Blair on *Today*." *New York Times*, December 25, 1974, p. 45.

LIEBERMAN, DAVID. "Paula in the Morning." *TV Guide*, March 24, 1990, p. 27.

"Life As an Also-Ran: CBS's A.M. Problem," *Broadcasting*, July 8, 1985, p. 36.

LIPINSKI, ANN MARIE, AND JOHN KASS. "For Dotson, Webb." *Chicago Tribune*, May 14, 1985, sec. B, p. 1.

LIPKIN, REBECCA. "Cast and Crew of *Today* Look Back and Ahead." *Back Stage*, February 19, 1982, p. 25.

LIPPMAN, JOHN. "CBS Tells Affiliates of Plans to Boost Rank Via Live Audience." *Wall Street Journal*, June 15, 1995, sec. B, p. 5.

LIPTON, MICHAEL L., WITH ANNE LONGLEY. "Making News." *People*, September 9, 1996, p. 113.

LOEB, KAREN. "*Today* Hosts with the Mostest." *USA Today,* January 27, 1987, sec. D, p. 1.

LOUIE, ELAINE. "Renovations at *Good Morning America.*" *New York Times,* December 1, 1994, sec. C, p. 8.

LUNDEN, JOAN. "I've Learned to Look for the Joy in Each Day." *Good Housekeeping,* April 1997, p. 86.

LUNDEN, JOAN, WITH ARDY FRIEDBERG. *Good Morning, I'm Joan Lunden.* New York: G. P. Putnam's Sons, 1986.

LUSCOMBE, BELINDA. "A Cold Front Willard Didn't Forecast." *Time,* May 8, 1995, p. 103.

LYMAN, JACK. "Five Who Survived." *TV Guide,* September 19, 1970, p. 56.

LYNCH, LORRIE. "Press-Shy Star Opens Up for Steinem." *USA Today,* June 19, 1986, sec. D, p. 1.

LYNN, ALLISON. "Gumbel Under Glass." *People,* July 4, 1994, p. 40.

MACKENZIE, ROBERT. "Review: *Today.*" *TV Guide,* April 30, 1977, p. 4.

MADDOCKS, MELVIN. "End of the Garroway Era." *Christian Science Monitor,* July 15, 1961, p. 7.

"Magid Firm Jumps from ABC to NBC." *Broadcasting,* January 2, 1984, p. 78.

MAKSIAN, GEORGE. "Bryant, Willard: Peace at Last." *New York Daily News,* March 8, 1989, p. 78.

——. "Gumbel, Scott: Face-To-Face, Cheek-To-Cheek." *New York Daily News,* March 14, 1989, p. 95.

——. "Nice to Bryant . . . for *Today.*" *New York Post,* March 1, 1989, p. 15.

——. "Not *Today.*" *New York Daily News,* March 6, 1989, p. 43.

——. "Showdown Will Have to Wait." *New York Daily News,* March 2, 1989, p. 72.

——. "Three-Way News Battle for Early Viewers Is Hotter than Breakfast." *Atlanta Constitution,* January 15, 1985, sec. B, p. 11.

MARGOLICK, DAVID. "Judge in the Simpson Case Eases Restrictions on Jurors." *New York Times,* November 9, 1994, p. 20.

MARIN, RICK. "TV Hosts Round Up POWs for Questioning." *Washington Times,* March 11, 1991, sec. E, p. 1.

MARIN RICK, AND YAHLIN CHANG. "The Katie Factor." *Newsweek,* July 6, 1998, 53.

MARION, JANE. "It's Brother vs. Brother for TV's Morning Viewers." *TV Guide,* July 14, 1990, 22.

——. "Mark McEwen, *This Morning*'s Weatherman: Dependably Breezy." *TV Guide,* September 30, 1989, p. 36.

MARRIOTT, MICHAEL. "Celebrities at Ringside: Better to See and Be Seen." *New York Times,* May 19, 1996, p. 37.

MARTON, JANE. "Being No. 1 Is Icing on the Cake." *TV Guide,* August 25, 1990, p. 24.

——. "Q. Can You Place This Face? A. He's *Good Morning America*'s Geography Editor." *TV Guide,* March 30, 1991, p. 15.

MATUSOW, BARBARA. "Heeeere's Katie!" *Washingtonian,* August 1990, p. 82.

MAX, D. T. "Sun Comes Up on *Today.*" *Variety,* September 28, 1992, p. 95.

MCCLELLAN, STEVE. "CBS Considers Sharing *This Morning* with Affiliates." *Broadcasting,* September 14, 1962, p. 25.

——. "CBS Revamps *CBS This Morning.*" *Broadcasting & Cable,* April 15, 1996, p. 40.

——. "Jane Pauley: Here at *Today,* Gone Tomorrow." *Broadcasting,* October 16, 1989, p. 30.

———. "NBC Brings Back Nuell for *Today*." *Broadcasting*, September 25, 1989, p. 30.

———. "NBC News Withdraws *Today* Offer to Nuell." *Broadcasting*, January 1, 1990, p. 108.

———. "NBC Takes *Today* Public." *Broadcasting & Cable*, June 27, 1994, p. 30.

———. "Reichblum to Be *GMA* Executive Producer." *Broadcasting & Cable*, November 1, 1993, p. 21.

———. "Rollins Exits *Today*." *Broadcasting & Cable*, November 22, 1993, p. 26.

McDARRAH, TIMOTHY. "Gumbel Fumbles Making Up with Willard." *New York Post*, March 7, 1989, p. 10.

McFADDEN, ROBERT D. "Fire at 30 Rockefeller Plaza Sends NBC Programs to 49th Street Sidewalk." *New York Times*, October 11, 1996, sec. B, p. 3.

"Meet the New Boss." *Harper's Magazine*, October 1995, p. 22.

MEISLER, ANDY. "A Real Man's Got to Know If He Should Carry a .357 Magnum—or a Bottle of Skin Bronzer." *TV Guide*, March 14, 1987, p. 8.

"Memo May Turn Viewers Off." *USA Today*, March 2, 1989, sec. D, p. 3.

METZ, ROBERT. *The Today Show*. Chicago: Playboy Press, 1977.

MIFFLIN, LAWRIE. "Emmy Nominations for News." *New York Times*, July 23, 1996, sec. C, p. 10.

———. "New News for the Morning." *New York Times*, April 10, 1996, sec. C, p. 18.

———. "News Instead of Cartoon." *New York Times*, December 4, 1996, sec. C, p. 18.

———. "TV Notes: A Morning Show Delay." *New York Times*, June 12, 1996, sec. C, p. 18.

MILES, LAUREEN, WITH KATHLEEN WALL. "Condom Conundrum." *Mediaweek*, June 12, 1995, p. 23.

MILLER, HOLLY G. "Joan Lunden: 46, Fit & Feisty." *Saturday Evening Post*, October 1, 1996, p. 38.

MILLER, MERLE. "Old Buttoned-Up." *TV Guide*, December 25, 1971, p. 10.

MILLER, MICHAEL W. "Tiffany Network's Farm Team Achieves Special Effect: Gilding Lillehammer's Lily." *Wall Street Journal*, February 14, 1994, sec. A, p. 14.

MILLSTEIN, GILBERT. "Meet the Man Who Succeeded Garroway." *TV Guide*, January 20, 1962, p. 10.

MOORE, FRAZIER. "Bryant Gumbel's Yesterdays, *Today* and Tomorrow." *News Journal*, December 27, 1996, sec. D, p. 3.

———. "Matt Lauer Gets Set for Dawn of a New *Today*." *Los Angeles Times*, December 31, 1996, p.14.

———. "*Today* Show Moves Into Own Glass House." *Washington Times*, June 16, 1994, sec. C, p. 18.

MORGAN, AL. "Around the World in 3640 Hours." *TV Guide*, May 24, 1969, p. 24.

"Morning Becomes Pauley." *Broadcasting*, June 2, 1986, p. 103.

"*Morning News*." *Variety*, January 16, 1952, p. 28.

"The Morning Program." *Variety*, January 21, 1987, p. 82.

"*The Morning Show*." *Variety*, March 17, 1954, p. 15.

"Mother Teresa." *Chicago Tribune*, December 27, 1985, p. 4.

"Mr. Dole's Smoke Rings." *New York Times*, July 4, 1996, p. 18.

MUELLER, GENE. "Even Though the Tears May Flow, I'll Keep On Enjoying My Lobster." *Washington Times*, June 20, 1994, sec. B, p. 7.

MURPHY, MARY. "Lauer's Hour." *TV Guide*, July 4, 1998, p. 17.

MURPHY, RYAN. "Good Morning, Joan Lunden." *Saturday Evening Post,* September 1988, p. 58.

"Musical Chairs on Morning Shows." *Advertising Age,* March 5, 1990, p. 32.

NAGOURNEY, ADAM. "Dole Criticizes Role of Press and Foes in Tobacco Debate." *New York Times,* July 3, 1996, p. 1.

"NBC Announces Co-Host on *Today* Won't Return." *New York Times,* April 5, 1991, sec. C, p. 24.

"NBC." *Television Digest,* August 17, 1992, p. 9.

"NBC News Responds to 'Gumblegate.'" *TV Guide,* October 3, 1992, p. 31.

"NBC News Shows Strength at Both Ends of the Day." *Television/Radio Age,* August 18, 1986, p. 54.

"NBC Reshuffles Slumping *Today* Show." *Washington Times,* May 16, 1990, sec. A, p. 2.

"NBC's Morning Man." *Broadcasting,* February 23, 1987, p. 95.

"NBC's Pauley Takes a Look at the Morning." *Broadcasting,* April 20, 1987, p. 60.

"NBC's *Today* Won the Three-Network Morning News Race for the Week Ended Feb. 7." *Broadcasting,* February 17, 1992, p. 72.

"NBC *Today* Program to Be Shown Every Day." *New York Times,* December 6, 1991, sec. C, p. 34.

"NBC-TV's Willard Scott: Making *Today* a Little Brighter." *Broadcasting,* January 8, 1986, p. 207.

"Neighbors Briefing." *Philadelphia Inquirer,* November 10, 1994, sec. CC, p. 3.

NEILAN, TERENCE. "Signoff: Bill Kurtis—Anchor, Producer, Idea Man." *New York Times,* July 28, 1996, sec. L, p. 51.

NESBITT, JEFF. "Disney Chief Keeps Deal Quiet as a Mouse." *Washington Times,* August 4, 1995, sec. B, p. 7.

"Network News in the Dark of Night." *Broadcasting,* September 27, 1982, p. 44.

"New Life in Morning Competition." *Broadcasting,* July 8, 1985, p. 38.

"New Studios in Rockefeller Center." *New York Times,* May 29, 1994, sec. J, p. 1.

O'CONNOR, JOHN J. "*A.M. America.*" *New York Times,* January 7, 1975, p. 57.

———. "'Easy-to-Swallow-with-the-Orange-Juice' News." *New York Times,* February 13, 1972, p. 71.

———. "Something for Viewers More Interested in the News Than in Personalities." *New York Times,* July 7, 1974, sec. D, p. 15.

———. "TV: A 7 O'Clock Debut." *New York Times,* November 4, 1975, p. 71.

———. "TV: ABC Picks Breezy Format for *AM America.*" *New York Times,* January 22, 1973, p. 77.

———. "TV: An Early-Morning Appraisal of Calley Trial." *New York Times,* April 7, 1971, p. 87.

———. "TV: Week-Long Irish Holiday via *Today* Show." *New York Times,* October 4, 1972, p. 91.

OLDENBURG, ANN, AND CHARLES SALZBERG. "The One Thing Paula Zahn Can't Do." *Redbook,* February 1995, p. 48.

"The Opinions of Martha Maples, Mother-to-Be." *Washington Times,* September 29, 1993, sec. A, p. 10.

ORR, JACK. "Good Morning, This Is *Today.*" *TV Guide,* February 8, 1989, p. 30.

PALL, ELLEN. "Will a Morning Star Continue to Shine at Night?" *New York Times,* June 24, 1990, sec. B, p. 29.

PANITT, MERRILL. "*CBS This Morning.*" *TV Guide,* May 14, 1988, p. 40.

Park, Jeannie, with Alan Carter. "With Big Bucks and a Big Job, CBS's Paula Zahn Wants to Grab Some ZZZs." *People,* July 9, 1990, p. 58.

Park, Jeannie, with Alan Carter, Gavin Moses, Sue Carswell, Michael Mason, and Marilyn Balamachi. "Two Was Company, Three a Crowd." *People,* November 13, 1989, p. 114.

"Patching Up a Family Feud on *Today.*" *USA Today,* March 13, 1989, sec. D, p. 3.

"Paula Zahn Leaves ABC." *Washington Times,* February 16, 1990, sec. A, p. 2.

Peters, Ida. "What's Happening: *CBS This Morning.*" *Washington Afro-American,* February 11, 1995, p. 4.

Petrucelli, Alan W. "Down-to-Earth Katie Couric." *Working Mother,* July–August 1996, p. 14.

Peyronnin, Joseph. "Olympics on CBS." *New York Times,* March 17, 1994, p. 22.

Pfizer, Beryl. "She Was Happy to Put Her Best Face Forward, But No One Could Agree . . ." *TV Guide,* July 8, 1961, p. 4.

Pina, Phillip. "Shut Out of O. J. Interview, Gumbel Ponders Future." *USA Today,* October 11, 1995, sec. D, p. 3.

Plaskin, Glenn. "Yesterday, *Today* and Tomorrow." *American Health,* March 1990, p. 71.

Plott, Monte. "CBS *Morning Program* Rises But Doesn't Shine in Premiere." *Atlanta Constitution,* January 13, 1987, sec. C, p. 1.

———. "*CBS This Morning* Debuts Monday under News Division." *Atlanta Constitution,* November 11, 1987, sec. B, p. 1.

———. "*Morning Program*'s News-Comedy Mix Leaves Television Critics Ill." *Atlanta Constitution,* February 1, 1987, TV supplement, p. 5.

———. "NBC News' Foray into China an Inspiring Success." *Atlanta Constitution,* September 28, 1987, sec. B, p. 7.

Polskin, Howard. "Who's Top of the Morning? Who's Got Egg on Their Faces?" *TV Guide,* August 19, 1989, p. 19.

Power, Jules. "*A.M. America* in Russia—Pro and Con." *New York Times,* November 30, 1975, sec. B, p. 31.

Pratt, Steven. "Weight-Loss Book Is Joan Lunden's Gain." *Philadelphia Inquirer,* May 1, 1996, sec. F, p. 1.

"Professor Garroway of 21-Inch U." *Time,* December 28, 1962, p. 35.

"The Program that Sounds Reveille." *TV Guide,* June 15, 1963, p. 12.

Pruden, Wesley. "Here's a Salute to the 'Brilliants.'" *Washington Times,* March 7, 1990, sec. A, p. 4.

Rader, Dotson. "The Quiet Rebellion of David Hartman." *Parade Magazine,* August 24, 1986, p. 4.

Randolph, Carol. "NBC's *Today* Show Smells Like Soap Opera." *Washington Times,* October 18, 1989, sec. B, p. 1.

"Rating for Quinn-Rudd." *New York Times,* August 25, 1973, p. 55.

Reed, J. D., with Alan Carter. "Her Uncertain Future Settled at Last, NBC's Jane Pauley Discovers There is *Real Life* and Normal Life After *Today.*" *People,* August 13, 1990, p. 66.

———. "*Today*'s Desperate Search for Tomorrow." *People,* August 13, 1990, p. 70.

Reed, Roy. "Daley Defends His Police; Humphrey Scores Clashes." *New York Times,* August 30, 1968, p. 1.

REILLY, RICK. "The Mourning Anchor." *Sports Illustrated,* September 26, 1988, p. 72.

"Remembering . . . with Jane Pauley." *Good Housekeeping,* July 1990, p. 46.

RENNERT, AMY. "*Today* Looks Bright to Pauley." *Dallas Morning News,* March 16, 1985, sec. C, p. 1.

"Restyled *CBS This Morning* Names Three New Co-Anchors." *New York Times,* May 9, 1996, sec. C, p. 20.

"Review: *The Morning Show.*" *TV Guide,* October 9, 1954, p. 20.

"Reviews: *Good Morning.*" *TV Guide,* April 28, 1956, p. 18.

"Reviews: *The Morning Show.*" *TV Guide,* July 9, 1954, p. 22.

REYNOLDS, BARBARA. "I've Been Blessed with Love of Family, Friends." *USA Today,* August 21, 1987, sec. A, p. 13.

RICE, LYNETTE. "CBS Stations Looking Local." *Broadcasting & Cable,* October 7, 1996, p. 50.

RICHMAN, ALAN. "Willard Scott Is Blowing His Top." *People,* March 20, 1989, p. 44.

RIFKIN, GLENN. "The Quiet Life as Pursued by David Hartman." *New York Times,* August 20, 1995, sec. H, p. 29.

ROBINS, J. MAX. "Showdown at Sunrise?" *TV Guide,* July 13, 1996, p. 26.

———. "Zucker—On Living in a Glass House." *Variety,* September 19, 1994, p. 39.

"Rollins Rejoins *CBS This Morning.*" *Washington Times,* July 24, 1992, sec. A, p. 2.

ROSEN, GEORGE. "Garroway *Today* Off to Boff Start as Revolutionary News Concept." *Variety,* January 16, 1952, p. 23.

ROSENBERG, HOWARD. "Food Lion, ABC and Tricks of the Trade." *Los Angeles Times,* January 24, 1997, Calendar section, p. 1.

———. "Goodbys from Heart to Hartman." *Los Angeles Times,* February 21, 1987, sec. F, p. 1.

———. "*Morning* Is Looking Up at CBS News." *Los Angeles Times,* September 4, 1985, sec. F, p. 1.

———. "So Who's Really in Charge in These Interviews?" *Los Angeles Times,* October 6, 1995, Calendar section, p. 1.

———. "The CBS Morning Agony: Digging into a Grab Bag." *Los Angeles Times,* August 4, 1986, sec. VI, p. 1.

———. "The Jerry and Jesse Show." *Los Angeles Times,* August 23, 1985, sec. F, p. 1.

———. "TV Hucksters on a Roll." *Los Angeles Times,* May 24, 1985, sec. F, p. 1.

———. "What's News Is Old in *Morning* Format at CBS." *Los Angeles Times,* December 14, 1987, sec. F, p. 1.

ROSENTHAL, ANDREW. "Focus Is Elusive for Bush." *New York Times,* July 2, 1992, p. 1.

ROSENTHAL, HERMAN, AND ILEANE RUDOLPH. "It's Christmas Time at the Morning Shows." *TV Guide,* December 21, 1991, p. 14.

ROUSH, MATT. "David Hartman Is Out as ABC's *Morning* Man." *USA Today,* October 2, 1986, sec. D, p. 1.

———. "Getting to the Heart of Gay Weddings." *USA Today,* November 7, 1996, sec. D, p. 3.

———. "Papal TV." *USA Today,* August 18, 1987, sec. D, p. 3.

ROUSH, MATT, AND BRIAN DONLON. "NBC and ABC Look Ahead." *USA Today,* August 13, 1987, sec. D, p. 3.

ROVIN, JEFF. "Jane's Search for Tomorrow." *Ladies' Home Journal,* July 1, 1990, p. 86.

———. "Joan Lunden: Now She's Got It All." *Ladies' Home Journal,* April 1987, p. 82.

ROYKO, MIKE. "Gary, Cathy and TV Bland Flakes." *Chicago Tribune*, May 16, 1985, p. 3.

———. "We're All Lost in the Mourning." *Chicago Tribune*, October 2, 1986, p. 3.

"Ruth Batchelor, Songwriter, 58." *New York Times*, July 29, 1992, sec. D, p. 19.

RYAN, MICHAEL, AND SALLY BEDELL. "Can a Host Still Be a Journalist?" *TV Guide*, May 14, 1977, p. 15.

SACK, KEVIN. "Perot Is Tangles in Contradictions in Debut of His Revived Campaign." *New York Times*, October 6, 1992, p. 15.

SAFIRE, WILLIAM. "Digging Deeper in Iraqgate." *New York Times*, July 6, 1992, p. 13.

SAFRAN, CLAIRE. "Joan Lunden: Good Morning, Heartache!" *Redbook*, August 1992, p. 80.

"Sally Quinn to Join *The Times* in Washington." *New York Times*, January 16, 1974, p. 67.

SANDERS, MARLENE. "How *Today* Really Lost Jane Pauley." *Good Housekeeping*, February 1990, p. 46.

SANDOMIR, RICHARD. "Albertville '92: CBS Winter Vacation Ends after 32 Years." *New York Times*, February 2, 1992, sec. 8A, p. 13.

SAXON, WOLFGANG. "S. M. Kritsick, 42, Veterinarian Gave TV Advice on Pets." *New York Times*, January 18, 1994, sec. D, p. 23.

SCARBOROUGH, ROWAN. "NBC News Chief Quits over Latest Firestorm." *Washington Times*, March 3, 1993, sec. A, p. 1.

SCHINDEHETTE, SUSAN, WITH KATY KELLY, ALAN CARTER, AND LEE POWELL. "Two Stars Vanish in a Blink of the CBS Eye." *People*, February 26, 1990, p. 30.

SCHMITT, ERIC. "With Copter Pilot's Return, U.S. Will Send Oil to North Korea." *New York Times*, January 6, 1995, p. 7.

SCHMUCKLER, ERIC. "ABC." *Mediaweek*, April 10, 1995, p. 8.

———. "NBC News Shows Mount Comeback." *Adweek*, February 28, 1994, p. 12.

———. "*Today* May Get Longer." *Mediaweek*, May 2, 1994, p. 3.

SCHNEIDER, KAREN, WITH SUE CARSWELL. "Live Wire." *People*, August 9, 1993, p. 70.

SCHNURNBERGER, LYNN. "The Look of Lauer." *TV Guide*, July 20, 1996, p. 8.

SCHOGOL, MARC. "The Scene in Bucks and Montgomery Counties." *Philadelphia Inquirer*, June 20, 1996, sec. B, p. 2.

SCHOOFS, MARK. "Lauer Power." *TV Guide*, June 18, 1994, p. 25.

SCHULTE, LUCY. "Roker the Rain King." *New York*, August 17, 1987, p. 20.

SCHWARTZ, TONY. "*Good Morning America* and *Today* in Fierce Competitive Duel." *New York Times*, November 4, 1980, sec. C, p. 17.

———. "Living for *Today*." *New York*, May 6, 1985, p. 28.

———. "NBC Hopes to Rise in Ratings on Wave of *Shogun*." *New York Times*, September 20, 1980, p. 43.

———. "New Programming Helps CBS and NBC in Ratings." *New York Times*, October 8, 1980, p. 27.

SCHWARZBAUM, LISA. "Matt Lauer of the *Today* Show: Hunka Hunka Mornin' Love." *Entertainment Weekly*, July 8, 1994, p. 43.

SCIOLINO, ELAINE. "Documents Warned in '85 of Iraqi Nuclear Aims." *New York Times*, July 8, 1992, p. 10.

SCOTT, SOPHFRONIA, WITH WENDY COLE. "Here We Go Again." *Time,* April 15, 1991, p. 57.

SCOTT, WILLARD. "Living on the Sunny Side." *Saturday Evening Post,* December 1983, p. 65.

"Secretary Shultz Interviewed on the *Today* Show." *Department of State Bulletin,* November 1982, p. 42.

"Secretary's Interview on *Today* Show." *Department of State Bulletin,* November 1986, p. 64.

"The Secret Life of Dave Garroway." *Look,* October 4, 1955, p. 36.

SEIDES, GILBERT. "Review: *The Dave Garroway Today Show.*" *TV Guide,* May 29, 1961, p. 23.

——. "Review: *The Today Show.*" *TV Guide,* September 23, 1961, p. 16.

SELIGSON, TOM. "The Truth About Jane Pauley." *Parade Magazine,* September 20, 1987, p. 4.

SERVAAS, CORY. "Harry Smith: Man with a Mission." *Saturday Evening Post,* May–June 1993, p. 40.

SHALES, TOM. "Even Without Phyllis, *CBS Morning News* Is Bad." *Chicago Tribune,* September 30, 1985, sec. E, p. 5.

——. "George Says She Meant No Offense." *Los Angeles Times,* May 17, 1985, sec. F, p. 19.

——. "Hartman Bright Enough to Shine in TV Ratings." *Chicago Tribune,* January 22, 1985, sec. E, p. 7.

——. "Kurtis Says George Adds 'Class' to Morning News." *Chicago Tribune,* January 17, 1985, sec. E, p. 9.

——. "Portrait: Bryant Gumbel." *Life,* August 1982, p. 19.

——. "Suggestion to Embrace Puts George on Hot Seat." *Los Angeles Times,* May 16, 1985, sec. F, p. 11.

——. "Will Panic Grip Huggable *CBS Morning News?*" *Chicago Tribune,* June 13, 1985, sec. E, p. 13.

SHANLEY, JOHN P. "Early Bird on TV." *New York Times,* August 31, 1959, sec. B, p. 9.

SHARBUTT, JAY. "After 10 Years, Hartman Still Shines in *Morning.*" *Los Angeles Times,* November 7, 1985, sec. F, p. 1.

——. "Anchors, Producer on Stump for *Morning News.*" *Los Angeles Times,* January 20, 1986, sec. F, p. 5.

——. "Atlanta Affiliate Pulls Away from CBS—Temporarily." *Los Angeles Times,* August 13, 1986, sec. VI, p. 1.

——. "Bell: Goodbye to *Good Morning.*" *Los Angeles Times,* December 20, 1986, sec. VI, p. 10.

——. "CBS and Phyllis George: It Just Didn't Work Out." *Los Angeles Times,* September 4, 1985, sec. F, p. 1.

——. "CBS Makes Big Splash of Its News." *Los Angeles Times,* May 24, 1985, sec. F, p. 1.

——. "CBS Maps Course to Brighter Mornings." *Los Angeles Times,* August 13, 1986, sec. VI, p. 1.

——. "*CBS Morning News* Revamp Is Promised." *Los Angeles Times,* May 24, 1986, sec. F, p. 1.

——. "CBS' *Morning* Survives First Tough Year." *Los Angeles Times,* November 20, 1988, sec. F, p. 1.

——. "George Out of Morning Show at CBS." *Los Angeles Times,* August 31, 1985, sec. E, p. 1.

——. "Gibson and Mudd Make It Official." *Los Angeles Times,* January 30, 1987, sec. F, p. 1.

——. "Hartley Makes an Early Exit from CBS' Ill-Fated *Morning Program.*" *Los Angeles Times,* November 11, 1987, sec. F, p. 9.

——. "Jumping from Print to TV Journalism." *Los Angeles Times,* January 31, 1985, sec. F, p. 1.

——. "McGrady Will Produce Walters' ABC Specials." *Los Angeles Times,* July 12, 1986, sec. V, p. 12.

———. "NBC Expanding *Today* Show to Sundays Come September," *Los Angeles Times*, May 6, 1987, sec. F, p. 1.

———. "New CBS Morning Show to Bow Jan. 12." *Los Angeles Times*, November 20, 1986, sec. B, p. 12.

———. "New *Today* Dawns for Steinem," *Los Angeles Times*, July 22, 1986, sec. F, p. 1.

———. "Rodgers in as CBS A.M. *News* Chief." *Los Angeles Times*, October 30, 1985, sec. F, p. 1.

———. "Rose Gets News Slot." *Los Angeles Times*, August 22, 1986, sec. VI, p. 27.

———. "Rx for Ailing *Morning News*." *Los Angeles Times*, August 17, 1985, sec. F, p. 1.

———. "Shanks Hired for CBS Morning Show." *Los Angeles Times*, September 5, 1986, sec. F, p. 20.

———. "'Stars of Tomorrow' on *Today*." *Los Angeles Times*, July 5, 1985, sec. V, p. 1.

———. "Sullivan to Co-Host New CBS A.M. News Show." *Los Angeles Times*, October 1, 1987, sec. F, p. 10.

———. "The Ins and Outs at *CBS Morning News*." *Los Angeles Times*, June 1, 1985, sec. E, p. 1.

———. "The News Arrives in 2 New Packages." *Los Angeles Times*, November 30, 1987, sec. F, p. 1.

———. "*Today* Show Tops Ratings." *Los Angeles Times*, March 29, 1985, sec. VI, p. 24.

———. "What's Next for CBS Morning Lineup?" *Los Angeles Times*, April 26, 1987, sec. F, p. 1.

———. "Winston Objects to CBS Plan for *Morning News*." *Los Angeles Times*, July 29, 1986, sec. F, p. 1.

———. "Winston Says Goodbye to CBS Morning News." *Los Angeles Times*, July 30, 1986, sec. VI, p. 1.

SHAW, JESSICA. "Deaths." *Entertainment Weekly*, December 15, 1995, p. 24.

SHEPARD, RICHARD F. "Chancellor Is Set as Host of *Today*." *New York Times*, July 5, 1961, p. 67.

———. "Comes the Dawn—and Garroway." *New York Times*, July 24, 1960, sec. B, p. 11.

———. "Garroway Resigns as Host of *Today* after Ten Years." *New York Times*, May 27, 1961, p. 47.

———. "The New Newsman on *Today*." *New York Times*, August 13, 1961, sec. B, p. 13.

SHERMAN, BETH. "TV Host's Mild Workout." *Newsday*, March 20, 1995, sec. B, p. 16.

SHERMAN, ERIC. "*Good Morning America* Turns Fifteen." *Ladies' Home Journal*, November 1990, p. 132.

SHERWOOD, RICK. "Willard Scott Doesn't See Clouds in Life." *Los Angeles Times*, January 12, 1988, sec. F, p. 1.

SHISTER, GAIL. "From the ABC News Ranks, A New *Good Morning America* Chief." *Philadelphia Inquirer*, December 11, 1995, sec. D, p. 8.

———. "*GMA* and *Today* Both Have a Claim to Be No. 1 in the Morning." *Philadelphia Inquirer*, October 21, 1993, sec. F, p. 8.

———. "Gumbel's 35-Page Wish Is Coming True: *Today* Is Going to Zimbabwe." *Philadelphia Inquirer*, November 11, 1992, sec. F, p. 4.

———. "It's a Race in the A.M., and *Today* Is on a Roll." *Philadelphia Inquirer*, November 10, 1994, sec. E, p. 1.

———. "Morning Shows Cancel Their Hillary Rodham Clinton Interviews." *Philadelphia Inquirer*, December 23, 1993, sec. E, p. 6.

———. "New *Good Morning America* Boss Glad of Chaotic Days at Channel 3." *Philadelphia Inquirer,* November 3, 1993, sec. E, p. 4.

———. "Ratings Make It a Good Morning for *Today.*" *Philadelphia Inquirer,* February 15, 1992, sec. C, p. 6.

———. "*This Morning* Gains in Ratings, Not in Respect." *Philadelphia Inquirer,* April 7, 1993, sec. D, p. 6.

———. "Turnabout in Air Play: *Today* Is No. 1 for First Time Since Nov. 2." *Philadelphia Inquirer,* July 16, 1993, sec. F, p. 4.

———. "Words Fly Over ABC's Latest Travel Deal for *Good Morning America.*" *Philadelphia Inquirer,* April 1, 1993, sec. E, p. 6.

"Showdown at Sunrise." *Fortune,* March 4, 1985, p. 10.

SIEGEL, ED. "The CBS Morning Blues." *Boston Globe,* February 11, 1985, p. 21.

SILVER, SUSAN L. "*This Morning's* Paula Zahn." *Saturday Evening Post,* January–February 1993, p. 39.

"Singing a Different Song." *TV Guide,* May 11, 1957, p. 28.

SKLAR, ZACHARY. "Is It News? Is It Show Biz? It's *AM America!*" *New York Times,* January 5, 1975, sec. B, p. 1.

SMITH, DESMOND. "The Lock Look in the Morning." *New York,* April 19, 1982, p. 31.

———. "The Third Man," *New York,* January 31, 1983, p. 27.

SMITH, LAURA C. "'Hello, I'm Barbara Walters.'" *Entertainment Weekly,* December 16, 1994, p. 88.

SMITH, LIZ. "Costner's Catch of the Day? Joan Lunden of ABC." *Philadelphia Inquirer,* August 7, 1995, sec. G, p. 2.

———. "Scoop du Jour." *Vogue,* April 1987, p. 332.

SNOW, SHAUNA. "Morning Report." *Los Angeles Times,* May 9, 1996, Calendar section, p. 2.

SPORKIN, ELIZABETH. "She's the Very Model of a Fashion Reporter." *USA Today,* December 29, 1983, sec. D, p. 3.

STAYON, ROBERT LEWIS. "Dave Garroway Tomorrow." *Saturday Review,* July 15, 1961, p. 34.

STEIN, LISA. "Will Katie Couric Be Deborah Norville's Substitute—or Successor?" *TV Guide,* December 29, 1990, p. 25.

STEWART, NORMAN. "Dan Rather's Newscast Signoff Not Original." *Washington Times,* January 5, 1990, sec. F, p. 2.

"Still the Chimp." *TV Guide,* July 19, 1975, p. 2.

STONE, JUDITH. "Jane Pauley's Charmed Life." *McCall's,* April 1987, p. 152.

STONE, SALLY. "McEwen: 'They're Actually Paying Me to Do This.'" *Indianapolis Recorder,* October 22, 1994, p. 16.

STORY, RICHARD DAVID. "Willard Scott: Sunny and Warm." *USA Today,* October 4, 1985, sec. W, p. 4.

"Sullivan May Be Off CBS Morning Show." *New York Times,* February 9, 1990, sec. C, p. 28.

SUMMERS, CAROL. "Forecast for *Today:* Cloudy—Letter." *New York Times,* July 1, 1990, sec. F, p. 4.

SWASY, ALECIA. "After You've Been a Beauty Queen and a News Anchor, What's Left?" *Wall Street Journal,* October 22, 1986, p. 35.

SWERTLOW, FRANK SEAN. "Brokaw May Replace Hartz as Host of *Today* Show," *TV Guide,* June 12, 1976, p. A1.

———. "Lindsay's Interview with Shah Raises Questions on ABC." *TV Guide,* August 7, 1976, p. A1.

——. "*Today* Dropping Walters in June, Seeks Replacement." *TV Guide*, May 15, 1976, p. A1.

"Tele Follow-Up Comment." *Variety*, March 5, 1952, p. 22.

"Tele Follow-Up Comment." *Variety*, April 2, 1952, p. 19.

"Tele Follow-Up Comment." *Variety*, August 18, 1954, p. 15.

"Tele Follow-Up Comment." *Variety*, July 26, 1961, p. 31.

"Tele Follow-Up Comment." *Variety*, September 12, 1962, p. 43.

"Tele Follow-Up Comment." *Variety*, July 1, 1964, p. 43.

"Tele Follow-Up Comment." *Variety*, May 26, 1965, p. 48.

"Tele Follow-Up Comment." *Variety*, September 5, 1984, p. 42.

"Tele Follow-Up Comment." *Variety*, April 10, 1985, p. 41.

THOMAS, CAL. "Getting the Pre-Emptive Hook at ABC." *Washington Times*, June 29, 1989, sec. F, p. 3.

"*Today*." *Variety*, January 21, 1959, p. 18.

"*Today*." *Variety*, April 8, 1959, p. 15.

"*Today*." *Variety*, April 30, 1959, p. 14.

"*Today*." *Variety*, January 17, 1962, p. 23.

"*Today*." *Variety*, April 1, 1964, p. 45.

"*Today*." *Variety*, September 30, 1964, p. 81.

"*Today*." *Variety*, November 16, 1966, p. 56.

"*Today* and Tomorrow." *Time*, January 28, 1952, p. 64.

"*Today* Gives ABC Morning Sickness." *Advertising Age*, February 10, 1986, p. 3.

"*Today*'s 30th—Growth in A.M." *Back Stage*, January 22, 1982, p. 39.

"*Today*'s Woman." *TV Guide*, January 16, 1960, p. 28.

"Town, Fooled by Hoax, Wants Willard Scott." *Atlanta Constitution*, August 4, 1988, sec. C, p. 4.

TOWNLEY, RODERICK. "He Must Learn to Be More Comfortable with Dolly Parton." *TV Guide*, December 5, 1987, p. 37.

——. "Today a Lady in Cleveland Turns 100 and . . . Oh Yes, It's 41—in Detroit." *TV Guide*, December 11, 1982, p. 22.

"Travel Trouble Keeps ABC Show at Home." *Chicago Tribune*, April 12, 1986, p. 4.

TRESCOTT, JACQUELINE. "Waking Up with Charles Gibson." *Atlanta Constitution*, June 21, 1987, p. 4.

"Truman, 'Kibitzer,' Gets on a TV Show." *New York Times*, July 2, 1953, p. 16.

"TV Newspaper." *Time*, September 15, 1952, p. 104.

"TV Producer Andrea Smith Named Book Editor of *Today* Show." *Publishers Weekly*, September 20, 1991, p. 17.

"TV's *Today* Show Originates Here." *Chicago*, May 1982, p. 14.

VAN GELDER, LAWRENCE. "Erma Bombeck Dies at 69; Put Howls into Humdrum." *New York Times*, April 23, 1996, sec. B, p. 9.

——. "Victim's Wife Files Lawsuit in NBC Killing." *New York Times*, September 21, 1994, sec. B, p. 2.

VEALE, SCOTT. "In an Uphill Ratings Battle, Bryant Gumbel is *Today*'s Man of the Earlier Hour." *People*, July 5, 1982, p. 43.

VIZARD, MARY McALEER. "A Newcomer Roils a Lake Community." *New York Times*, September 9, 1990, sec. J, p. 3.

WAGGONER, DIANNA. "Di's Brother: New Man on the Beat." *People*, March 2, 1987, p. 22.

WALLEY, WAYNE. "ABC Ties Ads, Themes on Morning Show." *Advertising Age*, April 30, 1990, p. 51.

———. "Morning Shows Rise and Shine." *Advertising Age,* July 17, 1989, p. 38.

WALLS, JEANNETTE. "Strong Faith." *New York,* March 4, 1991, p. 16.

"The *Washington Times* Guide to Has-Beens of the '80s." *Washington Times,* November 24, 1989, sec. E, p. 1.

WATERS, HARRY F. "If It Ain't Broke, Break It." *Newsweek,* March 26, 1990, p. 58.

WATERS, HARRY F., WITH NEAL KARLEN. "Crunch in the Morning." *Newsweek,* September 13, 1982, p. 84.

WATKINS, JIM. "Reruns." *New York Times,* November 19, 1995, sec. G, p. 40.

WEBER, BRUCE. "At Home with Katie Couric: A Morning Cup of Regular." *New York Times,* April 9, 1992, sec. C, p. 1.

WEBSTER, KATHARINE. "Animal Lovers Boiling Over Killing of Lobster." *Washington Times,* June 13, 1994, sec. C, p. 3.

"Weddings: Al Roker and Deborah Roberts." *New York Times,* September 17, 1995, p. 56.

"Weddings: James Merlis and Jennifer Richardson." *New York Times,* June 5, 1994, sec. I, p. 13.

"Weddings: Jeffrey Zucker and Caryn Nathanson." *New York Times,* June 2, 1996, p. 47.

WEISMAN, JOHN. "ABC Divisions Fight for Services of 'Soulful' Newsman." *TV Guide,* August 20, 1977, p. A3.

WELLER, SHEILA. "*Today*'s Man: The Double-Edged Charm of Bryant Gumbel." *McCall's,* June 1987, p. 69.

WESTOVER, TED. "Rating TV's Morning Show Hosts." *TV Guide,* May 10, 1986, p. 51.

"What a Hunk." *Honolulu Advertiser,* December 13, 1997, sec. F, p. 4.

"WHDH-TV Plans to Drop *CBS This Morning*." *Broadcasting & Cable,* February 7, 1994, p. 65.

WHITESIDE, THOMAS. "How ABC Buttered Up the Russians—and Maybe, Why." *New York Times,* November 11, 1972, sec. B, p. 1.

———. "Profiles: The Time Is Twenty-One After." *New Yorker,* September 5, 1959, p. 39.

WHITNEY, DWIGHT. "TV Teletype: Hollywood." *TV Guide,* May 1, 1965, p. 21.

"Whooping Cough Vaccination." *Harvard Medical School Health Letter,* July 1982, p. 1.

"Why Garroway Signed Off." *Life,* June 30, 1961, p. 102.

WILKINSON, JACK. "It's Low Comedy on the High Seas as *Today* Sets Sail." *Atlanta Constitution,* May 22, 1986, sec. C, p. 1.

———. "Weatherman for All Seasons." *Atlanta Constitution,* May 28, 1986, sec. B, p. 1.

———. "Wake Up, Forrest, It's 2:45 in the Morning." *Atlanta Constitution,* October 11, 1985, sec. C, p. 1.

WILLENS, MICHELE. "Super Agents of TV News." *Los Angeles Times,* November 13, 1994, p. 3.

WILLIAMS, JEANNIE. "Joan Lunden, the Jokester." *USA Today,* October 6, 1987, sec. D, p. 2.

WILLIAMS, LENA. "The Woman Who Replaced Jane Pauley's Replacement." *New York Times,* April 8, 1991, sec. C, p. 11.

WILSON, CRAIG. "Dr. Art Ulene: He Pays House Calls to Millions of Viewers." *USA Today,* February 23, 1987, sec. D, p. 4.

WINES, MICHAEL. "President Angrily Contests Charges Over Loans to Iraq." *New York Times,* July 2, 1992, p. 1.

——. "White House Interprets Bush's Comments on Iran." *New York Times*, October 15, 1992, p. 24.

WINSLOW, THYRA SAMTER. "Daytime: Looking & Listening." *Variety*, July 13, 1960, p. 42.

"Who's the Girl of *Today*?" *TV Guide*, December 4, 1953, p. 21.

WOLF, JAIME. "Jackie Chan, American Action Hero?" *New York Times*, January 21, 1996, sec. F, p. 22.

WOLFSON, CYNTHIA. "Linda Ellerbee: The Wry Side of *Today*." *USA Today*, May 16, 1986, sec. WE, p. 5.

——. "The Gumbel Machine Rolls On." *USA Today*, May 16, 1986, sec. WE, p. 4.

WOODSON, MICHELLE. "Jane Kisses *Today* Goodbye." *Entertainment Weekly*, December 22, 1995, p. 86.

YANDEL, GERRY. "Hartman Has TV Interview with Gadhafi." *Atlanta Constitution*, October 16, 1986, p. 19.

——. "Hartman Signs a New Contract, Will Leave *GMA*.'" *Atlanta Constitution*, October 7, 1986, sec. B, p. 1.

"Zahn Joins *CBS This Morning*." *Broadcasting*, February 26, 1990, p. 70.

ZOGLIN, RICHARD. "Miles in the Morning." *Time*, March 23, 1992, p. 66.

——. "Minding Their Q's and A's." *Time*, July 13, 1992, p. 77.

——. "Miscues in the Morning." *Time*, February 24, 1990, p. 59.

——. "Surviving Nicely, Thanks." *Time*, August 20, 1990, p. 76.

ZOGLIN, RICHARD, WITH WILLIAM TYMAN. "Exit Jane, Amid Turmoil." *Time*, October 23, 1989, p. 81.

"Zucker Returns to *Today*." *Mediaweek*, August 1, 1994, p. 2.

INDEX